REPORTING METHODS

REPORTING METHODS

[For Degree/P.G. Diploma Courses in Journalism and Media Communication]

By

S. Kundra

ANMOL PUBLICATIONS PVT. LTD.

NEW DELHI - 110 002 (INDIA)

ANMOL PUBLICATIONS PVT. LTD.
4374/4B, Ansari Road, Daryaganj
New Delhi - 110 002
Ph.: 23261597, 23278000
Visit us at: www.anmolpublications.com

Reporting Methods

First Published, 2005

PRINTED IN INDIA

Published by J.L. Kumar for Anmol Publications Pvt. Ltd., New Delhi - 110 002 and Printed at Mehra Offset Press, Delhi.

Contents

Preface

"Reporting Methods" as a paper is being taught at the various diploma, graduate and post graduate level in 'Media Communication and Journalism' at various universities and institutions. This book is designed as an introductory text to the above paper, encompassing vital information on all pertinent aspects. Thus the material presented here would be of interest as well as of great use to the students, teachers and professionals of Media Communication and Journalism. This book will provide complete knowledge of the news values, structure, methods of writing a news story, leads, sources of news, principles of writing, traits of reporter, interview techniques, news writing skills for covering—conference, press conference, seminar and different kinds of reporting like—crime, sports, courts, accidents, science, etc. to the students.

The major topics dealt in this book are—Introduction of News; News—Structure and Nature; Lead and News Supply; Sources of News; Traits of a Reporter; Interview—Technique; Presentation and Newscasting; Brodcast News Writing; Reporting and News-gathering Tactics; Different Types of News Reporting.

It is hoped that all those will benefit from the contents of this book for whom it is meant. The author will feel amply rewarded, if motive is achieved.

Author

1

Introduction of News

In two centuries of independent journalism, the art of divining the meaning of the news has been at once the most challenging and the most frustrating to seasoned professionals. William Bolitho once compared the process to "seeing through a brick wall," which has nothing whatever to do with the relatively easy business of differentiating between events and pseudo-events. It is, inessence, the separation of the truth from the news.

This is, by all odds, the least likely of all the journalist's practices to win him thc administration of a mass public in these dangerous times, although it is one of the most essential. If he is right, he is, as the saying goes, only doing his job, and what is so remarkable about that? Yet, when he is wrong, his detractors take pains to point out for his benefit that scholars are still worrying about the, meaning of events in the seventeenth century, with perhaps a bit of apprehension over what happened in ancient Greece, so why all the rush? As for those timid souls who invariable do not know or cannot say, and have access to no one who might be able to help them, they are not journalists. This may seem utterly unreasonable, but it is a recognized way of journalistic life and some actually enjoy doing it.

In those shrinking areas of primarily Western civilization where the journalists still is permitted reasonable liberty of movement and expression, his work necessarily involves him in difficulties that are almost unavoidable. The gathering and distribution of the news in a reasonably impartial and accurate manner are in themselves complicated processes, as a rule. It takes somewhat more than good will and academic honours including the Ph.D. to cope with the basic reporting of the ordinary processes of life and self-government in an open society and the administration of justice, let alone such extraordinary events as civil disturbances, panics, disasters, national emergencies, and wars. When the journalist in addition is called upon to disseminate instant wisdom while great events are unfolding, he knows that he is often laying himself open to 'furious challenge, primarily from his own kind. Therefore, unless he is a syndicated columnist or another imposing personality who commands the unique trust of his proprietor and editor, the system under which he operates requires him to qualify, to hedge, and to dredge up un-persons as his, sources. There is, unfortunately, no way of hedging gracefully. Taking refuge in the cliches of American journalism, many back into the interpretation of events with an apologetic. It is believed ...or, "It is said.." Others, seeking support from threadbare mystery, adopt the time-worn formula of crediting or blaming the up-person with such expressions as, "Sources here indicate ..." or "In authoritative circles it is felt... " Finally, a few will take a bolder line by forthrightly stating the opinion of impartial observers, generally meaning themselves. Only a handful can be read with the admiring exclamation of a Ralph Waldo Emerson, upon perusing The Times of London in the mid-nineteenth century: 'It is so!"

The ailment is endemic to the journalism of the space age, when the generalist may be rendered helpless by events he does not understand and the specialist may be too muscle-bound to move quickly enough to service the news media. In one sense, the American journalist superbly fulfills his function by quickly organizing and presenting the factual developments surrounding great events, from space shots to war, and from national elections to the civil rights crisis. As long as the news is hard and hot (shop talk terminology that makes sense to the journalist if no one else), he usually does his work with consummate professional skill. But where the news is based on rival propaganda claims, exaggeration for striking effect, or deliberate untruths put forward by eminent persons, groups or nations, then the press is at a disadvantage because it has as yet devised no machinery for consistently dealing with such matters. Occasionally, a newspaper simply will refuse to publish mendacious material, regardless of the prestige of the source. In one instance, celebrated within the profession, a determined reporter crumpled a statement handed out by a distinguished American ambassador and told his colleagues in cold fury. "This is a goddam lie and I refuse to send it to my paper." But generally the rule that is followed, as stated in various forms by authorities from John Milton to John Knight requires publication of truth and falsehood alike on the hopeful assumption that the public will recognize the former and turn its back on the latter.

Aside from these ethical considerations, the news itself is often difficult for the average citizen to comprehend (and that sometimes includes the average editor) It is not un-known for sources to add to the complications by deliberately putting a construction on the news that is favourable "to some particular interest, public or private. Moreover, the journalist himself may add to the process of distortion quite innocently with his selection of a fact to be featured and headlined in a complicated article. Or, he may omit comparatively dull material that is important but requires too much space or time to explain. The two-line quote, the brief angled description, the loaded word or phrase, and misplaced emphasis all can be dangerous. But the journalist who sins the most against the public interest is the one who writes or speaks to appease his superiors' set notions of what is going on or to conform to the policies of his organization.

When the Angle is the Message

There is no question that experienced journalists are generally able to handle these difficulties in their daily routine, but even they cannot hope for perfection. As for the television newscasters, the demands of the clock and the lack of picture possibilities restrict their interpretive reporting in regular news programms. A minute or two is not sufficient to explain the meaning of such things as the struggle in China the decline of NATO, the meaning of "black power," or the "death of God," and the machinery of Medicare. But it is in the news magazines, which generally do not receive sufficient credit for their good work, that the temptation is greatest to make the angle the message.

Sometimes the angling is harmless and even amusing. Newsweek's cover story on Pop Art, a passing fad of the mix-sixties, began with a breathless glorification of the trivial in this manner:

> It's a fad, it's a trend, it's a way of life. It's pop. It's a $5,000 Roy Liethenstein painting of an underwater kiss. It's a $1 poster of Mandrake the Magician....It's 30,000,000 viewers dialing 'Batman' on ABC every week. It's Superman zooming around on the Broadway stage. It's Pow! Bam! commercial on TV..."

The historic cure for this kind of writing is to force the culprit to read it out loud before an audience of fellow journalists and take the consequences. It has no dubious intent nor can intelligent people take it very seriously. Usually, it can safely be ignored or, once read, forgotten.

But the same exaggerated techniqu , applied to a serious subject, can have a quite different result. As Great Britain was wrestling with a grave economic crisis. Time gaily head-lined a cover story: "London: The Swinging City." In glib and colourful language, the account reported as follows on the state of affairs in the capital of the United Kingdom.

It was one thing for one of Britain's angry men, John Osborne, to equate the highest British values with down-and-out vaudeville in his play. "The Entertainer," It was quite another for Time to present the image of Britannia in a miniskirt, an aging and hefty grand dame miscast in the role of a go-go girl. The British were not pleased by the effusive, schoolgirl prose in the leading American news magazine.

Henry Fairlie, a British journalist who attracted an admiring following of American editors because of his talent for insult, responded with measured invective: "If I were given to conspiracy theories, I would believe that there is a plot to denigrate Britain by praising everything in it which is mindless and nasty, which is senseless and corrupting, which is meaningless and deadly. "It was perfectly true, he agreed, that a small section of highly publicized British life was giving the impression that Britain seems destined to sink giggling into the sea" "But he argued that it was a distorted picture. The headlines announcing the Wilson government's devaluation of the pound soon confirmed his astringent analysis. It was just about as accurate for Time and others to cast all Britain in the Beatie mold in the late 1960s as it had been for the Hearst newspapers and others in the 1930s to welcome John Bull into the Cliveden Set as an appearer of Hitler.

When Prime Minister Wilson clapped on a wage-price freeze, it became difficult if not impossible fof any responsible publication to sustain the happy and carefree image of a swinging Britain American tourists, curtailing their own spending, found the British people anything but switched on. The fact was that the British were deeply concerned over the chronic economic problems of their great and ancient land; with money tight, and little hope of relief in sight, the average Britisher was as far from "the scene" as his quiet neighbourhood pub. Of course, extreme fashions were being vended with promotional skill on Carnaby Street and a thin, bony teenager dubbed Twiggy caused American fashion houses to fall over themselves to engage her services as a model. There were prostitutes in Soho and effeminate, long-haired boys in Piccadilly. Strip clubs were operating and most Britishers continued to be enthusiastic smalltime gamblers. But none of this was really news.

The daily newspapers, of course, have their own troubles with both the glorification of trivia and the dangers of distortion in dealing with the news. While no one can know all the faults and virtues of 1,750 newspapers at any particular time, it is readily apparent from the most sketchy and unscientific examination that not all editors are bemused by great events and even fewer are patient with seemingly insoluble issues of overwhelming importance. In considering the future of disarmament negotiations, for example, some editors published a column by Holmes Alexander on the subject which began: "Genocide is a horrid crime but sometimes it is tempting. What a better world we would have if we could put a merciful quietus on our Utopians, those persons who look for perfectability in man."

Even in the prestige newspapers there can be awkward moments, such as Ambassador Edwin O. Reischauer's fare well interview in Japan which the Washington Post headed "Reischauer Backs U.S. Viet Policy," while The New York Times headline was, "Reischauer Critical of Viet Policy," The ambivalence of editorial thought, as evidenced in New York and Washington, produced a certain amount of grim humor in a Senate Foreign Relations Committee hearing room when it was publicly displayed by Leonard Marks, director of USIA.

The hard-working wire services, always comparatively easy targets because of the tremendous volume of news they handle under great pressure and tough competitive conditions, also have made their share of errors for various reasons. When James H. Mereditch was shot by a roadside sniper in 1966 outside Hernado, Miss., United Press International correctly reported he had been slightly wounded and taken to a hospital while the Associated Press through a reportorial misunderstanding filed a bulletin that he was dead. The erroneous information was retracted after a half-hour.

The failure of both American wire services and Reuters, the British agency, to file prompt reports on the death of United Nations' Secretary General Dag Hammarskjold in 1961 was an even more striking instance of reportiorial error. Newsmen at the airport at Ndola, Northern Rhodesia, (now Zambia) had mistaken a visiting British official, Lord Lansdowne, for Hammarskjold and had a bulletined his arrival on a Congo cease-fire mission at a time when he already was dead. As the agencies discovered to their chargin hours later, the Hammarskjold plane had crashed before he had ever reached Ndola. It was sadly recorded in the AP Log thereafter that AP men should' 'never assume to be a fact what they did not know to be a fact"

Although the Hammarskjold case emphasizes the vulnerability of the independent news media to wire service errors, this has given rise too few signs of concern either among journalists or the public at large. The disposition is to accept the occasional factual error as "just one of those things". Actually, it would be a mistake to assume that the relatively rare instances of bad factual reporting on major stories has hurt the credibility of the American news media. The evidence is all to the contrary. The celebrated nature of each of these cases, and the controversy that surrounded them, points up the comparatively isolated nature of factual errors that mar the reporting of big-news in the United States.

These are generally not the things that bother the journalist about his news organizations and their performance. Nor do many knowledgeable persons inside or outside the profession take stock any longer in the outdated criticism in Upton Sinclair's Brass Check. As Walter Lippmann once stated the position: "If the press is not so universally wicked, nor so deeply conspiring, as Mr. Sinclair would have us believe, it is very much more frail than the democratic theory has yet admitted. It is too frail too carry the whole burden of popular sovereignty, to supply spontaneously the truth which democrats hoped was inborn."

There are several ways in' which this frailty of the press manifests itself, one of the most important being the treatment of the substance of a controversial issue in the news columns. A. T. Steele, a distinguished correspondent in the Far East for many years and scarcely a devotee of the Brass Check school of criticism, has singled out the coverage of Communist China for close examination. He believes that the editorial orientation of a newspaper is a "factor of importance" in the handling of news about China. "Indeed", he contends, "it can be argued that the generally conservative attitude of the American public on China is more attributable to this influence than to any other Newspapers of conservative outlook—and they are predominant in the smaller cities and towns-tend to give prominence to news and to background stories that favour their point of view. They also tend to use columnists of a predominantly conservative viewpoint. The total impression of China conveyed week after week to the readers of such a newspaper is likely to be different from that conveyed by a militantly liberal or independent newspaper".

As for television, there is so little of substance that appears on the networks outside the regular news programms and their hasty expansion for big stories that every innovation is greeted with somewhat muted applause. Thus, a documentary on China, the Middle East, the Cong, Harlem, Watts, or Appalachia becomes a matter for enthusiastic comment. A long and perhaps wearisome documentary on foreign policy may be regarded as just short of a triumph. Where so skimpy a diet is generally available, a small addition makes the regular fare seem like a banquet—and perhaps sometimes it actually is. Yet, few can doubt that the burden of presenting the substance of the news, fairly or not, is still the job of the press.

The "Background" System

Because this is so, what thoughtful journalist do and say about their own situation becomes something more than mere shop talk to a discerning public. It is a matter of record, documented at professional meetings and other public occasions too numerous to mention, that those not under compulsion to remain silent are becoming increasingly concerned, not only over slanted interpretations of the news but also over the manner in which such material is obtained. The "background" system, under which officials and others freely offer their views of the news in return for a pledge of anonymity, has proliferated beyond anything imagined by its founder, Ernest K. Lindley The "background" session, originally intended to be a quiet private talk between an official and a reporter or small group of reporters at most, has become a weekly event in which large numbers of correspondents hear the Secretary of State or the Secretary of Defense State opinions, but not for attribution to them.

In a similar manner, Secretary of State Dean Rusk invented a, term called deep background Instead of the regular background, which could be attributed to an informed source or some other unperson, he held his "deep background" conferences only for an elite list of "trusties, " the British term for correspondents who are particularly in the government's confidence. In such sessions, the Secretary of State would cover extremely sensitive situations but only in return for the correspondents' pledge to use the material without any attribution whatever.

Such abuses of what was once recognized as a perfectly reasonable reportorial device have had serious consequences in Washington and elsewhere. Respected public figures of the stature of McGeorge Bundy and Bill Moyers have called for a more principled stand by both journalists and public officials in their dealings with each other. Some of the major correspondents for the better newspapers have refused publicly to use, for attribution to unnamed sources, the kind of material that should be labeled with the name and position of the official issuing it. As Max Frankel of The New York Times once told a State Department briefer at a White House background conference. "There's no reason why most of this can't be on the record. The Times will not print this story unless it's on the record." It went on the record."

Alan L. Otten of the Wall Street Journal called reporters who attended background conferences the "prisoners of the system." He pointed out that once they committed themselves, they were well-high obliged in most cases to rush into print with the government's unattributed material because of competitive pressures. Like so many others, he also ridiculed the supposition that any source in Washington could be kept secret for very long after putting out news or views that made major headlines. Nor could it be successfully argued that the device in all cases divested the government of responsibility for what was said and done under the fragile seal of journalistic confidence.

Dsespite the somewhat mild rebellion, it should not be imagined that backgrounders are out of style or that the practice is on the point of being abandoned. For both professional and personal reasons, some understanding must be maintained between the journalist and his sources that will make it possible for them to talk together, even to argue, without guarding the utterance of every word. Long before

Lindley dreamed up his World War II system of journalistic protocol, the better reporters and editors of the nation maintained such confidential relationships with some of the most important figures in public and private life. They still do. A negligible part of the many private conversations between reporters and their sources reaches print or the broadcast media in attributable form; under a kind of unspoken gentleman's agreement, which varies from source to source, the reporter generally knows what he can use and what he must pass up for the time being. If all background conference were abandoned, it would not hurt the skilled professional one bit because he has gained the trust of his sources and they are scarcely likely to abandon a beneficial two-way relationship. Under today's mass background conference routine, therefore, the only ones who really benefit are the junior reporters without sources, the lazybones who would rather pick an official's brains than use their own and do some independent work, and the numbskulls who worry more about the exact form of a quotation than the meaning behind it.

There is no law in the land that requires any source in government or out of it to trust all reporters; in fact sheer prudence would rule against it. True, formal announcements or other news developments must be given to all the media representatives on a fair and equitable basis; however, when it comes to discussing the meaning of the news, every source is going to pick the reporters be trusts and who are likely to be of most benefit to his interests. Those who are shut out will not like it. On occasion, they may kick up such a fuss that they will break their way into the circle of journalistic' 'trusties" on their own terms. That kind of rivalry always has existed, regardless of the growth of the system of handling out background information and opinion, and it is bound to continue.

Despite the abuses of the backgrounder, all available evidene indicates that the use of material derived from it is increasing steadily in the American news media and abroad. The wire services and the newspapers syndicates are making available a great deal more explanatory material today than they did a decade or two ago and many more newspapers are using it. Such interpretation may on occasion be faulty, windy, or difficult to understand, but editors need not run it if they do not approve of it. The imperfections of the system, in short are not sufficient reason for abandoning the effort to explain the news.

Of course, editors still exist in the United States who conceive it to be their duty to play Horatius at the Bridge and keep out of the paper all notions that run contrary to their own pure beliefs. They are a hardy breed; although their numbers are dwindling in the space age, they still have a considerable influence in the far right wing of American journalism. If there were a far left with more than token access to print, undoubtedly the situation would be the same but there have been no far left publications of significance in the nation for many years. In consequence, the play it safe" school of journalism flourishes primarily in places where editors either do not care about the meaning of the news or do not dare arouse local opposition by presenting views contrary to prevailing sentiment.

Interpreting the News

It is extraordinary, on balance, for so many inside the profession to adopt so critical an attitude on the problem of interpreting the news. In view of the long and undistinguished record of the American press in stubbornly facing down its critics, the movement toward greater realism in dealing with both the news and its sources is healthy and heartening. The mere acceptance of interpretation as a proper function of journalism, achieved after so many years of argument, is not enough. The methods of achieving it cannot be exactly defined; nor, for that matter, can they ever be expected to attain perfection. No computer is ever going to be invented that will emit acceptable explanations of the news at the touch of a button. No magic formula can be devised by science for clarifying, in one blind flash of revelation, the meaning of the convulsive upheaval of peoples and values in the world of the declining years of the twentieth century. Like the companion arts of exposition and illustration, interpretation has to be worked over, developed, and guarded against abuse and excess. Nor can it be assumed that everybody in journalism automatically inherits the right to interpret the news by the mere declaration that he is a journalist.

Conscientious editors rightly attempt to restrict the interpretation of events to those who have the ability, the background, and the experience to attempt it. Even so, there are many pitfalls before the qualified interpreter. What is true one day in a rapidly developing situation is not necessarily so the next, but often only the passage of time will cause the Ilifference to be revealed. It took two years for the Communist hierarchy in Moscow to dump Nikita S. Khrushehev as premier after his failure to keep Russian rockets in Cuba aimed at the United States. It was even longer before the average American editor realized that there really was a split between the Soviet Union and Communist China. On September 30, 1965, the Western correspondent who flew into Jakarta could assume with reason that Indonesia was becoming allied with Peking: next day, with the failure of a Communist uprising, the opposite was the case although it was some time before the new position was clarified.

Writing of an equally difficult stage of the Vietnam War, Vermont Royster pointed out in the Wall Street Journal: "The deficiency is inherent in the situation. Therefore, there is probably no way to remedy it." This is so often true that it is pointless to try to define precisely the position of interpretation between the function of reporting, on the one side, and editorializing, on the other. Many editors have tried to do it, some even believe the process can be compartmentalized. However, no set of compartments or definitions can dispose of difficulties that are, as Royster has said, inherent in the situation. For as all able journalists know, interpretation uses both the techniques of reporting and editorial writing without finally being either a report or an editorial.

The identity of the writer or commentator, and the integrity of his organization, are the only guarantees that can be provided to the public of the good faith behind the interpretation. Usually, it is sufficient. The notion that the public will be satisfied if an analysis is labeled as such really means very little, for the news columns are replete with unlabeled interpretation in the prestige press. More to be desired is the absence of any sign in the work of an analyst that he is an advocate of one cause or another, or that he has any special interest to advance. The same is true of his organization. There should be only one advocate—the editorialist. It is not seemly for the interpreter to try to persuade or to exhort: once he does, he sheds his assumption of disinterest which is all that separates him from the editorialist.

The current tendency to dramatize non-essentials, to oversimplify complex questions, and to imply U.S. importance one day and omnipotence the next has helped foster a national mood of confusion and frustration."

Such attitudes naturally encouraged some of the rivals of the daily newspaper, particularly the journals that aspired to give a more acceptable meaning to the news than the press. As a group they had long since adopted an adversary philosophy. Marya Mannes, a critic for The Reporter magazine, spoke for example of the "tragedy" of the "decline of public confidence in the daily press" and warned that the public would turn to television for something better. However, despite Miss Mannes's prophecy, there has been no perceptible mass movement to follow the intellectual leadership offered by either television or the magazines in the United States.

The Test: Civil Rights

The truth is that no element of the news media in the United States has any ground for complacency today. All are under critical scrutiny by informed public opinion as never before some more than others. If there is a single continuing issue that tests the public's belief in its news and communications system, it is by all odds the handling of the civil rights crisis. While there have been instances of superb work by all sections of the news media on this story in every part of the nation, the record on the whole is not one that satisfies most thoughtful journalists. More heat may be generated by the lively debate over free press and fair trial, but bench and bar are well able to fend for themselves in the rough and tumble of the democratic arena. This is not necessarily so as far as the protagonists in the turbulence over civil rights are concerned. Their leaders by and large, do not command the kind of respectful attention from the news media that is invariably accorded the American Bar Association and its distinguished spokesmen.

Some of the editors and publishers in the South have refused to let anything prevent them from telling the truth about non-compliance with the law in all its unlovely aspects. Some reporters, photographers, and newscasters of impectable Southern lineage have repeatedly exposed themselves to mob violence in order to cover the news of their own and neighbouring communities. Yet, there is no doubt that in the beginning and to some extent even today—many Southern newspapers have qualified before the rebellious majorities in their communities the threat of terrorism. Their editorial pages have condoned resistance to the law, even when it meant the endorsement of crimes up to and ineluding murder.

There are still resolute journalists in the South who uphold the tradition of personal responsibility - Ralph McGill and Eugene Patterson on the Atlanta Constitution. Barry Bingham and Norman Isaacs on the Louisville Times and Courier-Journal, Hooding Carter on the Greenville (Miss.) Delta Democrat-Times, J.O. Emmerich on the McComb (Miss.) Enterprise-Journal and others in a number of trouble centres. By their example, they have caused a substantial part of the press in the South to lift its standards in handling the news of America's great social crisis.

It is true that there is still little encouragement that can be given to the smaller and weaker papers in segregationist centres. Ira B. Harkey. Jr., a symbol of defiance in Mississippi, had to sell his Pascagoula Chronile and turn to teaching journalism. Hazel Brannon Smith, who made her weekly Lexington Advertiser respected every where except in Mississippi, led a precarious existence for years. Consequently,—relatively few cared to follow her forthright example.

Although a segregation-minded populace continues to buy complying newspapers in the deep South and patronizes their advertisers, this scarcely implies respect for the press. In a Germany where might made right, Bismarck also was able to force newspapers to do his biddsini but he referred to them contemptuously as the "reptile press," crawling on its belly before him. Naturally, the average Southern editor and publisher would consider such terminology a mortal insult, especially in the deep South where segregation remains an article of personal faith for the majority. But even a community of the most violent segregationists can measure the stature of a newspaper that prints only what its readers want to see and voices only editorial sentiments that can be applauded by the crudest and most vicious elements.

Rightly or wrongly, with the rise of civil rights violence across the land, the news media have often been as unwelcome in the ghetto as the police and other elements of the Establishment. This was particularly true in the Newark and Detroit riots of 1967. Reporters never know when they are likely to be jumped upon. Photographers with still or television cameras cannot be sure of their own safety, let alone their equipments. The relatively good record of most of the news media in covering disturbances does not seem to count for much. Nor have the excellent and often sympathetic documentaries about the civil rights movement on television made any significant impression on the militancy of the Negro masses. In effect, the lack of belief attached to the segregationist press in the deep South has also encompassed a considerable part of the press elsewhere among the ghetto-dwellers of the land. The difference in the motivation of the more liberal elements of the press has not loosened the growth of a belief among the extremists, white and Negro; that the news media constitute a symbol against which an effective protest may be registered.

The frailty of the press is very much in evidence in the civil rights issue. It is, in fact, no exaggeration to say that the press has been made a part of the issue. While accepting some of the failures in the South and the neglect of dangerous conditions in a number of cities elsewhere until they exploded into rioting, most working journalists do feel that they have done a decent and considerate job on the whole in telling the civil rights story. Outside the deep South, the record generally sustains them. But no one can persuade the militant Negro that this is so. He does not believe it. To him, the news means something entirely different than it does to the press he calls "white" because he will not acknowledge it as his own.

This state of mind, and the civil disorder it breeds, has shaken some of the complacency out of the news media and to some extent, forced its more progressive elements to re-examine their methods. What mob coverage does to inflame rioters to even greater acts of looting and sabotage will be examined later in this book, together with the general problem of controlling herd journalism.

A New Approach

Historically, journalism is not a profession that is founded on starry-eyed optimism It glorifies its Cassandras and ridicules its Pollyannas. It scorns the uplifter as much as it suspects the reformer, having had grievous experience with both in the course of its daily dealings with human affairs. As an echo to events, it cries woe's knowing full well that such an automatic reflex action has a better chance of being right than wrong. The journalist who predicted 19 times at the opening of League of Nations meetings that this one would be its last had the dubious satisfaction of seeing events bear him out at the 20th session. Such a philosophy glorifies the prophet of doom as he and his followers are being consumed by the flames they themselves have kindled.

Clearly, the journalist needs a different approach to the reporting of a controversy such as civil rights that goes to the very roots of national existence. As the position was stated by George Hunt, managing editor of Life, it is no longer sufficient to practice "blind adherence to news for new's sake, and playing it for all it's worth." Such lalssez-faire philosophy is out of date. Nor can it be propped up by some new gimmick in presenting the news, or a tricky method of writing interpretation to get more people to read it. What is required is a greater degree of editorial commitment—the decision, for example of editors in Rochester. N. Y. to go out and look for signs of progress in civil rights as well as the daily yield of bad news, the publication, as a further example of an enormous volume of material on crisis areas by editors in Los Angeles. Philadelphia, Kansas City, St. Louis, Hartford, and other cities. The telling of the Story of the City is the No.1 assignment in American journalism today.

What this means, in short, is that the more progressive journalists at length have realized that there are both civic and national responsibilities that come ahead of their normal professional duties. Merely telling and printing the news is not enough; nor is it sufficient to keep chanting a litany about interpreting the news without finding better people, better ways, more space, and more time to do it before a crisis makes it imperative. The journalist is no longer justified in wrapping himself in the guise of a philosophical anarchist and pretending that he is someone set apart with a mission beyond that of ordinary men. For the fact is that he no longer is a mere news gatherer; often, in the act of gathering news, he makes it and even influences the course of events. Surely, the time has come for him to recognize it. He is not part of a gigantic shadow play; he is one of the principal actors, and what he says and does can have a substantial influence on its outcome. He must face up to his responsibilities as a good citizen first, a good journalist second.

Whether the journalist likes it or not, this is the standard by which the public is judging him and will continue to judge him and his works. His are the responsibilities of the innovator and leader, not merely of the critic, and he must exercise all of them if he is to continue to exert his right to give meaning to the news.

❐

2

News—Structure and Nature

There has been no definition of it which is satisfactory to all. What passes for news in Indian newspapers may not be the product with which readers of British and American newspapers are familiar. And what appears in British and American newspapers may not be understood as news by the Indian reader. For long years before and after independence Indian newspapers featured speeches—speeches at public meetings, at conferences and in the legislative and local bodies—as news and devoted column after column of the daily issues to them. And they were the staple diet of the reader who was never satiated and wanted more of them. After speeches what occupied the space of the newspaper were reports of activities of Government—appointment of officials, announcements and notices and speeches of top officials—and these too were lapped up by the reader for whom the newspaper was only source of information about the alien government.

The obsession with speeches and governmental activities has continued to this day in this country with politicians and politics claiming a lion's share of the daily newspaper space to the exclusion of news of other aspects of life, except of course bad news like riots, natural calamities or major accidents. Apparently, Indian newspapers have not recovered from the hangover of colonial rule and the reader themselves have not been educated to expect or demand anything different from what they have been used to so far.

The definition of news, therefore, varies from country to country or from one continent to another but let us look are some broad definitions.

'News is anything out of the ordinary'.

'News is anything published in a newspaper which interests a large number of people'.

'News is what newspapermen make it'.

'Good news is not news'.

'For a long time it was considered that news was anything any big shot said'.

News and truth are not the same thing, wrote the great American journalist, Walter Lippmann. 'The function of news is', he said, 'to signalise an event; the function of truth, is to bring to light the hidden facts. The Press if it did its job well, could elucidate the news. It is like the beam of a searchlight that moves restlessly about, bringing one episode and then another out of the darkness into vision'.

An Indian journalist, Arun Shourie, made this comment on what is considered as news by Indian journalists today: "Today's journalism in India is a matter of contracts. The journalist's primary subject is Government; their primary source of information is Government and their primary audience is the Government. A good journalist—the envy of his peers—is one who has better contacts so that he can get the Government handout earlier than his colleagues. In such a situation one cannot fight a denial unless some other official for reasons of his own feeds one the information that would embarrass his official colleague. Contrast what the position would be if journalists were writing primarily about the people not about factotums in Government; if their principal source of information were the people, not the factotums in Government".

What the newspaper is constantly in search of is action, movement, new developments, surprises, sudden reversals, the ups and downs of fate, the cataclysms of nature and the perversities and follies of mankind. Says an American writer: 'Even sober-sided coverage of Government and politics is imbued with the search for drama and conflict. What most appears as news to the newspaper is often state stuff in the long history of human events. Much that transpires in the world—some of it of great importance—is not in the nature of action, motion; upsets, 'man bites dog' stuff. And these events or processes, certainly the absence of action, seldom rate much notice in the daily newspaper. Nothing is happening—although that in itself may amount to action as when a Third World country does not have a birth control programme or a city is not afflicted with high and rising rates of crime. Hospitals, mental institutions, schools and prison, all are usually not covered by the newspaper except when involved in sensations of some kind. The newspaper's concentration is personalities and surprises, natural though that concentration is made no doubt congenial to most readers, limits the usefulness and impact of the newspaper'

Lord Norihcliffe, the British newspaper magnate, said: "It is hard news that catches readers". People are interested in people. We are all gossip lovers and we want to know what is happening behind the scenes. To ascertain the facts, arrange them in proper order an present them to the reader is the task of the newspaper. To publish rumours but also because the reader will be deceived if they are not accurate.

The unusual will always interest people and therefore anything unusual is news. Mysteries, small or big, interest people and so mysteries are news. Events that affect people's lives are news, the more people affected the bigger the news. People like to read about things they have heard about but they also would like to read about something new. An essential feature of news is that it is new. News is a relative thing. It arises from the things people or groups of people have done, are doing, or plan to do.

News is often like an iceberg with only a small crag or pinnacle revealed to the public gaze, says a well-known writer. 'The professional newsman is constantly searching below the water level of community consciousness in an effort to bring all of the iceberg into view. In this search he uses his own and the newspaper's definition of news. It is the direct responsibility of the newspaper to find the news, develop it, interpret it and present it to the news consumer'.

Lord Northcliffe said there were two main divisions of news: *(1)* actualities: *(2)* talking points. The first is news in its narrowest. and best sense like natural calamities, accidents, crime, strikes and political happenings. The second is getting at the topics which 'people are discussing and developing them or stimulating them. News of the second sort, 'the talking points' Lord Northcliffe said 'does not fall into your basket like the other sort. It requires thought, initiative, looking ahead. It means a daily search by trained men of the world, directive by a News leader who has time to get about men and women, time to think—a daily search for subjects in the public mind or subjects that ought to be in the public mind'.

Who is to decide what is news—the journalists or the public? While ultimately it is the reader who will judge, and be the final arbiter, the answer must be found by the newspapers themselves. Those that discover the answer succeed and those that do not, fail to survive. The newspaper reader clamours for a rich variety of news which will not be interesting or significant to everyone. It takes all sorts of people to make a world and the newspaperman must cater for all. In so doing he has to handle much that is not of the remotest interest to him personally. As a British writer puts it: 'The journalist is a spectator, a commentator, not a participant. He sees the great game. Does he understand it? Can he interpret it? That is the real test of his efficiency'. An American Editor has said: 'News is not the event, it is the account of the event written for people who did not witness it'.

News values vary because newspapers vary. But it may be safely said that the broadest and biggest news is that which appeals to everybody; which stirs the deepest emotions and touches the profoundest interests of the people. To quote a well-known writer: 'what the public wants is news, news of human interest told in a natural way and presented in a manner agreeable to the eye and intelligent to the mind'. The highest news values are those which combine the elements of intrinsic importance or magnitude with surprise.

The varying nature of news is seen in the way newspapers handle the same story. While they may agree that a given sets of facts is news they may disagree on its character, the facts to be omitted and the stress to be laid on some others. A knowledgeable journalist has listed the five qualities that should characterise news.

1. News is any printable story which in the 'Opinion of the Editor will interest his readers. A story will interest readers (i) if it concerns them directly or (ii) it makes interesting reading.

2. News is always completely true or it is at least a set of facts that has been presented to the reporter as truth. It is the story of something that has just happened or something that has happened or it is a statement that has been made.

3. News has a quality of 'recency' about it. It is the story of something that has just happened or something being told for the first time. In short it is a story that possesses the appeal of freshly discovered material.

4. News has a element of proximity about it. People, generally speaking, are most interested in events that are near them in space, time and general background. This means that people are generally interested in stories from, their own city, state and nation, in stories related to their racial, social, cultural or national background. The element of proximity places special emphasis on stories of local in terest, current events and activities of racial, religious and national groups.

5. News must have some element of the unusual about it. The basic qualities of news are accuracy, interest and timeliness. To these must be added the qualification that the people must understand whatever is published. For, of what use is an accurate, interesting and timely report of a news event if the reader cannot understand it? Disasters, political crises and accidents are news no doubt but they are not the sole news. As one writer remarks, 'it is nonsense to imply

that the newspaper must have bad news to stay in business'. Positive news also has a role to play in the newspaper columns. Unfortunately this is not given its due importance in the Indian newspapers (especially language papers). Our newspapers must present a balanced view of the community, state, nation and the world beyond our borders. To do so it requires a certain amount of skill, patience and under standing.

We talk of news of reader interest. What are the things that will interest the reader? A general idea can be given:

1. Unusual events.
2. Mysteries and the unknown.
3. Prominent people, places and things.
4. Whatever people are talking about.
5. Statements by persons in authority.
6. All events that affects readers' lives.
7. Trends or continuing events that grasp the imagination of readers over a period of time.
8. New ideas-anything that is likely to be new to the general reader.
9. Conflict between man and man; between man and nature.
10. Natural phenomena; violence, calamities and disaster.
11. Tragedies and comedies that appeal to the human emotion.
12. The why of news; why things happen, what makes them happen, who pulls the strings.
13. Topics of health.
14. The environment.

Every newspaper has stock sources of news and these are covered by its reporters on beat or by the news agencies. Let us have a look at them.

1. Government and official news: news about the Head of the State, Cabinet, Parliament, State Legislatures and the administration.
2. Meetings of Parliament, State Legislatures, local bodies and subsidiary agencies of Government.
3. Functions attended by Minister, officials and VIPs etc.
4. Activities, movements, statements of people already known to they public or interesting to the public such as businessmen, leaders of industry, scientists, educators, sportsmen, film stars and cultural and religious leaders.
5. Accidents, crime, police and courts.
6. Health and hospitals.
7. Cultural and religious events.
8. Political meetings and news.
9. Money and business.
10. Science and economic news.

A newspaper may not have the staff or resources to tap all these sources of news every day. What can be done in that case is to have a news contact, an active and live contact, in some of these places who will contact the newsroom.if there is news. He may be paid a retainer or compensated in some other way. One of the most useful and fruitful sources of news is community or public service investigation. What sets people talking about your newspaper is the odd human story. Trivial news can be made interesting by clever handling and editing. Much heavy and dull material which reaches the reporter or the newsroom as news may contains gems of public interest for those who are alert and keen to detect them and describe them intelligently. Coming under this category are voluminous government reports, white papers, bluebooks and papers presented at seminar and learned bodies. They have forbidding exteriors and prosaic appearances but very often they contain much interesting news.

What is termed as risky news is generally of much interest to the reader. Where a political party meets in secret, or a commission enquiring into bribery charges or administrative lapses holds in camera sittings, the reader will be curious to know what happened and about the personalities involved. Much care and delicacy is needed in pursuing news of this sort. Anything reflecting on a person's character of reputation is dangerous although such news often has two chief qualifications which recommend it to the eyes of the curious reader namely, private history and a dash of scandal. This type of news has been appearing with increasing frequency in Indian newspapers and magazines in recent years. It would have shocked the older generation of journalists in whose code scandal, gossip and exposure of private lives had no place and were forbidden.

A major defect in our newspapers is the absence of local or city news both in quality and quantity. Surely in big cities people are saying and doing things that are interesting to others, establishing new relationships or breaking old ones and doing a multitude of things which are of interest to their neighbours. Our papers give the impression that people spend their entire time being governed or committing crimes of violence.

'The Press's lack of scepticism, its unwillingness to look behind official statements and claims, its too ready linkage of the powers of office with knowledge and ability, its assumption of official virtue where rigorous inquiry would have disclosed no virtue at all—these delinquencies could be charged to the press itself. This view was expressed by Tom Wicker, well-known columnist of the New York Times. Another writer had this to say about newspaper stories: 'Newspapers can use language with more precision. They can develop better definition of "news". They can recognise diversity. They can stop representing random and often bizarre opinions as the voice of the people. Above all, they can ignore the labels and stereotypes that are hung on people and things and seek out the reality of the human condition'.

Facts may be difficult to get hold of and a story may be causing more public interest than the newspaper can find news to satisfy the reader. But it still remains the newspaper's first job to be accurate. If it is decided to publish a report that is based on guesswork the Editor should make it clear that the facts are in doubt. A paper should not disguise speculation as information. Unfortunately too many Indian newspapers have erred in this respect. Unverified, speculative and highly improbable accounts have been passed off as news and contradictions and denials have followed.

The most important quality one expects from a newspaper is honesty. The most important way a newspaper can be honest with its readers is to make a clear distinction between what it reports and what it thinks. 'Reporting the news involves more than journalistic writing technique', says an American journalist. 'Responsibilities for informing the people have multiplied decade by decade in this century. Mere recording of 'happenings' is criminally inadequate. Today's citizen is infinitely more dependent on forces and institutions outside his direct control than was his counterpart 200 or 250 years ago. All three levels of Government (local, state and central) interfere with his life-from how long and where he shall attend school to how he provides for his retirement-in a degree not even dreamt of 50 years ago. His dependence on non-Government institutions has also mush-roomed. The modern citizen depends heavily on the reliability and competence of gas, electricity and telephones; his well being can be improved or damaged by trade unions or professional societies. All arms of the Press have moved towards meeting today's larger demands, some more than the others.

Whatever may be the position in other parts of the world, the newspaper reader in India implicitly believes what is published in his newspaper. Whether they do it intentionally or not the presentation and display of news in newspapers exercises great influence on the thinking and action of the readers. A paper which emphasises scandal, crime and sex compels the attention of the readers to such subjects. A more serious paper with a diet of more important national, state and local issues provokes community concern. Too often newspaper men are apt to think that leadership role of a newspaper is confined to the editorial columns. In fact headlines of news stories are more important in drawing the attention of the reader and helping him to form an opinion.

Who is a good journalist? Read this tribute to great American journalist, Ralph McGill by another in the same profession.

'He made you feel better about yourself and about the human race. He called out in you some strengths, some instincts for good you, may be, hadn't paid much attention to before and you found yourself wanting to do what he wanted done. He wasn't infallible. He wasn't God. He could be badly wrong about a lot of things and stubborn in his wrongness. Like the Vietnam war for instance. But he did the job a hero had to do. He stood in a hero's place and he stood firm'.

There are no prescribed qualifications for a journalist but not everyone can be a good journalist. A good journalist is sometimes born but more often he is fashioned out of the hard school of a newsroom where he undergoes rigorous tests and training and not accepted until he makes the grade of a full fledged journalist. He has to pass through the needle of the News Editor who never believes anything as the junior reporter in the following story found. The junior reporter gave the News Editor an unbelievable story of the miraculous escape of a man who fell from the top of a town hall to the pavement below. The man was wearing rubber soled shoes and alighting on his feet he shot up to half the height of the building. Again he fell, catlike on his feet and this time bounced to a quarter of the eight and at length by falls scaled down by half every time he subsided on the pavement, unhurt. When the reporter expected exclamation and delight, the News Editor shook his head and dropped the copy into the waste paper basket. "That's not our kind of new", he told the reporter. "It is only what might have been a serious accident story. If the man had broken his neck that would have been news".

Nicholas Tomalin, the veteran London journalist described in the Sunday Times the attributes of a successful journalist.

'The only qualities', he wrote, 'essential for success in journalism are rat like cunning, a plausible manner and a literary ability. The rat like cunning is needed to ferret out and publish things that people don't want to be known (which is and always will be the best definition of news). The plausible manner is useful for surviving while this is going on, helpful in the entertaining presentation of it and even more useful in later life when the successful journalist may have to become a successful executive on his newspaper. The literary ability' is of obvious use'.

Other helpful qualities Tomalin mentioned were: A knack with the telephone, trains, and petty officials, a good digestion and a steady head, total recall, enough idealism to inspire indignant prose (but not enough to inhibit detached professionalism), a paranoid temperament, an ability to believe passionately in second are objects; well placed relatives; good luck, the willingness to betray if not friends, acquaintances, a reluctance to understand too much too well, an implacable hatred of spokesmen, administrators, lawyers, public relations men, politicians and all those who would rather pervert words than policies; and the strength to lead a disrupted personal life without going absolutely haywire. Also desirable is the capacity to steal other people's ideas and phrases.

Tom Wicker of the New York Times wrote: 'Your Journalist) biggest weakness is that too many of you want to believe in people and things you are too lazy to question. Every now and then you do go wrong and put a good man down and a bad man up-how is that different from anything else in life? Reporters, one should presume, are normal human beings with the samte ambition, competitive fire, desire for status and affluence, fear, caution, ethics, honesty and guile like any other human being. They can be, therefore, and are often manipulated, threatened, rewarded and punished, cajoled and conned into doing what their news sources want them to do sometimes even without realising that they have been any of the above.

In the West, especially in America-and, one fears, in India too manipulating access, not granting or withholding social preference is the most standard means of striking and threatening a reporter and by all odds is the most effective even against told and independent reporters. The best journalists, it has been said, are those who are friendly, easy to talk to, not shy, yet certainly not brash. A journalist has to move at all levels of society and it is therefore important not to be too unconventional in dress or oveirly conspicuous in any way. "Anyone who wants to be journalist"; says a wellknown writer, "is more likely to succeed if he possesses naturally good manners. Your manners must be good enough to get you through the front door and once inside you should not offend people by your behaviour. The journalist is the newspaper. Everything you do or say or look reflects back on the reputation of your newspaper."

Journalists as a class the world over are proud of their professions, their lives and achievements. Their feelings are reflected in this confession by one of their tribe: 'I am proud of my business and grateful to it for a satisfying life as a reporter. I would rather cover a President than be a President. I would rather cover the country courthouse th n be the town banker. I would rather be club editor than bc president of a country club to which a reporter couldn't belong.

Journalists have to deal with people all the their and someone who is shy or easily paralysed with fear is not likely to be very successful. To be a good journalist you have to steel yourself and learn to ask what would be considered very impertinent question by anyone nicely brought up. 'The classic function of the aggressive reporter and editor-a part of the responsibility they owe to the public is to open doors with the power of the press-pry them open, blow them open'. Clifton Daniel of the New York. Times who said this added: 'Stripped to essentials the responsibility of the reporter and the editor is simply to serve the public not the profession of journalism, not a particular newspaper, not a political party, not the Government, but the public.'

NATURE OF NEWS

What are the psychological processes that determine the news reading choices of the individual readers? One of the best explanations we have, that of Wilbur Schramm, is reproduced in part, below. You should read it carefully, for you will be asked some questions based upon it.

I think it is self-evident that a person selects news in expectation of a reward.

This reward may be either of two kinds. One is related to what Freud call the Pleasure Principle the other to what he calls the Reality Principle. For want of better names, we shall call these two classes immediatere ward and delayed reward.

In general, the kinds of news which may be expected to furnish immediate reward are news of crime and corruption, accidents and disasters, sports and recreation, social events, and human interest.

Delayed reward may be expected from news of public affairs, economic matters, social problem, science, education and health.

News of the first kind pays its rewards at once. A reader can enjoy a vicarious experience without any of the dangers or stresses involved. He can shiver luxuriously at axe-murder, shake his head sympathetically and safely at a tornado, identify himself with the winning team or (herself) with the society lady who wore a well-described gown at the reception for Lady Morganbilt, laugh understandingly (and from superior knowledge) at a warm little story of children or dogs. News of the second kind, however, pays its rewards later. It sometimes requires the reader to endure unpleasantness or annoyances—as, for example, when he reads of the ominous foreign situation, the mounting national debt, rising taxes, falling market, scarce housing, cancer, epidemics, farm blights. It has a kind of threat value. It is read so that the reader may be informed and prepared. When a reader selects delayed reward news, he jerks himself into the world of surrounding reality to which he can adapt himself only by hard work. When he selects news of the other kind, he retreats usually from the world of threatening reality toward the dream world.

For any individual, of course, the boundaries of these two classes are not stable. For example a sociologist may read news of crime as a social problem, rather than for its immediate reward. A coach may read a sports story for its threat value; he may have to play that team next week. A politician may read an account of his latest successful rally, not for its delayed reward, but very much as his wife reads an account of a party. In any given story of corruption or disaster, a thoughtful reader receives not only the immediate reward of vicarious experience, but also the delayed reward of information and preparedness. Therefore, while the division of categories holds in general, the predispositions of the individual may transfer any story from one kind of reading to another, or divide the experience between the two kinds of reward.

But what is going on psychologically beneath these two kinds of choice of news?

The kind of choice which we have called immediate reward is simple associational learning, or problem solving. A stimulus is presented; a response is made; the response is rewarded. When the stimulus is again presented, there is a tendency to make the same response: If it is again 'rewarded, the tendency to make that same response' is progressively reinforced. If it is not rewarded, the tendency is progressively extinguished. The stimulus in this case, of course, is the news item. The response is the decision to read or listen to the item. The reward may be either a reduction of tension or discomfort. (*e.g.* curiosity, worry) or an increase in satisfaction (*e.g.*, from a vicarious enjoyment of the achievements of the winning team).

But what is the process which leads a reader or listener to select a news item, even though he knows it may not reduce tension, but actually increasetension; not relieve discomfort, but actually increasediscomfort; not. bring satisfaction, but actually bring dissatisfaction and worry? We have alleady suggested that these two kinds of reading are related to what Froud called the two principles of mental functioning, the Pleasure Principle and the Reality Principle. That is the immediate reward choice is learned through trial and error because it succeeds in reducing drives and tensions. The delayed reward choice, on the other hand, is made not because it is pleasant, but because sit is realistic. It is not pleasant to be afraid or to anticipate danger; but it is necessary, if one is to avert harm and avoid danger.

O.H. Mowrer, in his reinterpretation of conditioning and problem solving, has advanced a concept of learning which is extremely suggestive to any student of the process of communication. He points out that there are really two aspects of learning, related respectively to the two nervous systems. The central nervous system is the one chiefly through which we affect society; the autonomic nervous system is the one chiefly through which society affects us. The Central system is the one through which habits—that is, learned responses of the skeletal musculature—are formed. The autonomous system is the one through which attitudes or emotions—that is, learned responses of glands, smooth muscle, and vasomotor tissue—are formed. Habits, of course come into being to reduce drives and solve problems. Attitudes and emotions, on the other hand, are themselves drives or problems, and call forth skeletal reactions on the basis of which the central nervous system may go into action and develop habits.

Therefore, responses to the two kinds of news corresponds to what Sherrington calls anticipatory and consummatory responses. One is made as the consummation of a drive and with the expectation of immediate reward. The other is made to set up a drive, and in expectation of danger or delayed reward. One reduces a drive and is therefore pleasant; the other sets up a drive and may be painful. The two responses are not always cleanly differentiated. For example, the dramatic quality in a foreign news story may give an immediate reward, while the content arouses only fear or anticipation of danger. But learning may take place through either method. Gordon Allport gives an example of learning through the anticipatory response; "Suppose I mispronounce a word in a public speech and suffer mounting shame and discomfort. Tension has been created, not reduced; dissatisfaction and not satisfaction has resulted; but in this sequence of events I shall surely learn.

When a child starts to read a newspaper he usually begins with the comics and the pictures. He proceeds to the sports news, the human interest stories, and sensational stories of crime and disaster, all before he makes much use of public affairs news. It is interesting to conjecture how a child begins to read public affairs news. Perhaps he has an experience in which he is able to make not-too-long-delayed use of something he has read in the paper. Perhaps it helps him to answer a question at school, or to take his raincoat and avoid a soaking, or to avoid a street which is closed for repairs—in other words, to avoid trouble by being informed. He looks at the paper with respect. It reading the particular item was of benefit to him would it not be well for him to read other items also? As his understanding broadens, he perceives more of the causative and repetitive relation of events in society.

Thus the time when he comes to read public affairs news is an important point in his socialization. Most of the news in the immediate reward group is important to him individually because of the individual satisfaction and drive-reduction it accomplishes. But the news in the delayed group is important to him because it arouses the tensions and anticipation that are necessary for survival and development, that help him to be more effective, better prepared, socially.

If we accept tentatively the theory that there are two general classes of news, two patterns of reading, and two aspects of the learning process involved, then another variable important. Within each kind of news, what determines the likelihood that a given item will be selected? What determines the attractiveness of a given item to the reader?

Leaving out chance, conflicting mental sets, and the qualities of presentation which call attention to one item over others or make one item easier to read than others, we can hypothesize that a person chooses the items which he thinks are likely to give him the greatest reward. The exact yard-stick by which he measures this predictive value is an individual matter based on experience and personality structure, and powerfully influenced by the momentary situation. But in general there seems to be greater expectation of reward when there appears to be greater possibility of the reader identifying himself with the news.

This may be what the textbooks mean by proximity as a news value, but is not to be interpreted as mere physical proximity. For example: a fight in an American city may be physically nearer than a battle in the South Pacific, but if a mother has a son in the battle then how much more easily can she identified herself with the distant battle than with the nearer fight. On the other hand, the American scrap is likely to seem closer to the average reader than a Dutch coup in Indonesia, although one may ultimately have large repercussions for the colonial system and for international trade, whereas the other will doubtless pass out of the realm of important affairs as soon as the participants sober up. Similarly, it is a greater reward to identify oneself with the local team which is winning a championship than with a faraway team that is equally good. One of the startling accomplishments of mass communications has been to bring far comers and faraway people almost next door, so that it becomes relatively easy for a reader to identify himself with the personal affairs of movie stars in Hollywood, and for thousand of sports fans who have never been in South Bend to feel like alumni of Notre Dame. It is also easier to identify oneself with an event which is vividly described and which has a minimum of indirection. But I think it is safe to say that the individual world of the reader will for the most part determine the ease with which he can identify himself with the given team, and this in turn will powerfully affect the probability of the item being read.

Exercise: 1. In which of the following news stories (synopses) would you have a high interest? A low interest?

(a) A prominent clubwoman was biaten and choked to death today by her 15-year-old son, who said she had engaged him ever since he was arrested for trying to chloroform and photograph a girl friend.

(b) The erstwhile Soviet Union threatened to resume testing atomic and hydrogen bombs unless France stops nuclear tests in the Sahara.

(c) An 18-year-old youth was executed today for a murder shot he did not fire-despite a dramatic appeal for his life to the governor.

(d) There's a farmer near here who makes more money selling water than he makes from the eleven oil wells on his farm.

2. Below is a list of twenty reasons that people have assigned for their choosing to read a particular news story. For each of the four news stories above check as many of the reasons as you would apply to the choices you made of the stories you would read (if any) and of the stories you would reject (if any).

(a) This might be amusing.

(b) Somebody should do something about this matter.

(c) This needs explaining.

(d) I know someone who'll want to hear about this.

(e) I dislike such stories.

(f) I'm tired of reading about this.

(g) I know something about this that's not in the papers.

(h) This makes me feel sad.

(i) This will help me keep up with what's going on.

(J) This may affect me personally.

(k) This is disturbing.

(l) I can imagine this happening.

(m) This might be exciting.

(n) This might give me something to talk about.

(o) This is something I should be concerned about.

(p) I always read stories like this, but I don't know why.

(q) This information might be useful to me.

(r) This looks like good news.

(s) I'd like to find out how this happened.

(t) I know how that person must feel.

Audience Type

Merrill Samuelson presented sixteen synopses of news stories (of which the news stories in Exercise I above are representative) to a sample of readers and asked them *(1)* to rank the stories in an order of interest (*i.e.* preference) and *(2)* to apply to each story one or more of the reasons for reading that are listed in Exercise 2 (above). By factor analyzing these data, he was able to differentiate five different types of readers.

One type (D) had high interest scores on such stories as the Soviet. Union's threat to renew bomb testing and very low interest scores on crime stories and the trivia-puzzle type of story such as the one about a farmer making more money selling water than from his eleven oil wells. Moreover, the reasons assigned for the preferences were mainly "The needs explaining" "This may afrect me personally, " and "This is something I should be concerned about. " On the basis of the interest scores and the reasons given, he categorized this type of reader as one who reads mainly for delayed reward.

A second type (A) had high interest scores on many of the same news stories on which Type D readers had high interest scores, but they did not give as many of the same reasons as did the Type D readers. This type of reader, who was more highly educated than the other types, was less involved in the events he preferred to read about than were Type D readers.

The interest scores of a third type (B) and the reasons they assigned enabled the experimenter to categorize them as an immediate reward type of reader. This type preferred the stories that were puzzles and- which supplied a complete and early solution, such as how a youth could be executed for a shot he did not fire and how a farmer could make more money from selling water than from the eleven oil wells. The main reasons this type gave were. This needs explaining," "I'd like to find outhow this happened," and "This gives me something to talk about. " This type of reader is less concerned with the environment he lives in than are Types D and A, and is less interested in the deferred solutions to the long span problems that are inherent in international politics and social problems.

Readers of a fourth type (E) selected both immediate reward and delayed reward kinds of stories, although they had a low preference for crime stories. The main reasons they gave were. "This will help me keep up with what's going on," This needs explaining, "and I' d like to find out how this happened," The main reasons given for rejecting stories (mostly about crime) were. This is disturbing" and "This is something I should be concerned about.

The preferences, rejections, and reasons of a fifth type (C) did not form a pattern that could be explained by the experimenter.

As research into news reading behavior continues we may learn more about the motivation of different types of readers. As the studies presented in this chapter suggest, the explanations are in the personality structure of the individual reader. Researchers need to develop better personality measures that would be appropriate in this area and to include in their studies more questions than have so far been asked.

> **Exercise 1.** How would you categorize each of the stories in Exercise 1 on page 30—as immediate reward or as delayed reward?
>
> 2. An editor to whom you have applied for a job asks you to write an explanation of not more than 150 words on why people choose to read a particular news story and reject a particular news story. Write your explanation.

Reading in a Role

Although the news that one selects to read is determined by his basic personality needs and drives and his life history, it is also related to one or more of his roles in society. As a voter and a taxpayer, the reader is interested in some of the news about government, and newspapers accept an obligation to inform him in that area. As a housewife, a reader is interested in news about prices of consumers goods. As a parent, a reader is interested in news about education and juvenile delinquency. As an investor, a reader is interested in some of the news about business; most investors are forty or more years old and most are men, although an increasing number of women read business news. As a member of some group, a reader is interested in news about that group and about the matters with which the group is concerned for example, religion. Most readers have one or more hobbies for example, sports and bridge and the newspaper cater to their interests. So many people have some community of interest that specialized magazines are published about the interests; the amount of space that a newspaper can devote to each of these special interests, however, is limited.

The same news story is sometimes read by some persons in one role and by other persons in a different role. An example of such a story: "The United States Supreme Court ruled yesterday that natural gas pipeline companies may use a 'short cut' procedure to increase gas rates without consent of their customers. The decision brought a surge in the price of major natural gas stocks on the New York Stock Exchange." Some readers were interested in this story as consumers of natural gas and some as investors in a natural gas pipeline or local gas distributing company. A wire service which reported this decision tied into the decision the effect on the stock market, and a local newspaper tied in an interview with the local gas distributing company which purchased its gas from a pipeline company. The competent newspaper and wire service editor analyzes every event with the view to supplying answers to questions which will come to the mind of readers who will read in different roles.

Some Dimensions of Interest

There have been many definitions of news, but none is quite satisfactory. Perhaps as good a definition as any is that of Turner

Catledge, executive editor of the New York Times: "News is anything you find out today that you didn't know before.

Since, however, a newspaper's capacity for printing news compels it to be selective, an editor needs some kind of guideline or benchmark for estimating what will interest his readers. What he does, therefore, is to look for the presence in each event of certain elements which he believes to be interesting. Although he thinks of a story as being about some subject matter, such as crime, labor, or death, he also looks for an additional dimension which makes the event different from similar events of its class sometimes this element is odd, eccentric, or bizarre, but most often it is merely unusual. Some examples:

> A St. Paul man today shot and killed his second wife,
>
> 12 years after he killed his first wife.
>
> Cancer killed bandleader Jimmy Dorsey, today, less than seven months after the death of his brother Tommy [also a bandleader].

The first story was a crime story about an obscure retired postal employee. The second story not only had a similar unusual element, but it concerned two persons who were well known. Thus, if we were designing some calculus of reader interest, we would say that the second story has three interest elements: *(1)* death, *(2)* well-known person, and *(3)* singularity.

Well-known Persons

When a participant in an event is well known, the event is more news-worthy than when the participant is not well known. Some persons are prominent because of their high status in society and others because of the frequent exposure of their name or face or voice to newspaper readers or television viewers. Personalities on the television screen, for example, become so familiar to the viewers that the viewers come to feel they know them well. The following Associated Press story was well displayed in San Francisco newspaper:

> LAKE SUCCESS, N.Y. — Television personality Arlene Francis suffered a brain concussion yesterday when her convertible went out of control on the Northern State Parkway and collided headon with another car. A woman in the second auto was killed.
>
> Authorities at Harkness Pavilion said she was being treated for a minor concussion, a fracture of the collar bone, a cut on the scalp and bruises.
>
> Miss Francis is a regular panelist on the TV show, "What's Myline?"

The points to be noted in the foregoing story are that injuries to the women were of two different orders but that the orders of prominence were reversed, If neither woman had been prominent, regardless of the order of the injuries, the event would have been a "constant".

Proximity

Readers identify easier when events are near to them. Schramm's defines the nature of news proximity as being psychological, not merely physical. An event that happens in our own community has higher news value than an event that happens a considerable distance away. But, as Schramm said, a mother whose son was in military service in the South Pacific would be more interested in a battle in that area than in a fight in an American city. Readers are also interested in events that happen in places in which they have formerly lived or have visited.

An editor whose newspaper is read by most of the people in his community always assumes that the presence of a local element in any story makes it more interesting than a story in which the local element is absent. Thus, a news story about a fatal automobile accident in another community has a higher news value when one of the persons killed was a resident of the editor's community.

Editors also are alert to "local angles" in wire-service stories. An example; a wire service reported the explosion in Berlin, New York, of a propane gas tank truck which killed two persons and injured fifteen others. This despatch generated a' 'could-this-happen-here story in a California sub-urban newspaper in which local fire marshals and highway patrolmen were quoted as to the California laws which regulate the transportation of propane on highways.

If you should ever work for a wire service, you would learn early in your employment about the importance of the "points" on a wire; a "point" is one of the cities in which a newspaper receives the wire report. Thus, you would include in a story a reference to any person living in any of the communities and any reference to any of the communities. Whenever a wire service correspondent in World War II wrote about some soldier or sailor involved in a military action, he included the name of his city and, when available, his street address.

Other Dimensions of News

Our knowledge of the news value of the two dimensions of interest we have just discussed—well-known persons and proximity is soundly based in psychological theory. Perhaps psychological theory also tells us some—thing about the interest value of certain other kinds of news, such as news about cute children, animals, and money, but we have little objective evidence to support some of the dicta that have been mentioned by textbook writers. Below, however, is a list of about fifty mutually exclusive categories of news elements that were developed for a content analysis, and it might be interesting to speculate about the degrees of interest readers would have in some of them. Only a few are defined here. Keep in mind that each news story is likely to have two or more of these elements. Thus, a particular news story might be classified as "Our Community Crime" or "Persons Well Known Labour". These categories fit only the content of the particular issues of the newspapers which were studied. For an analysis of other newspapers at other times a few of these categories would be dropped and perhaps certain new categories would have to be developed.

Persons Well Known. Persons presumed to be well known to most readers of the particular newspaper because of their fame or notoriety or particular accomplishment.

Persons Not Well Known. Persons in the news because of their particular accomplishments or activities or position, but not well known to the usual reader of the particular newspaper.

People in Groups. Persons in the news because they are officers or committee members of their clubs, lodges, societies, fraternal organizations, Boy Scouts, and other non-govemmental groups; pallbearers, etc.

Hollywood. Persons not otherwise well known who are associated with the Hollywood entertainment industries. Excluded: activities of those persons classified as "Persons Well Known."

Our Community, Our Region. An element with which all members of the newspapers community (or region) identify themselves because of the place of the community in the news item or the effect this news may have on the community.

Our Nation. An element with which almost all readers of United States newspapers might identify themselves as members of this nation.

This does not imply that all events happening within the boundaries of the United States have this element; nor does this element apply only to stories taking place within these boundaries.

Our Allies. During a "cold war" period, some political and economic events in a country formally and informally allied to the United States have a peculiar meaning to an American reader because they are or seem to be related to the security or welfare of the United States. Excluded: news in which American men or equipment are directly I involved or in which the United States interest is directly stated.

Our Enemies. Most politicaland economic events in the Communist controlled nations affect the American reader in a different way than do events in other foreign countries. Such events may be threatening or reassuring.

Other Nations. *(a)* News about happenings in foreign countries other than those mentioned in "Our Nation," "Our Allies," and "Our Enemies." *(b)* Also those happenings in the countries included in "Our Allies" and "Our Enemies" which do not directly or indirectly affect the welfare of the United States.

Governmental Acts	Social and Safety Measures
Politics	Race Relations
Rebellion	Alcohol
War	Money
Defense	Health, Personal
Atomic Bomb-Atomic Energy	Health, Public
Diplomacy and Foreign Relations	Science and Invention
Economic Activity	Religion
Prices	Philanthropy
Taxes	Weather
Labor, Major	Natural Deaths
Labor, Minor	Transportation
Agriculture	Education
Judicial Proceedings, Civil	Children, Welfare of
Crime	Children, Cute
Communism in the U.S.A.	Animals
Sex	Marriage and' Marital
Relations	
Accidents, Disasters	Amusements
First Order	The Arts,—Culture
Second Order	Human Interest
Third Order	

For Class discussion: 1. Which combinations of two or more elements in a news story would speculate would generate the highest interest? The lowest?

2.These news stories evoked tremendous reader interest at the time they were published: Lindbergh's flight across the Atlantic, Gertrude Ederle's successful swimming of the English Channel, and Floyd Collins' entrapment in a Kentucky cave. What common element did they have that evoked so much interest.

SOME KINDS OF NEWS

News may be classified in various ways as to origin, subject matter and treatment. Here are a few kinds of news that get published, this list of categories, however, is not exhaustive.

Chronicle

Much of the news is taken from records in public offices and from reports by police and other officials. It is a kind of news that is easy to get: a newspaper just assigns a reporter to the police station, courthouse, city hall, and federal building.

In small cities, nearly all of this kind of news that is available is published, but in large cities only the news that is important or interesting is selected by editors. Much of this kind of news could be called a , 'consant', because it relates to something the reader has often read before with only the names of the participants being different. Most accidents and crimes are constants. The reaction of readers is often' 'I'm tired of reading about this" or "I always read stories like this, but I don't know why." Some newspapers publish this kind of news only as a record.

Editors would like to cover a wider range of readers' interests than they do but have not developed an adequate technique for finding out about a different kind of news. It is the practice of

London popular newspapers to pay informants for tips about news, but few American newspapers have done that. The Council Bluffs (Iowa) Nonpareil, however, developed a list of persons who often supply tips on "off-beat" news sources. Reporters contact them daily, weekly, or monthly. One example: a story that the federal building was tilting and was scheduled to be demolished; the tip came from an architect.

Sometimes it is possible for the news writer to organize the facts in a chronicle type of news story so that reading the story is emotionally rewarding. One way is to organize the facts in a climatic order when the facts justify that form of news story. Some chronicle type items are highly read.

Background News

In 1922, Walter Lippmann said it was the nature of news to signalize an event; that is, to report (only) some overt act. News, he said, is "but the report of an aspect that has obtruded itself. The news does not tell you how the seed is germinating in the ground, but it may tell you when the first sprout breaks through the surface." Thus, a labour dispute doesn't get reported until there is an overt act, such as a strike, and most white readers could not have been aware of the frustrations and aspirations of Negroes until the Negroes had conducted public demonstrations of protest.

Since Lippmann wrote in 1922, however, newspapers and wire services have been perceiving news as more than just "spot" news. They are reporting facts that may indicate what is going to happen. They are trying to supply more background about over events and the people who participate in some of the events, and they try to report change in society. As students of history know, social change is brought about by new technology and new ideas. Editors are now more habituated to perceiving change and the causes of change as something to be reported—what James B. Reston has called the reporting of "quiet revolutions". Newspapers also are reporting changes in manners and morals.

For Class discussion: 1. What is your evaluation of this statement: "Because of the excellence of our newspapers and magazine Americans are the best informed people in the world"?

2. A competent foreign correspondent who is a Latin America specialist has said that most American editors were surprised by the success of the Castro revolution in Cuba because, instead of publishing the "what's behind the news', kind of news they had been receiving from Cuba, they substituted the more dramatic' "spot", stories received from Cuba and other parts of the world. If this is true, whose fault was it?

"Give Lift" News

Since newspapers report so much news about conflict, most editors would like to report more news about people who exhibit courage, sacrifice, and compassion—news (to paraphrase William Faulkner) which suggests to readers that man's spirit will endure and prevail over the : basic animal drives. Such news gives the reader a "lift" spiritually and suggests to him that we do not live in a jungle world. Here are two examples of such local news stories that the Associated Press thought were worthy of being included in its daily report; the stories were widely used by newspapers.

CHRISTIANS HELP TO REMODEL SYNAGOGUE

LAWRENCE, KAN.—Somewhat to the surprise of the 35 Jewish families in Lawrence and about 80 Jewish students at the University of Kansas, a quiet campaign is going on to raise funds for remodeling the Jewish community center into a synagogue.

"We did not know about it; we did not organize it," said Herman Cohen, president of the community center.

"Who did? Some Christians, One of them, O.O. Ringler, explained the project was started because the Jews are the only religious group in Lawrence with no place to worship. The closest synagogues are in Kansas City and Topeka.

"It gives a person a wonderful feeling to have something like this happen, "said Cohen. "It is a fine thing to have others trying to help us.

KNOW ANYBODY SALVATION ARMY HAS HELPED?

KINGSPORT, TENN.—The newsboy kept walking past the Salvation Army Christmas collection kettle. Each trip he dropped in two cents.

An Exchange Club member, helping man the kettle station, finally figured it out. The 9-year old lad was donating his two cents profit from each paper sale.

Just to be sure, the clubman went up and purchased a paper and gave the boy a nickel tip. A few minutes later the lad was back at the kettle. This time he dropped in seven cents.

"Do you know anybody the Salvation Army has helped?" a club member asked the newsboy.

"Yes, sir. We got a Christmas basket last year," the boy replied.

Wednesday, the Exchange Club had the newsboy as its special guest at a luncheon. He left with a new bicycle, wearing a new jacket, and with a savings account book showing more than $60 on deposit for his future education.

> He was introduced only as Gary. The club said it wanted to publicize the deed rather than the boy and his family.
>
> Salvation Army records showed that Gary is one of five children, aged 2 to 13. The parents have worked irregularly this year with the top income for one month about $57.
>
> Gary's third—grade teacher said he almost never misses a day of school and often shares what he has with some youngster less fortunate than he.

How When, and Where the Newspaper is Read

The newspaper, like the telephone and the automatic washer, is a utility. How, when, and where is it used? A 1961 study has supplied some answers to these questions. The study revealed that readers use their newspapers in these ways:

50.4% Proceed through most of the paper one page after another and read whatever is interesting.

14.2% Proceed through the paper page by page, but scanning quickly:

20.0% Turn first to some specific item (*e.g.* the stock market tables or a particular column) and then proceed through the paper one page after another;

12.6% Turn first to some specific item and then proceed page by page, but scanning quickly;

2.8% Turn to a specific item but do not look at or read anything else.

These findings indicate not only that the newspaper is read rather thoroughly but also that a large majority of readers expose themselves to a synopsis, at least, of everything in the newspaper. This fact explains why some readership studies have turned up news stories on the inside pages which have had higher readership than any story on the front page. The findings are confirmed by the "reader traffic" data obtained from several hundred readership studies: a large majority of readers go clear through the paper; whether they read or do not read something on each page depends upon what is on the pages and the interests of the individual readers. Some readers scan but do not read anything on some pages; for example, some men are not interested in the content of women's pages. The amount of newspaper content that each reader reads is determined by *(1)* his needs and interests and *(2)* the amount of time available to him.

Mental Set

The reader has a different mental set when he reads a newspaper and when he reads a book or magazine. "Reading a book," says Irving Kristol, "is quite a different experience from reading a magazine. The original commitment by the reader is much more substantial. Picking up a book is an affirmation of more serious purposes. "There is also some difference in original commitment in reading a newspaper and reading a news magazine because they are read under different conditions.

For class discussion: Considering the fact *(a)* that the newspaper reader has a different original commitment when he reads opinion and when he reads news and *(b)* that most readers go through the newspaper page by page selecting to read those items that interest them, what is the proper location in the newspaper for the editorial-opinion page?

Ninety percent of readers of a weekday newspaper read it at home, 6 per cent at work, 3 per cent when visiting, and about 2 per cent on their way to or from work. This is a national average; it would not apply, for example, in New York city, where fewer newspapers are home delivered.

The average weekday newspaper is read at different times of the day. It is picked up and looked at 2.4 different times by each individual reader. The study which reported this finding also reported that the average reader spent 36 minutes a day reading his newspaper;

this is a self-estimate and is about the same self-estimate reported in previous studies.

The editor tries to produce a newspaper that will maximize the time a reader will devote to it. Nevertheless, the amount of time that a reader allocates to newspaper reading is determined, to some extent, by the readers individual living habits, such as the time he or she gets up in the morning, the time the children leave for school, the time the housewife does her marketing, and several other reasons.

The following tablets shows when people read a newspaper, listen to news on the radio, and watch television news:

	Real Newspaper	***Listen to Radio News***	***Watch TV News***
Early morning............	16%	25%	3%
Late morning..............	12	8	1
Midday......................	1	18	1
Early afternoon..........	7	5	3
Late afternoon............	21	9	3
Early evening.............	20	12	17
Late evening	20	12	17
Other, not specified.....	2	3	0
	87%	85%	45%

The table indicates that more people listen to news on the radio before nine O'clock in the morning than read a newspaper before that time. It also indicates that fewer people get their news from television than from the newspaper or radio. When respondents in this sample were asked, , 'Where do you usually get the news of the day first?' their answers were: radio, 52 percent; newspapers, 28 percent; television. 17 per cent; "can't say," 3 per cent.

THE QUALITIES OF NEWS

In modern journalism the way news is written is nearly as important as the news itself. The, easiest way to acquire "the nose for news" and develop the sense of "news value" is to "study" the news columns of standar9 newspapers and endeavour to understand the points emphasized by newsmen and the position allotted to the news story.

Proximity, *i.e.* nearness, plays a dominant part. The person who glances over a report that an earthquake in Agadir swept property worth millions and dragged hundreds to their instant graves under debris or skims a story saying that hundreds of Nationalists were killed in Algiers, is sure to jump with rapt altention to learn more and more when informed of his neighbour's involvement in an accident in the main street. The impact of propinquity in such cases is crystal clear. The events "nearest" are the most important ones in he world to every human being irrespective of caste, colour, creed and other considerations.

Sex is one of the most powerful qualities in news. It enters frequently in news stories of romances, wedlocks, separations mysterious suicidal cases, and sometimes murders. Experience indicates that the relations of men and women and their, eccentricities from a substantially heavy percentage of the news chosen for publication under the pretext of "human interest" material. The conflict and consequence of the influence of sex date back perhaps to the moment Adam, incited by Eve, ate the forbidden fruit.

Emotional appeal in the news is called the "human interest". An account with any strong feeling, as contrasted with straight news, is called the human interest story. Generally, such stories are either composed in bold face types or framed with ornamental types and "boxed" from four sides and branded as "box" stories. These are those stories in which interest is created in individuals about certain unusual happenings. Here, are examples of short, to-the-point readable newspaper reports which depict the determinants of human-interest stories:

A police official, it is reported, has been taken into custody in Jorhat for, it is alleged, picking a person's pocket. He is alleged to have stolen Rs. 1,000 from a man who went to deposit money in the State Bank—Statesman, Calcutta.

The Anti-corruption and Prohibition Intelligence Bureau of Maharashtra on Monday raided the Central Railway Police Station in Bombay and found four policemen drinking liquor—Indian 'Express, Bombay.

A huge pack of old records hurtled down—from a rack over a clerk seated at his table and sent him to his death in an office at Jamnagar. The clerk lay buried underneath the mass of records for some time until he was extricated by the emergency police who had been summoned for assistance.

The victim, who was immediately rushed to hospital, died shortly after his admission—Indian Express, Bombay.

Hundreds of dropping women voters, queueing up in ling lines under the burning mid-day sun in a South Madras polling booth, went thirsty as water cups were snatched away from their parched lips.

Strange but time, it happened when a candidate raised an objection that distribution of drinking water amounted to canvassing.

The polling authorities took immediate steps to stop distribution of water to voters-Sunday Standard, Chittoor.

A 125-pound defendant in a divorce suit in Des Moines, Iowa, U.S., described his wife as a "250-pound battleship", but denied that he had willingly deserted her.

Instead, he explained in a written answer to her divorce petition, he was "glad to get away from her" because the defendant is small and an individual of not great physical strength. The plaintiff is a female of great physical strength, violent temper and a prize fighter of the first rank who gave the defendant two severe beatings before he, recognising that discretion was the best part of valour, took himself away to preserve his own health, physical safety, and mental order The Hindu, Madras.

A young women has refused to recognise as her husband the man who claimed her as his wife, because he had no beard.

The man lodged a complaint that his wife deserted him, and that he wanted to keep her.

The woman told the Jammu Magistrate that when they were separated her husband was a Sikh youth with a beard. The man standing in the court and claiming her, she said, was clean-shaven.

The claimant said that he was a Sikh but had shaved off his beard recently.

Asked by the court to recognise her husband, the woman pointed out another man standing in the court and said: "He should be my husband"—Samachar, Mysore.

Analysis of these stories reveals that there is reader-interest in lives and welfare of others. The contents of perfect human-interest stories are age, animal, sex, conflict, money, children, beauty, combat, suspense, personal appeal, and sympathy.

METHOD OF WRITING NEWSPAPER STORY

The newspaper story in Modern Society has evolved to meet the requirements of everyday life as lived by everyday readers. It relies on the elements of novelty, directness, pace and variety, and it strives to convey its information in the form most in keeping with the tempo of our times. It aims to state its facts quickly and clearly.

A News Story has Three Parts

We can divide the newspaper story as it strikes our eye on the newspaper page into three parts:

(i) The headline;

(ii) The first paragraph;

(iii) The remainder of the story.

The headline first attracts us. It stands out in bold black type. Its message is terse, abrupt and often startling. It makes us stop and look. It tells us quickly what the story covers. Its primary function is to attract our attention. It corresponds to the beat of the drum outside the street show. But we will not consider the nimble art of headline writing here. As we have seen, headine writing belongs to the copyreader's province and not to the reporter's.

The First Paragraph or Lead. It would be difficult to overstate the importance of the opening paragraph or lead. Always this lead remains the primary concern of the newspaper writer. In any form of writing the writer tries to put his best food foremost. In journalistic writing this first stride has unique importance.

Because the present day reader resembles the man who both runs and reads; present day newspapers seek to facilitate his getting his information quickly. The convention has developed of telling the main facts of a news story in its first lead paragraph. Read any modern newspaper today and you will find that by glancing at the headlines and through each lead you get, substantially, all the important news, although you may miss many interesting details.

This convention requires that in the 'lead the reporter answers the questions which would occur to any normal person when confronted with'the announcement of an event. These Questions, called the five W's are:

Who?

What?

When?

Where?

Why?

and How?

Suppose the news story concerns a fire. In writing his lead- the reporter would answer the question, 'What?' "Fire broke out" he would write. He would answer the question, 'Who?' and 'Where?' by telling whose premises were burnt and giving their location. He would answer 'When' by telling the time the fire broke out and how long it lasted. 'Why?'—in this case the cause, the usual carelessly tossed cigarette butt. Our reporter can answer the 'How' in this story in several ways by describing the type of fire, "flames fanned by a stiff breeze", or by answering 'How much?' Here, he would estimate the probable financial lost and find out if premises had been covered by insurance and if so by what amount.

This simple illustration shows some of the things which a good lead is required to do. It summarises the story for the reader. It identifies the persons concerned. In this case it gives the full name of the owner of the premises and the address of his property. It fixes the locale of the story. It gives the reader the latest available—information in this case probably the extent of the damage. Yet so far, it has neglected another very important function of the lead. It has failed so far to stress the story's news "feature".

THE NEWS FEATURE OF A STORY

What is a story's news feature? It is that angle or twist which differentiates the story from what. may be called a run-of-the-mill item. Blazes of this kind unfortunately happen everywhere, everyday. But, suppose the burnt premises temporarily housed important works of art which likewise went up in smoke and were lost to the world: or suppose the building was the property of some well known person, a statesman, a business magnate, a prominent public figure; or suppose, again the next door to the burning premises stood a cinema building, crowded at the time by people unaware of the danger. Each of these suppositions would satisfy the story's news feature. Each would supply the necessary element of uniqueness.

But whether it be run-of-the-mill or outstanding in its impact, the lead should cover the story's essential facts. The city editor enunciated the alpha and omega of the craft when he shouted to his inquiring cub reporter:

"Spill the whole story in the first paragraph, and maintain the interest for the rest of the column".

The best-written lead not only satisfies the reader's initial curiosity, but wets his appetite to read more, Summing up, we may say then that the newspaper writer must see to it that his lead does five things: presents a summary of the story; identifies the persons and the place concerned; stresses the news feature; gives the latest news of the event; and, if possible, stimulates the reader to continue the story, And. the present day tendency is to achieve all this as quickly and as briefly as possible.

Rudolf Flesch, a consultant on readability to the Associated Press, insists that the traditional Who, What, When, Where and Why lead is antique. However, a great many antique,traditions still persist. Nevertheless, newspapers have been stimulated by the radio and television newscasts and also by the newspaper reports in this traditional technique with success.

A reporter may write his lead in a variety of forms. Editors welcome originality. Several types, however, have proved their readability, and have become almost standardised.

MAIN TYPES OF LEADS

(a) The Digest Lead. This lead summarises clearly and plainly all the principal facts. It remains the simplest in construction and forms a basic part of all lead variations. The typical news item or dispatch starts off with the digest or summary lead. The following is a fair example:

> London, Jan. 23—A silver cup nearly two feet high, standing on a bar at the Olympia Exhibition Hall here, awaits the winner as 375 bartenders from all over the world submit their prize original cocktail formulas in a contest for the world's championship that began today.

(b) The Direct Appeal Lead. This form borrows the interest compelling device of the personal letter. It addresses the reader directly or by implication as "you", and has the effect of making the reader a collaborator in what follows. It often begins with such phrases as "If you have .ever thought,", or "If you have ever seen or read". Here is a typical direct appeal lead:

> If you think you've got it tough when you have to listen to your little sister practice the piano, take pity on Alfred Jay Smith. In the last 30 years he's had to audition 20,500 child performers. And he likes his job.

(c) The Circumstantial Lead. Here we have a beginning which stresses the circumstances under which the story happened. It crops up usefully when the story has a human interest slant:

> Chester, Pa, Feb. 20—The cries of a pet cat into the mouthpiece of a telephone at a house in West Third Street today brought out a detachment of police and plain-clothes men bent on frustrating a burglary and possibly saving a life.
>
> A telephone operator at the central exchange called the police department and informed the desk seargent that cries of distress. were coming from the telephone -at the Third Street house. A patrol wagon full of policemen was hurried to the scene and they surrounded the house. Repeated knocks at the door brought no answer and they forced an entrance.
>
> They found the cat with one of its feet caught in an ice chest. In its struggles to get free it had knocked the receiver from the telephone, which was lying on the floor, and it was crying into the mouthpiece. The family was away.
>
> —Associated Press of America

Here is another circumstantial-type lead. Although' the body of the story is about a fatal auto crash in which two of the five sisters were killed, the emphasis in the lead is placed on the circumstances which lead up to the accident-the heart attack of the driver. Without this—emphasis on circumstances under which the story happened, it would have been just another "run-of-the-mill" account of an auto accident.

> A heart attack suffered by Mrs. Mary White 60 of 5 East 37th Street, Waverly, was believed by the police today to have caused her to lose control of her car in Cedar Village last night with resultant death for herself and one of the four elderly sisters who were with her. The three remaining sisters suffered severe hurts.

(d) The Statement or Quotation Lead. This type of lead starts out with an enunciation which, as often as not, occurs in quotation marks. In speech reporting particularly, a succinct, epigrammatic sentence often puts in capsule form the gist of the speaker's idea. When the reporter has added to this the inevitable five W's, the resulting paragraph coincides with the digest or summary lead.

> A "large percentage" of the persons 60 years of age in state mental institutions "do not belong there", Abraham Cohen of the Mayor's Advisory Committee for the Aged declared yesterday. He spoke at a plaque-dedication ceremony at the Walter S. James Community Cencer for the Aged, 23-12 Second Avenue.

(e) The Descriptive Lead. This form of beginning presents a picture. The reporter may set the stage for the action of his story or he may present in detail one or more of his chief actors. In other words, this lead can describe the scene or it can describe one or more of the people involved.

> Dressed in similar grey gabardine coats and grey fedoras and wearing false rubber noses attached to lenseless spectacles three armed young thugs invaded the third-floor offices of the Anderson

> Jewellery Company, 24 Main Street, Beverly, early yesterday afternoon, held up seven persons and escaped With £ 5920 in cash.

(f) The Suspended Interest Lead. This type of lead serves as a stimulator of interest. It gives the reader enough information to whet his appetite, and no more. After the lead, the story usually runs along in chronological form, so that the reader must read to the very end to get at the climax. Reporters use this type of lead chiefly for short bits, on the theory that if used on longer articles, readers would not bother to wade through paragraph after paragraph. Here is a typical suspended interest lead, used in a typical way:

The quick action of John Lowell, a baker, probably saved this city of 16,290 inhabitants from disaster today.

At 4 P. M. he noticed that the gas flames in his bread ovens had flickered out. Ten minutes later gas again hissed through the pipes, unlighted.

Lowell reasoned that many unattended gas appliances in the slumbering city might be pouring unburnt gas into homes and apartments. He called Fire Chief Charles Albert.

> Fire trucks, police cars and ambulances sped through the darkened streets, sirens screaming. A shield truck blared, "Check your gas Check your gas." Chief Albert said that the cacophony which woke the population saved many lives as his men found about 200 gas-filled homes and he personally awakened "at least fifty" groggy citizens. No one was overcome.

The light and heat company serving the area laid the gas interruption in an air pocket in the lines.

(g) Various "Stunt" Leads. All editors put a premium on novelty, and some even on the bizarre. Accordingly a variety of what we can call exclamation point leads crop up from time to time and have been dubbed, "astonisher", "punch" and "teaser" as the case may be—Originally one knows no pigeonhole and refuses the standardisation of definition beyond the generalisation that such leads are eccentric variations from the norm. When successful, a stunt lead has its own reward:

Bertram Walker today had a fishing table to top them all. Out of the icy, wind-hiped waters of La Crosse Channel, Centralia, yesterday, he caught a man-an all-weather swimmer who had been floundering in the fastrunning ebbtide.

> Robert Jackson, 57, a 170-pound hop carrier of 122 Manchester Street, North Port, was losing his fight against the currents when the fishermen heard his cries for help, uncorked a 50 yard bull's eye cast, "hooked" the swimmer and reeled him to safety.

Mr. Jackson was released after treatment at St. Mary's Hospital, Centralia, for exposure, submersion, cuts and bruises.

Mr. Walker, an electrical engineer for the Calco Engineering Company, went back to his fishing.

(h) The Tabulated Lead. Occasionally one runs into a story in which no one fact is-prominent. Each facet of interest has about the same value. In such instances, a practice has grown up of tabulating each item in the lead-one, two, three, four.

> A major scandal bas erupted in the 3rd Internal Revenue District, the World-Telegram learned exclusively today. It involves:

1. Suspension of a five-man "fraud squad" suspected of shaking down 12 firms for $50,000 to cover up income-tax discrepancies.

2. Implication of a high city official who is a Tammany stalwart.

3. Exhaustive investigation by intelligence agents of the Treasury Department. Their findings have been turned over to U. S. Attorney,

F. X. McGahey's criminal division for presentation to a grand jury. -N. Y. World-Telegram.

STEP-BY-STEP CONCLUSION

We start the normal story at its beginning and trace it step by step to its conclusion. The newspaper convention of the lead, however, makes the news story an exception to this general rule. This lead demands that in most instances the news story begin with its climax. Two reasons lie behind this formula: the desire to catch the reader's attention; the desire to save the reader's time.

The lead forms the springboard for the reporter's leap into the story. From a springboard wholly adequate, he can make a graceful dive; from one even partially defective, he may sadly flop. Often the impetus given by a successful lead carries him with fine tempo and gusto into the remaining paragraphs. Sometimes when fumbled over, the lead throws a disheartening shadow ahead.

This lead business makes even the practiced journalist pause. While covering a story he carries in the back of his mind the consciousness that a suitable beginning for the story must somehow evolve within him. He keeps on the watch for the element or those elements in the assignment which would make a good lead. A feeling of rare content creeps over him when he tucks the sought-for start away in his mind for eventual use; The best way to gain journalistic facility is to practice the writing of leads.

THE REMAINDER OF THE STORY

From the headline and 'the lead we come to the rest of the story. The reporter constructs the model news story after this pattern. He selects the most important incident or fact for his lead. Then he proceeds by selecting the next most important incident, fact or detail; then the next/important; the next important after that, and so on till he reaches least important phase of all. Guided by his idea of news importance, the story assumes graphically the shape of an inverted pyramid. To the most important element of the story, the reporter has given the greatest space and prominence. To the next most important he gives somewhat less prominence and space, so on down the story. He ends up at the apear of the inverted pyramid with the facts or incidents of least value.

Obviously, he can best shorten his story by cutting off the last paragraph. Herein rests the technique's chief virtue from the makeup editor's point of view. Most papers receive far more news than they have space to publish. Stories must often undergo a last minute shortening if important late news demands inclusion. The make-up editor knows that he can slice one, two or three paragraphs off any story written in this inverted pyramid form without depriving the reader of the story's chief new element.

The newspaper uses the word "story" as an omnibus term to cover all the items it publishes. Many of these articles are not stories at all in the sense that they have no narrative quality. Probably, an analysis of today's newspaper would show that it contained more exposition, interpretation and opinion than narrative. We may find that the greater part of the news articles have to deal with new Government policies that the paper strives to make clear; new judicial decisions the significance of which the paper attempts to indicate' new-scientific theories and inventions that call for explanation. For the majority of these articles, the paper will full back on the standard inverted pyramid form. In some instances it happens that all sections of the interpretation have equal value and importance. Here, we find no tapering off to an apex and no building up in time sequence. These interpretive stories fall into a graphic pattern of rectangular arrangement of equal sections.

The Final Shape

Back to his typewriter with his notes, the reporter starts to build his story. He already knows, because he has covered it whether his story will be exposition and interpretation or a chronicle of what happened.

If his Job is to explain, he knows from experience that all exposition calls for a definite plan, and that the time he now spends on making an outline will be more than saved when he starts to write.

Clarity is the goal at which all explanation aims. No matter how detailed or learned the explanation may be, if it leaves the reader muddled and puzzled, it has failed. The only way to avoid a confused story is to make a plan.

Suppose the writer's assignment calls for the explanation of a process. How will he construct his plan? First, he educates himself. He clarifies the whole process in his own understanding; mentally he takes the whole process apart and then reconstructs it. Only when he knows what it is all about himself, is he ready to start. First he considers the lead which must contain the news or the process alongwith any attention-getting devices the may have in his repertory. Then step by step, as he puts the process together in his own mind, he outlines it for the reader.

If on the other hand, his story is a typical news narrative, he knows the ingredients that go to make it interesting. He knows that it consists of the "and then" or story element, of description and a certain amount of suspense. The descriptive element comes logically enough into an narrative. The reader wants help in visualising the scene beyond the precise geographical location. Conversation too enters as a logical constituent of a story which deals with people other than deaf mutes. The reporter sees that this conversation can sometimes help him with his description, but he must realise that the best conversation actually steps in only to help the action along. He injects suspense by delaying the point of climax of his story as long as possible.

❐

3

Lead and News Supply

The beginning of the news story is called the lead or intro. For many years the beginning was a formless, rambling sentence or combination of sentences that led up to the account of the event. Here is an example from the report of a national political convention:

> This, the last day of the Republican jubilee, dawned as bright as the prospects of the great party of freedom, and remained throughout one of those days of brilliant sunshine which are set a long intervals as are the diadems in the early Summer. As on the previous day, the streets were crowded at an early hour with surging crowds.

The Summary Lead

Some time after the Civil War a definite from developed which summarized the what, who, when and where of the reported event.

It has been stated that the summary form of lead originated during the Civil War; that, because of the unreliability of the telegraphic services, some war reporters adopted the procedure of reporting a battle by sending a brief summary followed by a detailed elaboration. Their reasoning was that the summary would reach the newspaper speedily even though the more lengthy "body" of the story might be delayed.

We find the summary lead being used in the eighteen-eighties, first by wire services and later by local reporters. This way of reporting news had a particular advantage, in the opinion of Melville

E. Stone, the first general manager of the Associated Press: it virtually assured objectivity in reporting because it restricted the writer to the what-who-when-where formula. Since the Associated Press supplied news reports to newspapers supporting both political parties, Mr. Stone believed the Associated Press should establish a reputation for reliable factual reporting even though some inherently interesting events had to be reported in a colorless manner. This form also permitted a newspaper to eliminate all or a part of the body of an Associated Press dispatch.

The advent of the spoken radio newscast influenced newspapers to abandon the practice of having a summary lead for all news stories. Summary lead are still used for most routine news stories, but news writers now often write in the way that people talk. If a person talked in the way that some summary leads are written, lie would sound as if he was out of breath. The comprehension of the reader of a long lead is about the same as the comprehension of a listener to such a lead. A listener, in most circumstances, has the opportunity of interrupting a speaker with questions and of asking him to repeat all or a part of his narrative. Since a newspaper reader cannot employ this "feedback" he must regress in his reading. This is frustrating, and it sometimes causes the reader to abandon his reading of a news story just as he would turn the dial on his radio.

Length of the Lead Sentence

It is important for comprehension that the first sentence of the news story be fairly short. An easily comprehensible sentence has the effect of drawing the reader into the story of inducing him to continue reading. The average number of words in the first sentence of the Associated Press A-wire report is 23 words; Since the Associated Press makes a strong effort to achieve ease of reading, this score may be regarded as a suitable par for the local news writer.

The writer should summarize as much as possible in the first sentence without letting it be too long. In some instances he has to sacrifice; brevity to include a key fact, but he should try for brevity. The way he achieves this goal is by *distributing* some of the *Ws* in the first two or three sentences instead of including all of them in the first sentence. Here are two ways of reporting the filing of a damage suit:

> Irving Loring, 40, of 268 Brucker street, a passenger in a sports convertible that toppled off a Shoreline highway cliff last March 24, filed a $200,000 damage suit in superior court yesterday against the driver, Walter Patterson.
>
> Loring, a credit manager for a wholesale liquor company, alleges that Patterson, 22, of Piedmont, drove the car at a "wanton and reckless rate of speed" and was under the influence of intoxicants at the time the car went off the cliff.
>
> Loring says he suffered severe face and skull injuries that required 140 stitches.

As Rewritten:

What — A passenger in a car that toppled off a Shoreline highway cliff last March 24 sued the driver yesterday for $200,000 damages.

Who — Irving Loring of 268 Brucker street, a credit manager for a wholesale liquor company, alleged his facial and skull injuries required 140 stitches.

Where — In a complaint filed in superior court, he charged that the driver, Walter Patterson, 22 of Piedmont, was under the influence of intoxicants.

Why — He also alleged that Patterson was driving at "Wanton and reckless rate of speed."

The second version of this report is more easily comprehended because *(1)* the number of words in the first sentence is only 19 instead of the 33 words in the first version, and *(2)* most of the *Ws* are distributed through the first three paragraphs. Since the names of the principals are not well known, they are referred to as "passenger" and "driver" in the first sentence so that the reader understands the "what" without having to think about who they are while he is reading the first sentence. He may continue reading to find out whether or not the principals are persons he knows or has heard about. The first sentence in the second version also corresponds more closely to the way one person would tell another person about the event.

> Exercise: Rewrite this lead: "An early transfer of between 200 and 300 flights daily from the traffic jam at Chicago's O' Hare International Airport to Midway Airport on the southside was recommended yesterday by John E. Egan, former alderman from the Midway ward [13th] and for 17 years chairman of the city council aviation committee. Egan now is a sanitary district trustee."

Purposes of the Lead

The lead has three objectives. Whether a writer tries too achieve all three of them door only one or two depends upon the character of the event. The objectives are *(1)* to tell the gist, or substance, of the event, *(2)* to draw the reader into the story, and *(3)* to cause the reader to see the event.

Stating the Substance of The Event

Before a reporter or dictates a story he decides which aspect of the event to put in the lead. This decision is sometimes called "playing the feature" or "playing up the angle."

When the action reported has been completed it is often possible for the lead to be a single sentence.

> A juror in a burglary trial was himself arrested yesterday.

> A new way of producing atomic energy without either uranium or million-degree heat was announced today.

> "Go ahead and smoke-moderately", is the recommendation of Dr. William A Reinhoff, noted Baltimore surgeon, who discounts the idea that smoking causes lung cancer.

Multiple "Whats"

In some events the news writer perceives two aspects to feature. The second of these is an aspect that adds interest to the report.

> A labourer was sentenced yesterday to pay a $150 fine for stealing three chunks of copper worth $65 from a University laboratory.

> The State of New Jersey, which spent $1,200,000 to capture and convict Bruno Richard Hauptmann, executed him tonight with a penny's worth of electricity.

Some "whats" are so routine that they are barely newsworthy, but some circumstance, when added, may enhance interest in the report. An example: a woman sued an automobile driver for injuries she received when she dashed into the street to rescue her small son from the path of the car. She lost her suit for damages. One reporter wrote the lead this way:

> A verdict in favor of Samuel Howell, charged with negligence when his automobile struck Mrs. Nancy Farlow, was brought in by a circuit court jury yesterday.

Another Reporter's Lead Was:

> A mother, who was injured while trying to save her 4 year old son from the path of an automobile,

> was denied damages by a circuit court jury yesterday.

Not a great many readers of the first version would continue after reading the lead sentence unless they knew one of the principals. But a very large number of readers would continue reading the second version to get an answer to the "why".

Here is an example of a news story that left out of the lead an essential part of the "what":

> A Jonesboro man today sued the Universal Oil Co. and its employee, Ira Thompson, for injuries received in an automobile accident last November 6.
>
> The complaint, asking $10,000 damages, was filed in circuit court by Madison Wilson. He alleges Thompson was driving the company's car.

What is the "what"? Was this an accident in which two cars collided? Since it was not that kind of accident, the writer had to write a third paragraph to tell all of the "what." A better lead would have been:

> A Jonesboro pedestrian sued the Universal Oil Co. and its employee, Ira Thompson, today for $10,000.
>
> Madison Wilson filed the complaint in circuit court alleging he was struck by a company car driven by Thompson last November 6.

The second version is seven lines shorter than the first version. Since the key word' 'pedestrian', was the second word in the lead sentence the reader knew at once the nature of the event.

The effect of an action or an event is sometimes the principal 'what' in a lead.

Pedro Lopez, alias Peter De Lucci, age 34, entered the home of J.F. Foderer, 1548 Howard street, on January 19 (according to his own testimony) at about 5:20p.m., and stole a radio and some jewellry. He aided the police in recovering the loot. His attorney was Percy Jackson and the assistant district attorney was I.D. Matteis. Lopez was born in Puerto Rico. He had served two terms in San Quentin reformatory.

Burglary after sunset constitutes first degree burglary. Second degree burglary is burglary during daylight. Lopez was tried yesterday in superior court presided over by Judge Aylett Cotton. If he had been convicted of first degree burglary, he would automatically, under the statutes, have been a third offender and his sentence would have been 12 years to life. Second degree burglary carries a sentence of one to five years. Judge Cotton ruled that Lopez committed the burglary in daylight although the prosecutor conjectured that Lopez would certainly have been seen carrying away property in daylight. Sunset, it was stipulated in the evidence was 5:42 o'clock. The defendant was convicted of second degree burglary and sentenced to San Quentin for one to five years.

In the type of news story which reports changes, innovations, and developments in society, industry, education and other spheres of life, the best lead is often one of the concrete instances or examples of the matter being reported. The beginning of such a news story also, as a rule, presents a scene or a person doing some act or talking.

> LUBBOCK. Texas—Thousands of white-faced cattle with round, sad eyes and unsophisticated tastes nose about in long troughs filled with a green, flaky concoction.
>
> Nearby, workmen are finishing off a new 25,000 squarefoot meat-packing plant scheduled to begin handling 400 head of cattle a day next month.
>
> "We can do as good a cattle feeding job here as anybody in the Corn Belt—and do it cheaper,"

> boasts sportshirted Durward W. Lewter, part owner of Lewter, Inc.'s feed lot and packing plant here.
>
> "We have our choice of the best cattle here. We're in the heart of the grain sorghum area with its cheap feed. And right at hand is the cotton that supplies us with the meal and hulls for feed supplements."
>
> A Change on the Range Mr. Lewter's words sum up some of the reasons for a quiet but significant change taking place today on the western range lands—a change that already is having an economic impact in these parts and one that's likely to have increasingly wide repercussions on traditional patterns of raising and marketing beef cattle.
>
> Historically, cattlemen in the range lands stretching through New Mexico, west Texas, Okfahoma, western Kansas and Colorado have shipped most of their herds to other areas, principally the Midwest, for fattening on corn before they were sent to market. *(Wall Street Journal).*

Drawing the Reader into the Story

There are several ways of writing the lead sentence that induce the reader to continue his reading. One of them was mentioned before, *viz.*, generating surprise by adding an antithetic element to cause the reader to learn the "why." A somewhat similar device is the question lead. It prepares the reader to make a response in somewhat the way he is prepared to respond when personally addressed in a face-to-face relationship.

> Who should pay for the proposed addition to the Community Hospital—patients who would pay higher room charges or city taxpayers?

> The City Council will discuss this question tonight after it has received a report from a citizens' committee.

A lead which is a direct address to the reader—a "you" lead—is also calculated to induce the reader to continue reading because itinvolves him to some degree.

> If you've recently had a baby, bought a car, or moved, chances are your name is for sale.
>
> It's worth from a penny to a dollar in the expanding. market for mailing lists of people with special interests or needs.
>
> Such lists are purchased by advertisers from firms that cull names and addresses of potential customers from public records, newspapers, subscription rolls and other sources.

The quote lead. Beginning the story with a quotation is, in most instances, disapproved. The reason is that readers are mainly interested in action, not talk. Quotation may repel the reader instead of drawing him into the story. In some circumstances, however, a quotation can draw the reader into the story when the question is very brief. One instance is when it is a part of the gist of the story.

> "Under no conditions."
>
> That was Governor Cox's answer yesterday when asked whether he might change his mind and accept the Republican nomination for Vice President.

A quote lead is sometimes a good way to introduce a personal experience story.

> "My fingers were raw. We figured thatit we could hang on by morning, someone would find us."

"I kept hold trigger till no noise. Then saw blood."

So Takao Phillyaw, Japanese-born widow, explained how she killed her husband's cousin at her east side apartment last night.

When there is no other way to put people into a dull story a quote lead may draw the reader into the story. Reports of meetings of the city council, the planning commission, and the school board are often reported without a single name's being mentioned. The news story reports only the actions taken, and the action relate only to inanimate objects and abstract matters such as proposals, plans, and taxes. The reader is not able to visualize the proceedings. Here are two versions of a report of a planning commission meeting; the main difference is that a single quotation in the body of the first story has been transposed to the lead in the second.

80-FOOT DOME
SHOPPING CENTRE
PLAN PUT OFF

Action on a proposed hemispherical, 80-foot high, $550,000 shopping centre for Alto was postponed yesterday by the Country Planning Commission pending notification of nearby residents of the height of the building.

Samuel Nelder, Tiburon Peninsula property owner, had requested a use permit and architectural supervision for the shopping center on eight acres on both sides of Belvedere drive between Reed boulevard and Highway 101.

Architect John S. Bolles has planned an 80-foot high "geodesic dome" of aluminium.

"Isn't anyone objecting to the height of the building?" asked Commissioner Felix M. Warburg.

RD. Dobbs, principal planner, explained that the height was not mentioned in the notice to property owners.

Planning Director Mary Summers' pointed out that a country ordinance limits buildings to 45 feet in height unless a variance is granted.

"Isn't anyone objecting to the height of the building?" asked Country Planning Commissioner Felix M. Warburg yesterday.

The commission was considering Samuel Neider's application for a use permit and architectural supervision for construction of a 80-foot high "geodesic dome" of aluminium for his $550,000 eight-acre shopping center.

The commission decided to postpone action pending notification of nearby residents about the proposed height.

The dome was recommended by architect John S. Boles. The property is on both sides of Belvedere drive between Reed boulevard and Highway 101.

RD. Dobbs, principal planner, explained that the height was not mentioned in the notice to property owners.

Planning Director, Mary Summers pointed out that a county ordinance limits buildings to 45 feet in height unless a variance is granted.

For class discussion: Which version of the foregoing news story do you prefer, considering that the action taken by the commission was reported in the third paragraph of the second version?

There tends to be an overuse of quotation marks in both the lead and the body of news stories. Words and expressions carry unnecessary quotation marks.

> The Governor today characterized as "inaccurate" the legislative counsel's report on dividend tax withholding.

The main purposes of quotation marks in the lead are to indicate exact language, to set off an obvious error, a nickname, and a slang expression.

Conversion of a lengthy quotation in the lead to indirect quotation often facilitates comprehension.

This lead was written from a "handout":

> DETROIT—The United Auto Workers Union today announced a new collective bargaining programme for next year, which, it said, "features a division of profits above ten per cent on net capital before taxes between the corporate executives and the stock-holders; the workers and consumers.

As Rewritten:

> DETROIT—The United Auto Workers Union today called for a profit-sharing plan in next year's wage contracts, and postponed demands for a shorter work week.

Some Pitfalls

A few statements may be made about what do avoid in writing the lead.

1. A void the Say-Nothing Lead.

> Stanford University research scientists announced today they have uncovered surprising new information about the neutron, one of the small particles which make up the atom.

As Rewritten:

> Stanford University scientists plucked a secret from the heart of the atom today. They found a way to measure the size of neutrons—a key that may open doors to other mysteries of the atom age.

An empty lead sometimes results from the writer's abortive effort to introduce some kind of image into his reporting of a fact.

> With aplomb despite a hair disarranging wind, Mrs. Lyndon B. Johnson christened an 11,000 ton ship today. But because of the weather, the big cargoliner had to stay where it was.

A former editor of the London Daily Express wrote in his memoirs:

I saw the MS. of a reporter's story about Mr. Churchill's meeting at Woodford last night. It opened with an amusing incident about the electric lights failing. But, of course, it was a most important speech and the introductory angle was wrong. In fact, it sacrificed the substance for the shadow. It was rather like saying "Nibbling an olive and holding a glass of vodka in his hand, Stalin declared war on Britain last night."

2. A void The Cluttered Lead. Too many names and too many facts are sometimes crammed into the lead sentence. This can be avoided by distributing some of the names and some of the modifiers of the essential elements in succeeding sentences and paragraphs. One idea in the lead sentence is about all the reader can comprehend easily. Nevertheless, necessary qualifications that are omitted result in an over generalization that can mislead the reader.

> Charles F. Noyes Co., Inc., through Herbert C. Born, vice president, in a $350,000 transaction, has leased for Emily S. Geyer to Ninth Federal Savings and Loan Assn. of New York City, one of the largest in the nation with its main offices at Broadway and 42nd street, the property at the north-west comer of First avenue and 45th street, directly opposite the United Nations development a plot of 4,800 square feet, fronting 40 feet on First avenue, and 100 feet on 45th street, for a long term of years with options of renewal, on which the buildings are being demolished, as a location for its first branch office.

Exercise: The foregoing news story is an unedited handout that was published in the real estate section of a New York newspaper. Rewrite it for an a verage sentence length of 21-25 words.

A second example which was not a handout:

The Bridges trial jury was excused over the Thanks giving week-end to day as defense counsel Vincent Hallinan, supposedly chastised by a six month's contempt sentence, nevertheless raised a dispute over prior Communist hearings that provoked a day of argument.

Overstuffing the lead sentence may often be avoided by making two sentences of the lead paragraph.

> A 21-year old reformatory parolee, who said he wanted to "point up in equalities of the parole system, " set fire to a newspaper pressroom and fired a shotgun blast in a radio station last night.

As Rewritten:

A youth on parole from a reformatory set fire to a newspaper pressroom and invaded a radio station with a shotgun last night.

He said he wanted to "point up in equalities in the parole system."

3. The Lead Sentence should not Present a False Tone for the News Story. The lead sentence is a lens through which the reader looks at the rest of the story. A frivolous lead sentence, for example, is inappropriate to serious subject matter. The following sentence began a story for which the lead was appropriate; it signals the reader that the event is humorous.

An optimist attempted to cram himself and a tuba he was carrying abroad one of New York's jammed subway trains today. He didn't make it. He should have taken up the piccolo.

If the man with the tuba had been killed or injured, the lead would have been inappropriate.

Helping the Reader to See the Event

The reader of a news report, unlike viewing some television news shows, is often two or three degrees removed from reality. The police reporter, for example, gets most of his facts from policemen who have gotten them from eyewitnesse and participants. The reporter translates the words he has heard into written words. The written words are symbols of spoken words. The reader, in consequence, reads only the symbols.

An appropriate choice of words can enhance vividness. But the news writer, with respect to some events, may also enhance vividness by reconstructing the event for the reader in one or more sentences in the lead. He adds the dimension of visualization.

> A school bus carrying as estimated 38 children struck a wrecker, sideswiped an automobile, then plunged into the Levisa fork of the Big Sandy river today.
>
> A construction dredge, under tow in wind-whipped Lake Michigan, early today dipped under high waves and plunged to the bottom, taking the lives of eight of the 18 men abroad.
>
> A driverless butane gas truck, belching flame, struck a mailbox Friday and headed straight down a sidewalk into the front door of the Hillcrest Haven rest home, killing three elderly patients.
>
> NEW YORK—The crowded Lock-heed Electra crashed into a dike, flipped on its back and plunged, blazing, 500 feet along a swamp; Seventy-six passengers and crewmen hung head downward, pinned in their upsidedown seats by safety belts as flames closed in on the cabin.
>
> But not a life was lost today when American Airlines' Electra Flight 361 crashed at the end of a runway to New York's LaGuardia airport.

In some instances, it is better to make the lead sentence longer by adding a few words than to strive merely for brevity. This is justifiable because the headline has already reported the substance of the event and that information has been stored in the mind of the reader before he started to read the lead. In the fourth lead quoted above one newspaper's headline was" AIRLINER CRASHES, BURNS; ALL 76 ABROAD SAFE" and a four-column picture showed the upside-down plane. Another example:

> FORT WORTH, Texas-An angry mob yelling "get those niggers" tonight hung an effigy of a Negro from a tree in the front yard of a Negro barricaded in his home.

Here are two ways of reporting a certain kind of event. The writer of one of the stories, however, has an advantage over the second writer because he wrote the story for the succeeding news cycle and had more time for both writing and for obtaining one or two additional facts.

The Syntax of the Lead Sentence

The lead sentence, generally, should be in the normal sentence order. The normal sentence order is *(1)* the subject, *(2)* the finite verb, and *(3 or 4)* indirect object or direct object. Thus: *(1)* Stanford University scientists *(2)* plucked *(3)* a secret *(4)* from the heart of the atom.

Of the sixty lead sentences quoted in this chapter, all but four are written in the normal sentence order. One sentence begins with a conditional clause ("If you've recently had a baby ...,"); one is an interrogatory sentence; one is in ellipsis with the normal sentence order implied ("Under no conditions..."); and one begins with an adverbial clause modifier ("With aplomb...").

The subject of the lead sentence is usually the "who" ("A passenger in a car...") or the , 'what" (''A verdict in favor of Samuel Howell...,"). It is nearly always easier to write a lead sentence in the normal places automatically. Moreover, since the normal sentence order is fixed in the English language by our habits of speech, a sentence in the normal order facilitates the reader's comprehension.

The writer should deviate from the normal sentence order only when he wishes to emphasize a sentence element other than the subject. The beginning of the sentence and the end of the sentence are the emphatic parts. When, therefore, the writer wishes to emphasize the time aspect of the event—the "when"—he begins with the time.

> Five minutes before the legal deadline, Mayor George Wilson today filed for re-election.

> Six days before he was scheduled to retire on a pension, an Air Force officer was given a dishonourable discharge from the service today.

There is no justification, however, for this kind of lead:

> Meeting at noon today, the Rotary Club heard Governor Morris defend his tax programme.

You may already have noticed in the leads that have been quoted in this chapter that "today" and "yesterday" were nearly always "buried" inside the sentence. The "when" aspect of the event is seldom important or interesting. In some news stories the "when" is reported as far down in the story as the fourth or fifth paragraph, so that the reader can concentrate on the more important or more interesting aspects.

To stress immediacy, newspapers and wire services "update" the lead of a news story for the succeeding news cycle (called a second-day lead); for example, they change the lead in an afternoon newspaper of a news story that was first written for a morning newspaper. Believing that readers are more interested in fresh news, they rewrite the lead to give the story that appearance. Because this effort has sometimes led to absurdity, now there is less stress on the "when" in the second-day lead. Here is an approved example of "updating" in the afternoon news cycle:

> NEW YORK—Novelist Virgil Payson was in Bellevue hospital today for psychiatric observation.
>
> City Magistrate Joseph Martin ordered Payson committed after the author was arraigned yesterday on a charge of simple assault brought by his wife, singer Margaret Newsom.

Obituaries often are "updated" for the second-day lead in this form "Funeral services will be held today for ..., who died yesterday."

The "where" element of an event is sometimes worthy of emphasis:

> Within 100 yards of the road intersection at which his wife met death in an auto accident last year, a Jonesboro man was killed in the same way last night.

Also sometimes worthy of emphasis are the "why" element ("Because he was discharged, a labourer yesterday shot...") and the "how" element ("Caught in a collapsing slag pile,...was crushed to death yesterday").

To emphasize some unusual aspect of the event or to hedge a prediction, the writer begins the lead sentence with a modifier.

> Barring unforeseen developments, the local baseball club will be sold to Kansas City interests.
>
> Even though he killed his wife for their joint insurance, the policy of William and Henrietta Fleming is valid, a pleading filed in circuit court today avers.
>
> Alive but incoherent, a wrong-way turnpile driver was the only survivor of a head-on collision that killed seven persons last night.

Exercises: 1. Below are several leads containing one or more of the following errors: *(a)* main feature buried under unimportant details; *(b)* sentences overloaded with details; *(c)* when or where put before the who or what when unjustified by relative importance; *(d)* editorial comment introduced; *(e)* style used too rambling; *(f)* wordy phrases used at start.

Rewrite each of these leads in a clearer, more effective and concise form.

(a) In a survey to learn something about the effects of television on the American home conducted by the Business Administration students at Wester State University, using 1,000 local television fans as "guinea pigs, " it was found that the average televiewer spends three and one-half hours per day at his television set on the occasions when he stays home.

(b) Disclosure that local post officials are conducting a drive to discover the identity of the largest distributors behind the Irish Sweepstakes ticket-selling in this vicinity, plus the revelation that last May's winners have not been paid off have already resulted in blocking the sale of at least $250,000 in tickets and the disposal of 575,000 worth may be prevented.

c) During a meeting recently of Phi Pho Nu, national social sorority, elections were held for the coming year. After counting of ballots by election officers, it was discovered that the new secretary will be Hermina Knox. Other officers include Donna Snell, first vice-president; Illene Kennedy, second vice-president; and social activities directory, Gwen Scheively. Alice Niffern will serve the group as president again, having held that post last year.

(d) Among the many fine firms exhibiting in this year's county fair, which continues through Sunday, March 28, in Woodland Park Auditorium with admission free to all, is the Wiere Jewellry Company, which is displaying 250 antique and unusual watches and clocks, many of which date back 200 years or more.

(e) At a meeting of the Greene County election commissioners held last Tuesday, the recent school trustee election was held null and void, due to a technicality in the manner of conducting the alloting. As a result, Ivar Petrone, Leslie Siedbe, and Frank Malligan now find themselves no longer newly elected members to the trustee board.

2. Rewrite this cluttered lead to facilitate the reader's comprehension:

> Robert Rogers, Fremton police officer, testified in superior court today that Philip Snead, plaintiff in an assault and battery suit against Sam Vossler, bartender, was drunk and disorderly at the time of the alleged assault.
>
> Rogers charges came under the direct examination of Paul Ghezzi, attorney for the defendant. Rogers asserted that Snead was...

For class discussion: 1. Why was this lead written this way?

> AMES, Iowa (AP)—A rule of the college at Iowa State University requires that administrative officials retire on the July I after they reach 65 years of age. Dr. Charles E. Friley has bowed to the rule and quit office as president of Iowa State.
>
> The rule doesn't apply to teachers. Dr. Friley will, accordingly, join Iowa State's faculty as a teacher and researcher.

2. Which of these leads is better calculated to educe an image?

> Dr. Otis Barton, 48-year-old-undersea explorer, went farther under the ocean today than man had ever gone before when he dived 4,500 feet into the dark Pacific in a five-foot round steel ball.

A man in a steel ball saw weird and wondrous marine life 4500 feet down in the Pacific Ocean today, the deepest descent in history.

EDITORIAL DEPARTMENT

The Editorial Department is responsible for providing news and the reading matter for the newspaper. It includes news, art and many other subordinate sections. Reporters gather news from different places in the country and also from abroad. Photography section provides photographs. Cartoonists supply sketches of personalities and events. Editorial and special writers contribute articles, including feature articles. Editors also obtain special articles, illustrations and features from outside the organisation for publication in their newspaper.

Division of the Duties

The editorial staff provides material for publication and prepares the subject-matter called 'copy' for the printer and the engraver. Big newspapers have elaborate editorial staff consisting of many editors and sub-editors as incharges of various sub-sectiors, designated as Editor, Managing Editor, News Editor, Sunday Editor, Sports Editor, Women's Editor, Picture Editor, Society Editor. Drama Editor, Literary Editor, Music Editor, Art Editor, etc. Small newspapers combine many of these positions, or drop some altogether, and have an editorial staff consisting of ten to fifteen persons. The editorial department is the record section of a newspaper. It also maintains a library, where, beside other relevant books, extensive files of clippings and photographs are maintained.

The Editor

To be the editor of a daily newspaper with a nation-wide circulation is an ambition which very few journalists can attain. There are however occasions when many intelligent reporters and correspondents are satisfied with the excitement and thrill of their job and do not relish to have the ambition of a more ordered routine of an indoor job of the editor, 'even though it may bring them greater name and fame.

Dynamic Role. Like the newspaper itself the functions and responsibilities of the editor keep on changing. When there were few newspapers the editor was regarded as a potentate who ruled by the force of his personality and was a terror for his opponents. The editorial board of a large newspaper carried more power than it does now. Present day newspapers are more led by the public opinion than they lead it. The reason is that a newspaper has become a commercial organisation rather than a political institution as it used to be in the olden days. The editor, in order to maintain and increase the circulation day-by-day, month-by-month and year-by-year, has to compute the public mind and express opinions in the light of popular trends prevalling from time to time. If any of the major newspapers were to take an elitist approach, it may be classified as an anti-people newspaper and many of its readers may not only stop buying it but also build public opinion against it. For this reason most of the editors give out their ideas and opinions on current issues after gauging the public mind. Moreover, there is a great limitation on modern editorial control. The individual opinions of an editor are subject to all the views of his colleagues, correspondents and members of the editorial board. No newspaper allows one man control, however intelligent the editor may be. The editorial policy of a newspaper is usually guided by an editor-in-chief, a managing editor, assistant editors the news editor and half a dozen specialist editors. The first three of them usually form the real editorial trio. They mutually decide upon the programme and policy of the newspaper regardirig interviews of national and international personalities and write leader articles on important subjects or events.

Public Relation Duties. The Editor of a Newspaper must have patience, human sympathy, a working acquaintance with type and how to use it; the faculty of being able to distinguish between public right and public wrong as well as private right and private wrong. He must be an all round intellectual, knowing the essentials of the history of the world and of human nature. He should be able to discriminate be ween honest publicists and smooth-tongued propagandists. Above all be must possess a courageous heart which enables him to say "yes" or "no" at the right time.

He should be able to inspire confidence in his staff whom he can presumbly trust. He should not build an iron curtain around himself through which he emerges only on rare occasions. In the editorialship every member of the crew has his job to do and there is nothing more depressing for the able-bodied seaman or the cabin boy than to realise that the captain does not know him either by name or by sight. The good Editor makes it a point of honour to know his staff and to recognise personally a notable piece of work. There is no harm in an occasional descent from the Mount Olympus, as the Editor's room as nicknamed, to visit the reporter's room to see the paper 'put to motion'.

Perhaps the greatest lesson one could learn in newspaper life is that unless the spirit of good companionship prevails, the workers labour largely in vain. If a grave issue of any kind arises it is the Editor's duty to take the final decision without fear or favour, however much any member of his staff may differ from it. As long as they know that he has discussed the pros and cons with his advisers around him and not merely retired behind his iron curtain, he will retain their respect and esteem.

Round-the-Clock Routine. From early morning to midnight, the Editor is on duty either in the office or on his round of visits and even then he is never certain that his sleep will not be disturbed by the arrival of a vital piece of news. Yet no Editor of a daily newspaper ever wishes to change his job-unless, possibly, to migrate to another newspaper. For he enjoys the thrill of knowing that he is helping to make history. His burden is lighter when he knows that he has at his elbow one or more assistant editors ready to take some of the strain from him when life gets too hectic. His assistants who specialize in particular fields such as home and political news, the news from overseas and the financial news, are usually eager to divide the burden with him.

Field Duties. The horizon of the Editor of a daily newspaper is not limited by the walls of his office. He must keep in touch with public opinion by mixing with the leaders in every walk of life. His life is so hectic that his luncheon table has to become an adjunct of the editorial desk. An hour or an hour and a half over luncheon can be a great help to a newspaper man in straightening out his views on an urgent public issue; an action contemplated by a Minister of the Cabinet or a dispute in industry. There are also occasions when the conscientious Editor travels far afield.

Writing of Leading Articles: There are divided views as to whether the Editor himself should write leading articles or whether he should confine himself to briefing other members of his staff. In any case, in the opinion of many, the Editor should not write regularly. A leader from his pen should be an event of special importance and should be reserved for very important occasions. Most leader writers are able to assimilate very quickly the ideas which the Editor has passed on to them before they begin to write, and it is always the Editor's privilege to revise the article and, if he is really dissatisfied, to re-write it. But the leader writer who feels that he is frozen out when the big moment comes, after he has been writing on a subject week after week, will soon become disheartened and will not give his best. On a national newspaper the leader writer may not contribute more than two or three articles a week, but he has plenty to occupy his time if he is to keep abreast of life in that part of the world with which he is dealing. The more newspapers and official reports he 'studies the more valuable he becomes to his Editor. On some of the newspapers there are leader writers who seem to be able to turn their hands to almost any subject in any part of the world.

Writing of the 'Light Leader'. It is another important item of a newspaper. Many newspapers now include an article of this kind as a relief from the serious and some editors of noted newspapers have achieved a world-wide reputation. But it is not every editor who can create humorous comments, inoccuous and interesting. In this field, there are more misses than hits. Obviously, no one writer could easily maintain a daily supply of light article or column. One of the best writers of light leaders of the present generation once expressed the view that the essential requisite of a light leader writer is a neat literary beginning and a witty closing sentence which produces a smile on the readers' face and which makes him regret that the light leader was not long enough.

THE NEWS EDITOR

The News Editor is one of the most important person who plan a daily newspaper. His role in any newspaper office-whether it be weekly or daily—is all pervading. To a national newspaper an active, intelligent and enterprising news editor is the vital spark which energises its news coverage and outlook. He is responsible for a steady and continuous inflow of up-to-the-minute news into newspaper office. Although most of the news supplied is a mechanical process covered by daily routine, but like all machinery of news gathering, the news editor is responsible for watching its smooth functioning. The news editor keeps a careful eye on the routine side of his news collection as well as on the other side of his work on the news desk which calls for more imaginative emulation.

Functions of a News Editor. An ideal news editor manages to get all the obvious stories into his paper with a good proportion of them as exclusives. While the selection of obvious stories is important, greater importance is attached. to the original ones produced by his team of correspondents. The number of words received on the teleprinter in a newspaper is so large that if each word were to be printed, the newspaper will have to run into hundreds of pages each morning. The news editor is called upon to use his discretion, discrimination and imagination in reading the public mind and select the stories which have real news value and can be called important by his readers—quite a large number to be allotted a "splash" position on the main news pages according to the subject matter on field of activity they are concerned with. All this has to be done with an alertness to ensure that the kind of stories readers seek shall be found in his newspaper.

There are some fundamental. stories which no newspaper can offord to miss as they go into all the daily newspapers without exception. While they are important and have to be included, there are others called exclusive which only an alert news editor can discover from the large ocean of copy that has been pouring into the office during the day. An intelligent news editor has to make a judicious follow-up of a seemingly promising paragraph or sometimes even make further enquiry before finalising the story and give it the perfect shape he wants.

Exclusive Stories. The news editor gets good satisfaction from the stories which are exclusive to his own newspaper. If he can manage to get into every issue a dozen or more minor stories with good news value but exclusive, he feels elated. The news editor is also responsible for final scrutiny of important news stories submitted by different correspondents, feature writers and outside correspondents. He gives special attention to the facts and figures included in the write-ups and wherever he is in doubt, he takes pains to check-up their accuracy from the authentic source. Any slip on his part can land the newspaper into trouble. Hence good newspapers have highly experienced and intelligent news editors.

Organising Ability. The hurry and scurry of daily routine makes heavy demands upon the organising ability of the news editor and his decisions, specially when time is short yet there has to be accuracy. The exigencies of the case may sometimes mean even deputing different correspondents to different parts of the country to piece together the links of a promising story.

There are certain qualities that the News Editor must possess. He must have an infinite amount of patience and a, keen interest in news of all kind.He must have a good general educational background with a fair amount of historical, political and economic knowledge. He must try to keep himself abreast and informed on every important development in the work-a-day world. He must enjoy reading the newspapers, the weeklies, and the magazines. He must not think that he can keep normal working hours, for it is more true of the News Editor than of anybody else that he is always on duty whether at home or in the office. He must be a good mixer, he must be on the lookout for news all the time, he must learn to scan the newspaper, and perhaps the most important asset of all he must be able to retain his sense of humour however depressing the situation may be.

His Daily Routine. His working day begins early. Once he gets to his office there is so much to be one that he has little time to examine thoroughly his own paper and those of rival managements. Therefore, he must begin his reading with his early morning cup of tea and continue it on the way so that when he gets to his desk he has a fair idea of the contents of the morning papers. His assistant will have arrived earlier and will have prepared a list of his papers, exclusive news items and a more depressing list, that of the stories which the paper has missed. He will probably regard the 'scoops' as in the natural order of things, but he will certainly want to hold an inquest on the news which has been missed, primarily to satisfy himself that there is not a fault in the paper's methods of news gathering which needs to be eradicated.

Having dealt with the past he must immediately concern himself with the future and launch his plan of campaign for the next issue. Probably his first task will be to decide whether there is anything in any of the papers which needs to be followed up. It used to be Lord Northcliffe's dictum that a first-class news story will always stand up to one or two 'follow-up' stories, and the reporters can be put on to these right away. Next he must mark the diary and assign the reporters to attend meetings which ought to be specially covered and not left to the news agencies. He must also allot men to the news stories which have cropped up and to enquiries which may not produce immediate results but which may be the preliminary step towards a first-class article a few days later. But he must watch his man-power closely. He must not fritter it away and he must not be left in the position that if later in the morning big news comes in, the reporters' room is empty. It is certainly not false economy to have one or two reporters sitting idle; if they are wise they will spend their free time in reading newspapers, books, or periodicals which can always be borrowed from the office library. It is the great thrill of the News Editor's life that the can never guess when the big news will break. One News Editor certainly will never forget the moment when a pale-faced messenger tore an item off the tape machine and put on his desk the first news of the death of Lal Bahdur Shastri.

Morning News Conference. Assuming that the morning is a normal one the News Editor, having allotted the reporters their assignments turns his attention to the preparations for the morning news conference, for which he is primarily responsible. This is generally attended by the Editor or one of his assistants, the Junior Editors and their assistants, the picture editor, the cartographer, a representative of the City Department, and a man from the circulating department which should always be kept in close touch with the news as it arises. This conference is usually of an informal character when ideas on the day's news and on space requirements are freely exchanged in preparation for the more important conference which will be held in the late afternoon.

The News Editor also remains in communication with many of the special writers, who do much of their work away from the office, and with the heads of other departments. He goes through the 'marked papers' in which the contributions from correspondents are brought to his notice. That is why it is held that the News Editor should not stick to his desk all the time because good contacts are necessary for the maintenance of a first class, news service. For that reason, most of the News Editors of the national newspapers are given an entertainment allowance and most of it is spent at the luncheon table.

Maintaining Contacts. The News Editor who is anxious to maintain his contacts lunches out of his office two or three times a 'week. On other days he is satisfied if he can snatch half an hour for lunch in the office itself.

By the time he returns to his room the pace has quickened. Copy is beginning to arrive in a steady stream and either the News Editor or his assistant goes through every line of it. News lurks from most unexpected places. The early editions of the evening papers need to be watched carefully, if such editions are brought out.

The programme for the editorial conference which is held in most offices in the late afternoon and which is really the central point of the day's activities, the custom differs in every office, but broadly speaking, the conference over which the Editor presides is attended by the head of every editorial department. The agenda for this conference is prepared by the News Editor and his staff, with a separate page prepared by the Overseas News Editor, dealing with all the news which has come in from his realm. The news of the day is listed as far as possible in its order of importance and it is the News Editor's job to explain it item by item. He must be ready to stand cross-examination on any detail, and the ordeal is usually a trying one, for he may have omitted to make himself familiar with the very point which other members of the conference consider to be the most important. It is then that the News Editor needs altertness land sense of humour.

Before the conference he has a talk with the Chief Political Correspondent so that he is able to report what is happening in the Lok Sabha and the amount of space which the Parliamentary Chief is asking for but does not always get. The hot news of the day having been examined, there is time for a brief examination of the other editorial features including the pictures, the entertainment page, the special articles, the city news and the sports page. It is also time that the Editor announces the subjects selected for the night's leading articles.

It is only after the conference has ended that the News Editor breathes a bit freely because his day's work is drawing to an end. A final glimpse at the evening papers; a perusal of the teleprinter, a visit to the reporter's room to see that everything is running smoothly and that the copy is not being held up; a talk with the Chief Sub-Editor to smooth out any difficulties which may threaten and then, most welcome sight, the arrival of the man who will relieve him, the Night News Editor. As the latter must remain on desk until the early hours of the morning it may have been impossible for him to attend the afternoon conference, so the News Editor informs him of all that lhas happened to ensure continuity.

NEWS SUPPLY

Where do newspapers get news which is processed and served to their readers every morning? The sources are many and varied and they cover the world. For news concerning the city from where the newspaper is published (this is called mofussil news) the paper relies on its own team of reporters and mofussil correspondents. For national or domestic news (that is news from all over the country outside its area of publication) and international news, newspapers depends on reliable, well established and reputed news agencies which sell news on a commercial basis and according to the needs and demands of individual newspapers. Most leading Indian newspapers have their own news bureaus at the national capital and correspondents in the state capitals and international cities like Washington, London and Tokyo, who cover all importants news and also send special dispatches not normally coming within the purview of news agencies.

In India there are two English news agencies, the Press Trust of India and the United News of India which are the main suppliers of domestic or national news to the Indian Press. They also provide international news but not in such quality or quantity as the reputed international agencies. Both these agencies are owned by the Indian newspaper and are entirely free from government control of any kind. They function as comeptitive organisations and it is for the newspaper to select the news they want to publish from either of them. There are newspapers which buy news from only one of these agencies but generally the major newspapers patronise both the agencies for they provide a wider choice and coverage and the chances of missing any important news are minimised. There are also two Hindi news agencies which cater to the language press.

The Press Trust of India (PTI) was born after India's independence as a successor to the famous Associated Press of India (API), which was a subsidiary of the international British news agency, Reuters and which dominated and virtually monopolised the supply of domestic news to the Indian-owned and British-owned newspapers in India during the British rule. The API was subsidized by the Government of India and it was accused by the nationalists fighting against alien rule of being the mouthpiece of the British Viceroy. It was officered and controlled by Englishmen although the journalists and reporters who worked for it were Indians some of them of outstanding calibre and efficiency.

Attempts were made to organise Indian news agencies to supply the nationalist angle but they could not make much headway owing to official hostility and the entrenched po :tion of the Government favoured agency. The Free Press News Service and the United Press of India (UPI) played a notable role during the freedom movement in espousing the cause of the nationalists and giving publicity to their activities and views but ther lives were short for lack of resources and the inveterate antagonism of the British rulers.

Foreign or international news agencies which supply news to Indian newspapers are mainly four in number, They are 1. Reuters; 2. Associated Press (AP of America); 3. Agence France Press (AFP); 4. United Press International (UPI). None of these agencies supplies news directly to the newspapers. They sell their news in bulk to the two domestic agencies PTI and UNI who in turn transmit them to their clients after making their own selection. PTI has an arrangement with Reuters and AFP and UPI for purchase of news, and UNI has a similar deal with AP Besides these tie-ups with established foreign news agencies, PTI and UNI have bilateral understandings with national news agencies of some important countries like China, Japan and Gulf countries, and Yugoslavia who supply them news from their countries in return for news from India. In recent years we have had the non-aligned news agencies pool intended to disseminate news from Third World or less developed countries of Africa, Asia and South America.

Out of the four main foreign news agencies who cater to Indian newspapers, the chief and most prolific supplier is Reuters followed by the Association Press and AFP in that order and the United Press International (UPI) being a very poor fourth. Reuters, which is perhaps the oldest news agency (it is named after its founder, Baron Von Reuter) has been supplying news to newspapers in India from its very inception 130 years ago. It has been the target of attack by nationalist newspapers in the early years of the Indian Freedom Movement. One of the charges against it was that it acted as the handmaiden of the British rulers in India and a Whitehall, London. Indian newspapers were forced to use Reuters service because there was no other agency to convey official and governmental news which occupied so much space in the newspapers of those days and also international news. The Association Press and the United Press International, which are purely American agencies, came on the Indian scene in the thick of the Indian nationalist struggle and during World War II when American eyes were turned to India as a base for operations against Japan. At one time major Indian newspapers were flooded with news stories from all these agencies who had arrangements direct with individual newspapers, each competing with the others in being first with the news and scoring scoops, It became a problem for the News Editors and the newsrooms to cope with the tremendous rush of material pouring in at all hours of the day and night and select and process news without duplication and confusion.

Domestic and foreign news are delivered to the newsroom through teleprinters which are automatic typing machines carrying messages which are transmitted through co-axial cable from the originating place by punched tapes fed to a transmitter. As the roll of paper with the typed messages flow into the basket or receptacle behind the machine in an unending stream they are collected, cut and sorted out and passed on to the various news sections to which they belong. The teleprinters are remarkable machines which require no supervision, watching or tending except when they go out of order or get stuck owing to faulty transmission. All that one has to do is to tear off the messages as they come out and if it is a flash or some outstanding news send it to the News Editor quickly and watch out for more. The news transmitted by the teleprinter if self-contained and complete and except where it is a running story, that is where the story is incomplete with developments occuring or anticipated or unreported, the newsroom has not much work to do beyond deciding if it should be used and how and where and what heading if it should be used and how and where and what heading should be given. This saves the newsroom from the trouble of putting out a story in proper language, order and sequence and in the desired narrative form with a lead, a middle and an ending. What the teleprinter supplies can be compared to cooked food emerging from the kitchen and all that you have to do is to select what you want, add spices to it, if you feel like, to make it more palatable and attractive and then serve it to the customer.

It was not always so. Before the advent of the teleprinter, agencies delivered the news to the newspapers through the post office by cables and telegrams. The messages received through Morse code at the post office were written in hand and sent to the newspapers through messengers in bulky packets at all hours of the day and night. The messages were in abbreviated English (cables as they are called by journalists) and there was every possibility of their being mutilated, senseless or just gibberish. In their anxiety to reduce cable or telegraphic costs the agencies adopted all kinds of methods or ruses to keep down wordage which very often caused a nightmare to the sub-editor at the receiving end, Writing about Reuters service in those early days the Editor of an English-owned newspaper in India said: "World news was furnished by Reuters Agency, an admirable objective service with the careful accuracy it always maintained but with cable charges of a shilling a word it was little more than a 100 words a day. Reduced to this pemmican form it was not infrequently unitelligible and Reuters representative would come round to the office with the plaintive enquiry whether we could make head or tail of some message". On one occasion Reuters Agency cabled a message to India which said: "Herbert Mills dead". Indian newspaper could not quite place Herbert Mills, who he was and what he had to do with India. One British-owned newspaper searched the Who's Who and decided the man referred to by Reuters should be Col. Herbert James Mill C.B. But it knew that Col. Mill was alive and healthy and he could not be the person mentioned. It was puzzled and did not know what to do with the message when an Indian-owned newspaper came to its rescue. It discovered that Reuters had mutilated the name and caused all the confusion. The deceased gentlemen it said, was "neither Col. Herbert Mills nor Col. Herbert James Mills. He was no other than Herbert Mills Birdwood who was born in Belgaum in the Bombay Presidency and was a judge of Bombay High

Court, Vice-Chancellor of the Bombay University and member of the Executive Council of the Governor of Bombay".

How sub-editors functioned in this welter of confusion and chaos and fashioned intelligible and fascinating news stories for the entertainment and education of the readers can form the subject of the book by itself. A much more serious hurdle for sub-editors in those days was posed by message of the British Official Wireless which was an official agency of the British Government in London. The B.O.W. messages supplemented Reuters by giving details of official speeches and statements of policy which were of great importance to India. More often than not the B.O.W. cable was more of a quiz than an intelligible message for it carried brevity and minimum wordage of absurd lengths. With the result, only the seniormost sub-editor handled it, elongating its cryptic words and phrases into meaningful sentences and identifying the names and places mentioned in it after checking them in reference books. Many sub-editors did not have the energy or patience to edit B.O.W. messages and threw them into the waste paper basket hoping they would not be hauled up for doing so.

News agencies are very careful in supplying news to newspapers. They check and recheck and make sure that what they transmit to the newspapers is a fact, not a rumour or a false story. If a news is based on rumour or got from unverified sources, the news agency say so and leaves it to the reader to decide what value he should place on it, making it clear that it had issued the report because of the importance of the subject matter of the news. The reputation and credibility of a news agency may suffer or grow depending on the confidence it in spires in the newspaper and its readers by the quality and dependability of news distributed by it. Reputed world news agencies and domestic agencies have had their bad days and awkward moments when they were taken for a ride.

Thus it happened that reuters reported the end of World War I in 1918 almost a month before it actually ended. Reuters had relied on an Amsterdam report which quoted another report that Germany had capitulated and the Kaiser had abdicated. Believing the report to be true; Indian newspapers wrote editorials hailing the allied victory. But the announcement of the Allied victory and termination of the war came many days later. An Indian newspaper's comment was: On another occasion in 1923, Reuters slipped again when it reported the death of the Gaekwar of Baroda on a train from Berlin to Amsterdam. All the world newspapers published the report and carried long obituary notices and Indian newspapers paid editorial tributes only to be total the next day by Reuters that the Gaekwar was alive and it was his son, Jaisinghrao Gaekwar who had died.

News agencies sometimes place newspapers in a fix by issuing contradictory versions of the same event they are reporting. In 1961 when the UN Secretary-General Dag Hammarskjold was killed in a plane crash in North Rhodesia, UPI filed a story on it. However, the AP carried a different version saying that the UN Secretary-General had been seen by its correspondent at an airport in a neighbouring country and was alive and well. It had to issue a correction later admitting that Hammarskjold had died in the air accident and that its correspondent had mistaken another airport passenger for Hammarskjold. On another occasion AP carried a report that the American civil rights leader, James Meredith was shot dead while on a protest march. It was later ascertained that Meredith had only been wounded in the head. The reporter who filed the story later said he thought he heard an official say Meredith was 'shot dead'.

Our domestic news agencies have also been responsible for occasional lapses. One was that which related to the passing away of the Dravida Munnetra Kazhagam (DMK) leader C.N. Annadurai in 1969. The Press Trust of India (PTI) flashed the news of his death in a hospital in Madras 12 hours before he actually passed away. The reporter misheard one of the partymen talking about Annadurai and concluded he was dead. He rushed to the phone to file his news and in a few minutes it was known in all newspaper offices and it was broadcast by All India Radio. One local newspaper had prepared a supplement to carry the news and would have been on the streets with the PTI news had not a sixth sense told its Editor to wait for confirmation from its own reporter keeping vigil at the hospital. The paper's reporter when contacted said the DMK leader was alive and PTI itself very quickly put out a service for its clients asking them to kill the Annadurai story. Annadurai died in the early hours on the following morning.

The news agencies' reports of the death of India's President, Zakir Hussain, in 1968, were again in conflict regarding the place where he actually died, in his bathroom or in the drawing room. A harassed News Editor of a prominent newspaper had to seek the assistance of its special correspondent in New Delhi to clarify the point: It is not unusual for one news agency to carry a report which will be contradicted by another news agency the same day or the following day from the same source or another source.

A news agency, domestic or international, must meet the standards of thousands of newspapers of all shades of though, religious beliefs, nationalities and sympathies. What may seem of special interest to a newspaper may be of no consequence to a news agency except when it is specially asked by a newspaper for coverage of what it desires. But what may seem interesting to a news agency does not always evoke a similar response in its clients. Newspapers being what they are it is difficult enough to satisfy one of them let alone hundreds of thousands at a time. A news agency therefore will be very particular in presenting all sides of a story that is controversial. It may not be the ideal way but it is the fairest way. News agencies clients do not expect them to take sides. They regard them as impartial purveyors of information. News agencies reports will be closely scrutinised in the newsrooms for any shade of editorialising (taking side) or slant (leaning to one side).

The news agencies begin their morning and evening service to the newspapers with a news budget which will indicate the main and subsidiary stories expected to be carried that day and their probable wordage or length and when they are likely to land in the newsroom. This will be of great help to the News Editor or Night Editor or whoever is in charge of the edition for it will enable them to allot space for the various stories and also decide how to and where to feature them. In the United States the news agencies' work have been computerised (as we have already noted) and even in the smallest state bureau the typewriter is all but obsolete, being replaced by the computer and VDT for story composition and filing. The newsrooms of their clients may get a daily four or five line abstract of the day's complete offering-foreign, national and state stories. Sub-Editors in the newsroom choose the stories they want from the abstract, then by using computer codes and symbols, receive those stories directly into the newspaper's computer at a rate of 1200 words a minute. Under this system the news agency can deliver up to the minute stories that are better written and better edited than those in the past. The subeditors are thus spared the trouble of ploughing though scores of stories which they do not want. And they have more time to devote their attention to edit and process the stories they have selected and also take care of material coming in from other sources like their own correspondents and news syndicates.

We in India, however, are a long way from computerised news agencies. Although Indian news agencies have greatly improved the scope and contents of their service, News Editors are not always happy with them and sub-editors spend many anxious hours every night with incomplete and often mutilated stories, not to speak of total black out of news on the teleprinter because of power failure or coaxial cable fault. It is not unusual for an important story which had landed earlier in the evening hanging in the air far into the night either because a vital correction had not been received or some crucial parts of the story had not been put on the printer. In such situations the desperate sub-editor, who is hard pressed for time, tries to patch up the story with material available from other news agencies or the paper's own correspondent who might come to his rescue.

A newspaper may not have the space or the inclination to use all the massive material that a news agency supplies it 24 hours a day and even where it used the agency stories it cuts and trims them to suit its needs. As an American writer remarks 'Copy-editors (sub-editors) do not boggle at turning an AP opus into a two-para short'. He adds that news agency reporters 'write stories that are designed to be cut from the bottom, usually at the end of almost any para.

These stories are written for news outlets all over the country with the assumption that someone will want the full length and everyone else can trim as necessary.' Sub-editors in Indian newspapers seldom rewrite agency stories or trim them. They either use them as they are or do not use them. They very often combine stories from rival agencies picking a paragraph from one and another from the other and give them a common credit line like this: PTI and UNI. We shall hear more about this later.

News agencies are firecely competitive. They keep logs on how often they beat their reivals on a story, how many minutes they were ahead and how many newspapers used their stories. Agencies if they come to know of an important news break, rush with the story although all the facts and developments connected with it may not be available at that moment. It may be a single sentence with the title: 'Flash, Flash, Flash'. And the sentence may be: 'Sanjay Gandhi killed in air crash'. This flash will be repeated a number of times in order that no newsroom misses it. The flash will be quickly followed by one paragraph additional matter called 'add' which will give a summary of the news as and when additional information is available. By the time this series is completed the agency will be ready to put out a complete story with a lead and which may go into many sections. If it is a running story or a story where developments occur from hour to hour (as in a natural calamity or a Cabinet crisis) the agency will put out new leads, add or delete earlier parts of the story in an unending stream of new material. We shall see later how a sub-editor deals with such a situation.

The advantage of a newspaper subscribing to more than one news agency is that the sub-editors can used the story from one service to check facts contained in the same story supplied by another service such as casualty figures, proper names and spellings. The sub-editor is free to use whichever version he like. In the newsrooms of competing newspapers a sub-editor of one may lean towards one agency while another in a rival paper may tilt towards another agency. Here is a glossary of words used by news agencies in their transmission of stories to newspaper:

1. Flash. Two or three word news announcement alerting the newsroom to a story of unusual importance.

2. Bulletin. A short summary of outstanding news, usually not more than a lead para of a major story. It is not intended for publication but to alert the News Editor of a major news break. It can of course be used in the paper if it comes as the paper is going to press. A bulletin may also be used to signal an important correction, such as a mandatory 'kill' of a story of an agency, which means that the story has been withdrawn and should not be used.

3. Pick-up. Used to indicate where story is to be picked up after a new lead insertion.

4. No Pick-Up. This means revised story contains all material sent previously.

5. Repeat. A re-run of a story for a client on request.

6. Round-up. An undated story involving more than one place of origin of the news.

7. Sidebar. A short feature intended to accompany a main story.

8. Wrap-up. A final comprehensive story combining stories and segments put on the printer previously.

The most common heading given to a news agency story is Lead which is like a head to a body, which fathers all the essential ingredients of a story and brings them to the top and this will be put on the printer as the last item after all the details have gone in first. In a constantly developing story with new facts and incidents emerging all the time one lead will not be sufficient and so the agency will go on changing the leads as the development of the story warrants and these will be titled First Lead, Second Lead, Third Lead and so on. This tendency of the agency to pile lead on lead is always a puzzle to newcomers to journalism and non-professionals in general. When circumstances change, when erroneous information is given and accepted in good faith there is nothing a news agency can do except to update the story. The easiest way to do that and draw the attention of sub-editors to it is to put out a new lead. Inserts are generally confusing to handle and difficult to place even with complete instructions. It is not always easy to find out exactly what happened when there is an incident or a natural disaster and a considerables time may lapse before the facts are established. The news agency has then to put out leads until the story assumes solid form.

Every newspaper has its own team of reporters to cover local, state, national and international news as mentioned earlier. The size, quality and number of places where they are stationed depends on the resources and reputation of a newspaper. Indian newspapers have fewer correspondents in foreign countries than British and American newspaper. In fact newspapers which have correspondents in neighbouring countries like Nepal, Pakistan, Bangladesh and Burma and even Sri Lanka are very few and not all correspondents are very active. The same is the position with regard to South-East Asian countries like Thailand, Malaysia, Singapore, Indonesia and the Arab countries, Africa, most of south America and Canada are closed continents for Indian newspapers. They have more correspondents in the capitalist countries of the West than in the communist countries and some of the prominent newspapers have no correspondents in Moscow. Indian news agencies are better placed in this respect but their correspondents are not as numerous or strong as those of the foreign news agertcies. As a result Indian newspapers have to rely almost totally on foreign news agencies for international news and comment and they are not always objective or sensitive to Indian needs and predilections. Also foreign news agencies mostly concentrate on news emanating from Western countries with Eastern or communist countries coming far behind and the Asian and African countries almost totally ignored unless there is a riot, natural disaster or military coup.

At the national level Indian newspapers including the bulk of language papers which are published outside the national capital have their own men in New Delhi who cover national events and keep their editors and readers well informed on the happenings and thinking there. The major newspapers have their own bureaus consisting of three or four correspondents who cover Parliament and various ministries of the Government of India. Their dispatches not only give the news but also interpret and analyse them which the news agencies cannot do. Since the agencies concentrate on the news they are able to achieve a wide spread and the newspapers use them as much as they want to supplement their correspondents' stories. Some of the newspaper correspondents (they are called special correspondents or special representatives where they are not given by-line) are very close to the Ministers or the bureaucrats and come into possession of exclusive news which in journalist parlance is called a scoop. A scoop by one correspondent spurs his professional rival in another paper to better him with one of his own and so the game goes on with the Editors happy or unhappy as the case may be and the readers greatly benefited by the disclosure, while the Government which is always the target of these 'newshawks' is embarrassed or just angry.

India is a vast country with as many as 22 states, some of them as big as many western countries, and it would require great resources for a newspaper to have correspondents in each state capital not to speak of the more important cities in them. There are very few papers which have correspondents in all the state capitals. But the major newspapers have their man in most of the state capitals who has the entire state to cover. The news agencies with their vast networks of correspondents all over the country supply news from all regions to the newspapers. News agency correspondents file their news to the nearest news bureau where they are edited and processed and put on the teleprinters of clients.

Within the state where it is published a newspaper has a correspondent at every district headquarter who will cover the entire district. They are called mofussil correspondents, that is correspondents outside the state capital or headquarter. The word 'correspondent' which is so much a part of the newspaper world had its origin in the coverage of mofussil news or news of the districts. The word came to be applied early to the non-journalist, either a white collar worker, petty trader to politician who sent a letter to the newspaper editors for publication. These letters might give news or they might start a controversy on some public issue or they might ventilate some grievance against an official or official policy. The editors published them and encouraged the correspondents to write more and in course of time they became regular correspondents of the paper giving news of official and non-official activities in their district and news of social functions. They were paid an honorarium by the better placed papers. An Indian editor said that the mofussil correspondent of those early days of Indian journalism had but a 'morganatic' connection with his paper. He was not on the payroll and he was not bound to render it regular service either. The editor said the truth of the matter was that the correspondent adopted the paper for purposes of his own and used his wits and opportunities 'to levy a tithe' in his pitch. He was a 'hail fellow well met' to all and sundry. Those were days, the editor said, when printed words cast magic spells and to be mentioned in a newspaper was an extraordinary distinction. (This is still so). The old stagers were past masters in the art of psychology and they knew to a nicety how far they might apply the 'toasting irons' to their victims. They also knew how far the papers they served with singular devotion to themselves would put up with their vagaries and irresponsibilities. Delicately balanced between the two they lived on the fat of the land. The editor said few newspapers at the beginning of the century were in a position to afford the luxury of paid correspondents even in important mofussil centres. When honorary correspondents volunteered to render service 'presumably in public interest' they were given the freedom of the paper within well defined limits. In later years the paid mofussil correspondent came into being on the staff of many newspapers but there were also other categories of mofussil correspondents. One saw their nomenclature vividly in the columns of the Hindu. These were first, 'Our Own Correspondent,' then, 'A correspondent,' 'An Occasional Correspondent,' and 'An Esteemed Correspondent' . All these types of correspondents provides a plethora of district news to the Hindu which achieved a distinction in this field even in those early days.

The team of local reporters or city reporters is the pride of a daily newspaper. These reporters are near the hub of news and their task and responsibility are greater because their readers are also in the arena of news and are both spectators and participants in them. The curiosity to know about events almost next door and about men and matters who figure in the news is more widespread and acute among local readers who will never for give a newspaper which leaves them unsatisfied or ignores news of importance. The rivalry among newspapers is also greater in the local area because this is where circulation is built up or lost. Therefore every newspaper will be interested in organising an efficient and alert corps of reporters who will ever be on the lookout for scoops or outstanding investigative reports. We shall have occasion to describe the activities and role of a reporter in greater detail later.

The strength of local reporters of a newspaper will depend on the size and importance of the city from where it is published. If it is the national capital or capital of a big state and if the newspaper's circulation is large it will be to the advantage of the newspaper to keep a big sized team of reporters for wider coverage of governmental and local news, official functions and special stories of significance and interest to the local reader. The local reporters have their routine beat, like the Government Secretariat, the police, courts, hospitals and chambers of commerce, hotels, railway stations and airports but they may also be given special assignments to cover a meeting or interview a Minister or VIP. The more important Indian newspapers now have on their staff reporters who are specialists in their subjects, like Agriculture, Education, Science and Technology, Industry and Medicine. These specialised reporters contribute every week to the newspaper's features on these subjects and they also interpret and analyse speeches and resolutions passed at conferences or official statements of policy relating to these subjects. Their expert knowledge and guidance are of great value to the editorial writers and also to the reader for they make it easier to follow and understand the language of scientists and professional men. In most newspapers in India there is a chief reporter, as we have mentioned already, who is the head of the reporters' section and who assigns and supervises their work. He acts as a liaison between the News Editor and the Reporters and consults and coordinates his work with the News Editor. He is in direct contact with the Editor and answerable to him. In this the practice differs from what obtains in Western newspaper where there is no Chief Reporter and it is the News Editor who controls and assigns works to the reporters. The News Editors and the Chief Reporter are the closest to the Indian newspaper editor and they are expected to work in harmony and complete understanding in the discovery and reporting of news, in following clues and digging up hidden news and in being one step ahead of the rival newspaper in coverage of local news.

❐

4

Sources of News

News is what everyone wants to know about. A newspaper office's main concern is to gather and report newslocal, state, regional, national, and international. The basic understanding about news is essential for any editorial work in a newspaper/news agency or a news magazine. In this chapter, we shall define news and try to understand all the elements which make news. We shall also discuss at length the significance of "news values" for a reporter. The sources of news are very important for a journalist. Therefore, we shall discuss the characteristics of various news sources in this chapter.

Before you proceed further, try to find out what you mean by news. Have you ever though about the nature of news? You must be listening to radio to update yourself with the happening of the country and the World. You must also be reading newspapers. Why do you read them? Your answer may be "to get information". And without the information you may feel that you are lost to the World. You would not be able to relate yourself with the society-politically, socially and economically.

You would not like to read Monday's newspaper on Thursday to update yourself. Do you? Of course, We go back to the old newspapers to confirm certain information, but definitely, in general, we do not do that every day.

There are several definitions of news. News may be defined as "anything timely that interests a large number of persons, and the best news is that which has the greatest interest for the greatest number". In other words, the news is the timely report of events, facts, and opinions and interests a significant number of people. The news is a new piece of information about a significant and recent event that affects the audience and is of interest to them.

Having situated ourselves in the world of the 'news', let us now try to put all our ideas and understanding of the news and see if we can have a definition of the news.

Now, we shall present to you some definitions of the news. But a world of caution. You will surely find them almost comprehensive and almost all encompassing but not complete. Therefore, we must remember that the news is relative. It changes with the changes in other factors related or connected to it. The definition of a news item is dependent on: the size of the community; the periodicity of the publication; the social character and economic base of the Community; the focus of attention or emphasis of the Community.

You must be aware of the famous definition of news developed by Jhon B. Bogart, City editor of the New York 'Sun'. He defined the news like this, "when a dog bites a man, that is not news; but when a man bites a dog, that is news". Jhon Bogart pointed out very correctly that unusual events fail under the purview of the news.

Later, another famous editor of the Sun, defined the news as, "...everything that occurs, everything which is of sufficient importance to arrest and absorb the attention of the public or of any considerable part of it". You must be familiar with the name of Joseph pulitzer, the publisher of the New York World. He defined news as, "original, distinctive, dramatic, romantic, thrilling, unique, curious, quaint, humorous, odd, and apt-to-be-talked-about".

The founder of the first School of Journalism, Walter William, defined the news as, "...News, in its broadest sense, is that which is of interest to the readers-the public...". The former managing editor of the New York Times said that the news was "...anything you can find out today that you didn't know before". We may provide you with some more definitions but we may do so at the risk of repeating ourselves or padding up this section unnecessarily.

Let us recapitulate the salient points of the news. The News is: perishable-When the event is understood and the tension is eased off- the news gets less informative and more of history; of interest to a large number of people; of unusual events and happenings; what is new to the public; an event put forward by a reporter-without a reporter, a news item does not exist.

However, you should remember that the general notion of the news varies with people and situations. Generally, though some of the points about news, may vary, but essential ingredients of the news are universally recognised.

Hard News and Soft News

The news is mainly divided into two main categories. Hart and Soft News. The Hard news is mostly event-centered. It is a narration of an event. The Hard news items are centered on, "What, when, where and why". Consider the following news item taken from the front page of "The Hindustan Times", Delhi Tuesday, May 20, 1997.

500 KILLED IN BANGLA CYCLONE

> At least 500 people were killed and several hundreds missing when a powerful cyclone hit Bangladesh's southeastern coastal disctricts today, report agencies.
>
> Official sources said that at least 400 people have been killed in Cox's Bazar and 100 others in Patuakhali. Storm, tidal surge and house collapse were responsible for the killings, the sources said.
>
> The cyclonic storm with a speed of 200 kph pounded the coastal belt this afternoon. Thousands of houses were flattened and trees and electric poles uprooted by the storm. The chittagong district control room sources said that the storm started hitting almost all the coastal areas of the district with light rainfall accompanied by gusty wind.
>
> Officials said about 3,00,000 coastal dwellers were evacuated to makeshift shelters.

No doubt, the major thrust of a daily newspaper is the hard news. The main task of the dailies is to provide information to the readers. But, another type of news more of analysis, reasons, background and interpretation is becoming a very important segment of the daily newspaper. Mere accounts of events do net satisfy the readers. They would like to enter beneath the upper crust of hard news. This type of news is called Soft news. Consider the following news item. This is taken from the edition of the Hindu as of the hard news.

CONFERENCES WITHOUT TRAVEL

> Videoconferencing equipment is playing a major role in a worldwide communications revolution. Time and travel costs have been saved by providing people with the facility to talk face-to-face with colleagues and customers anywhere in the world by operating videoconferencing equipment from their desks.
>
> The system, which over a keypad giving easy control over the audio visual link. Groups of people can be brought into a conversation by the system which also allows slides and illustrations to be displayed and common documents produced.

Videoconferencing technology will bring more efficient management control, quicker response time and better use of a company's resources.

It is bringing benefits in many different fields, including medicine and education. In California, for instance, it is being used for remote consulation and diagnosis between far flung medical establishments, meaning less travel for patients and rapid access to specialist advice for surgeons.

The Concept of News

News is one of the best known commodities in today's world. Everybody who understands a language and has access to mass media recognises it. The concept of news must have existed even before the beginning of the era of mass media. One may find relics of a Primitive system in remote tribal areas where people exchange local news during weekly markets just by talking to one another.

When two friends meet after sometime they exchange information which can be called personal news. Letters written to friends and relatives carry what can be described as news by the This kind of information exchange is continuing since early days of human society in one form or the other.

Everybody will agree that death makes news. If a person dies of a disease or an accident it makes news. The importance of this news is related to the importance of the person and/or deadliness of the disease.

Mrs. Indira Gandhi was assassinated. It was big news. If she had died of a heart attack or in an accident, even then it would have been big news. That news was important because of the importance of Mrs. Gandhi-other factors were there, but the biggest news value of that event was the person involved.

If a person dies in a road accident in madras it will be news in Madras; but if he dies of AIDS in a Madras hospital it will become news of not only national but of international significance. In this case the importance of news is because of the disease.

But even ordinary death of an ordinary old man will make news at least for those who know him and are related to him. It may not appear in a newspaper but it will be news to some people. Thus we can say that the concept of news in human society is as old as recognition of death as an event and its communication by any means to those whom the event would affect. Revolutions in transport and communication have led to various changes in significance and reach of the news but the basic concept is the same.

In this sense the concept of news may even be older than the concept of God. But as even today we do not have a universally agreed definition of God, there is no definition of news on which verybody agrees.

Before the era of newspapers and electronic media, news was communicated by word of mouth. Public announcements by those in power were communicated to the people by various kinds of drummers. Such announcements even now dominate the news coverage in the newspapers, radio and television in almost all countries respective of ideology. Radio and television stations become first targets in coups and those who snatch power from the old regime use these electronic drummers for their first announcements.

Though the concept is very old the word 'news' is relatively recent in origin. In English it appeared as "news" in 1423, "news is" in 1485 and evolved to "news" in 1523. It was only after 1550 that it became "news" and even in 1622 there was Butler's Weekly News in London while in 1685 we had such sentences as—"The amazing news of Charles at once were spread".

The four letters of the word news have been described as representing the four directions—North, East, West and South. News can come from any of these directions. But as we see every day all events do not make news. Only important and interesting events make news. Further, an event itself is not news—it becomes news when its account is available. Thus Bhagalpur Jail blindings made news several weeks after the event. Similarly, activities of Coomar Narain and Ram Swaroop were going on for quite some time before they made news 'when' the account became available.

History is also an account of important events. But it relates mainly to the past. News is in a way current history. Today's newspapers will be source material for historians of tomorrow as today historians consult newspapers of yester years in the archives. What is happening today may go down in history, but its account which media gives now is news.

But if new facts about an event of historical significance are brought out today then it will make news. What Richard Nixon wrote about the Indo-Pak war of 1971 made news more than a decade later.

Not only events but opinions also make news. Opinion of former prime minister Rajiv Gandhi about arms race in the world makes news. The opinion of the man in the street about the budget makes news. Editorial comments by important newspapers can also make news for other newspapers. Coverage of the Indian prime minister's visit in the media of the country visited will make news in India. What 'the Pakistani press is publishing about an event in India may be news for the Indian press. What the US press wrote about the Bhopal gas tragedy was news for Indian newspapers.

With these varying situations in mind we can attempt a definition of news: "News is an account of a recent event or opinion which is important or interesting".

Importance and interest are two factors that present unlimited variety and thus explain why an event is newsworthy for one newspaper or broadcasting station and not for many other newspapers and radio or TV networks; why one news item becomes world news while another may be fit for only a local daily.

VALUES NEWS

Importance and interest are often described as news values but in fact these represent the sum total of news values or intrinsic characteristics that distinguish news from non-news. Identifying and measuring these values is usually called news sense. It is commonly believed that reporters identify news by intuition. But this intuition, which should be called news sense, develops in news men who sub-consciously learn how to measure news values.

Change. It is a basic news value. If nothing happens there will be no change. But the world is not static. Every moment things are different from the moment before. The bigger the change and the more the people affected by this change the more important it is from the news point of view.

Conflict. Actual conflicts and even the danger of conflicts make news as they tend to bring about major change. All wars and threats leading to wars have proven record of newsworthiness. But conflicts of smaller dimensions like group or personal conflicts resulting in crimes, strike and demonstrations, etc., also make news.

Even conflicting ideas and resulting debates make up news. Tension and suspense often associated with conflicts are also regarded a news values.

Disaster. Be it a result of natural calamity like an earth-quake or a volcano eruption or be it a man made event like the Bhopal gas tragedy or the Kanishka crash-disasters always make news. It is also true of disasters of lesser dimensions like boat tragedies, small acts of sabotage resulting in loss of life or property or both.

Progress. Progress is also a news value as it is the positive result of efforts made by society. It improve quality of life. Through routine struggles of life frequently emerge shining successes. From laboratories after years of work emerge new devices, new inventions, new remedies. All this and its various dimensions make news.

Cause. Like consequence, the cause of a newsworthy event also makes news. Every event has consequences so has it causes also. The cause of a hotel fire may be known immediately it will make news, but if it is not known all efforts to find out the cause and possible interpretations will make news. Similarly, various theories and interpretations of Punjab crisis will keep on making news from time to time.

Consequence. The immediate and long-term consequence of an event also makes news. The more people it affects the greater the consequence. Fear of consequences of an event also makes news. Thus possible consequences of a nuclear war makes news and all efforts to avert it and failures or successes in that direction make news.

Consequence also serves as measure of conflicts, disaster and progress. The greater the consequence, the more the news value.

Eminence and Prominence. Involvement of eminent personalities in an event adds to its news value and it is directly proportional to the prominence of the person. Thus, if an eminent scholar says something on a problem it will have news value while the same remarks made by an ordinary person may go unnoticed.

When Mulk Raj Anand fainted while speaking at Lucknow it became national news. If this would have happened to a less known figure the importance of that event would have been reduced to that order.

Prominence is many a time built up by media. Media had a major role in bringing Jarnail Singh Bindrimwale, Charles Shobhraj, Billa and Ranga and Rajnarain into prominence. And then whatever they said or did, even if it did not have any other news value, got into newspapers just because of their prominence. People were interested. in them because they were familiar. A big chunk of news in media is about those who are known.

Proximity. News is meant for human beings. The prime concern of a man is himself then he is interested in his neighbourhood. If other things are equal, proximity becomes key news value. A traffic jam in Bombay will be more important for a newspaper published from Bombay but may not find a place in a Delhi newspaper. If the prime ministers visiting Madras his activities will get more space in the Madras edition of Indian Express as compared to the Chandigarh edition of the same newspaper.

Timeliness. It is also a basic news value as old news is no news. In a highly competitive world of journalism every medium tries to be first with news. News is a highly perishable commodity and therefore every medium tries to give the latest available to score a point over the other.

Novelty. If a dog bites a man, it is not news, but if a man bites a dog, it is news. This old newspaper saying recognises the news value of the unusualnovelty.

Human Interest: Almost everything in news concerns human beings, but this particular news value is the emotional context of the news event. Anything that appeals to everybody not because of interest in the subject but because everybody shares human experience has news value. Human interest is the element with which the reader identifies anything familiar that stirs his feelings. Crime stories often have a human interest angle that makes then readable.

Human interest content of stories is higher when ordinary persons are involved in extraordinary situations—an adventure, a disaster, a tragedy or a triumph. Human interest is also evolved when it depicts extraordinary persons in ordinary situations.

Evaluating a News Story

You know intuitively what a story is. Ever since you were old enough to speak, you have been telling stories and listening to stories. As soon as you could, you began reading them—mostly children's fiction at first, then factual stories as you grew older and began to read school books, magazines, and newspapers.

So you've been conditioned all your life to recognize stories. But when it comes to analyzing the components or putting together a story yourself, how well do you fare? Can you dash it off as quickly as you can tell it to a friend? Or do you freeze when you sit down at the typewriter?

If you are a would-be writer who freezes, chances are you have one or more of these problems:

1. You don't have all the necessary facts. You can't supply the specific who, what, where, when, why, and how that are the essential ingredients of every story.
2. You're a poor typist, and you're thinking less about the story than about where to put your fingers.
3. You have no clear picture of the person you are addressing. You can't identify his interests.
4. You don't understand fully enough the concept of "story."

Each point is important. Reporters always should have more information than they think necessary. They also must know what is important to the audience and have enough typing skill that manual awkwardness won't interfere with clear thinking. But above all reporters must have a good idea of what constitutes a story.

True, no all news appears in story form. Every newspaper publishes a lot of information as statistics of his stock market reports, weather readings, football and baseball standings, lists of births and divorces. News broadcasters, having less time than the newspaper has space, devote less attention to lists of names and numbers, but they too deal with a certain amount of nonstory material. News of this kind, however, can be gathered and recorded by anyone, regardless of talent or training. The reporter who expects to be more than a clerk must learn to put news in story form.

Stories: Fictional and Factual

The beginning reporter, exercising caution, can learn something about "story" from fiction. News stories and works of fiction differ, of course. News consists only of actual persons and events, with nothing invented, whereas fiction consists of imagined characters and scenes. The reporter's goals, too, usually differ from the fiction writer's. Most news stories are designed to inform or explain, whereas fiction is written to entertain, evoke emotion, or stimulate thought.

But the essential elements of the "story" are the same: people and action. Jaurnalists can use the analogy to fiction as long as they remember that the people they deal with are real and the actions they report are only those that could be proved in court.

Teachers of fiction define story as struggle. Call it conflict are merely action; the important thing is that something must happen. Without action, we have no story.

The simplest fiction plot involves are central character struggling to salve are basic problem. As the action progresses, the character encounters obstacles which require further action. In a good plot, the protagonist may move two steps backward for each step forward. At any rate, he or she keeps moving, struggling against obstacles are apposing forces. Struggle is the essence, and the story ends when the protagonist wins, loses, are quits. The reader is interested as much in the struggle itself as in its outcome.

In fiction are drama, the conflict may be either internal or external. The central character may struggle against a personal for against the forces of nature, against society are same segment of it, are against his own selfish impulses. In sophisticated fiction, the opposing force is seldom personified. It is only a situation, with no heroes are villains, against which a fallible human being struggles. This is the brand of fiction that mast closely resembles reality.

Fiction stories must include motivation and sequel-cases and effects. So should news stories. But perhaps the most important thing that reporters can learn from fiction is that all stories involve people individually are in groups-in action. Events never happen in a vacuum. People are always involved in them, and except for natural disasters-people usually cause them. The struggle may be anything but dramatic, the obstacles not even obvious, but struggles and obstacles are present in news as in fiction.

In its totality, news is the daily chronicle of mankind-people talking, arguing, fighting, trading, planning, building and destroying, winning and losing, making love and making war. It is the story of individuals and nations, humanity and inhumanity; and any definition that omits the human element mrisses the point entirely. All news concerns human beings. Even when a story is primarily about natural phenomena-storms, eclipses, droughts, floods, are earthquakes-we write about their effects on people are how people view them. We are human beings writing about human beings for human beings.

From all this, we can derive three rules for the beginning writer:

1. Put proper names into your story-names of individuals an organizations.

2. Use strong verbs-as strong as the action justifies.

3. Write mostly in the active voice, which stresses the actor. Most events dan't just happen; people cause them.

Avoid Overdramatizing

Before you charge off in a cloud of purple prose, bent on turning every story into a drama, a word of caution. No story is more than an abstracting from reality. It is never life itself. Until it is written, it isn't even a story. It is merely an event, an idea, are a set of Circumstances that becomes a story only through the reporter's preception and skill. And ethical reporters must always ask themselves whether they are seeinge "story" clearly and coolly are whether they are exaggerating the conflict and overdramatizing. Journalism has no place for the writer who "never lets facts stand in the way of a good story."

Life unlike fiction, is seldom melodramatic. It has few clearly defined heroes or villains, and even those can't be labeled as such. They can be characterized only through fair, objective reporting of their deeds and words. The "villain" in real life is seldom an individual or even an identifiable group. More often it is a situation that has developed over such a long period that the early causative factors-and the persons responsible for them-have been long forgotten. Society itself the circumstances under which it exists, its customs, and its restrictions is at the root of many evils.

Nor should the reporter seek out controversy. Like violence, controversy usually will make itself known. It is true, without conflict no story exists. But conflict doesn't necessarily imply either violence or controversy. For example, a scientist searching for a cure to cancer is engaged in a conflict against the forces of nature and the frustration of failures. This is by no means a controversy. Even when a controversy exists, the reporter must take pains to avoid portraying a simple difference of opinion as a confrontation.

Other Storytelling Limitations

As tellers of stories, journalists have several limitations. They have neither the time nor the space to develop a story as thoroughly and "realistically" as the fiction writer. Much of the minor action and physical description the fiction writer uses to make a scene vivid must be omitted as unimportant; the reader of news is more interested in the outcome than in the events leading up to it. Therefore, reporters seldom tell the story chronologically. Instead of keeping the audience in suspense, they being where fiction writers would end-with the climactic action and its net effect.

Nor do journalists have the fiction writers freedom of expression. They can't comment on the action or enter the characters' minds. They writer only what is said or done, not what a person thinks or feels, which means that they often must present action without fully explaining its motivation.

In fiction, the story usually ends when the protagonist wins, loses, or quits. In news, it's not that easy. First, we have no protagonist in the fiction sense, because reporters don't take sides. Second, there are few winners and few losers (except in the sports report), and sometimes you can't tell one from the other. Further, the action refuses to stop at a convenient place. Some human struggles seem to continue without end, and the only way journalists can approach the fiction writer's "satisfactory ending" is by quitting when they have presented all the facts available at the moment.

News is More Than Story

To the writer of fiction, the story is no a sense its own end. But to the journalist, the story is only a container, a form in which news is presented. And it is easier to define the container than its contents. People generally agree on what constitutes a story, but they differ widely over what constitutes news.

News must be timely, factual information which has some value to the reader or listener. It may be enlightening, instructive, or only entertaining. It may be only in interesting tidbit to store away in the mind, something that adds to a person's general knowledge, or it may be information that can be put to use immediately, such as announcements of future events. Regardless of its nature, it can be considered news only if the reader sees some benefit in it.

Indirectly, or course, the public may benefit from almost any current, factual information. The more a person knows, the more he or she can talk about. People more a person knows; the more he or she can talk about. People who gossip know this instinctively. And some people-salesmen, politicians, and others whose success depends partly on conversational ability-approach the news consciously with the goal of having something to talk about. (Reporters, too, can benefit from this approach. It they are well informed in several news areas in addition to their own, they seldom Jack an "ice-breaker" to open an interview.)

News has been defined as:

Anything You Didn't Know Yesterday. If it doesn't somehow add to what your already know, it isn't news.

Whatever Interests the Reader. If it doesn't' interest somebody, it's not news. On the other hand, some highly interesting information-gossip, for example-may not be news because it lacks significance.

Tomorrow's History Today. This is a good definition of the outstanding stories and even of some less attention-getting stories that are laden with statistics. But it gives news more importance than the bulk of it deserves.

Any Change in the Status Quo. This approach is based on the notion that something must happen, or there's no story.

The Status Quo Itself. The prevailing situation, which the public may ignore or take for granted, can be important news when it is made visible and analyzed.

A timely, factual report of events, ideas, and situations that interest the public—This may be the best definition of all. It combines timeliness and audience interest, and it is slightly less vague about subject matter. And, unlike the other definitions, it says that news isn't news until it is reporter.

The list could go on for several pages. But perhaps the best advice to beginners is that if it's timely, something the general public hasn't heard or noticed before, if it interests you or an identifiable portion of your audience, then it's news.

Many Publics, Mostly Local

Telling a story implies an audience. Defining news which is the content of the journalist's story involves determining the relationship between events and the interests of your public. Thus the concepts of story and news are inseparable from an awareness of audience or reader.

You may dream of writing the Big Story that will be read by everyone in the world, but it's only a dream. Even the most important international stories reach only a fraction of the world's population. And usually reporters write for a far more limited audience: the readers, listeners, or viewers in a precisely defined geographical area. The newspaper or broadcast station's first goal is to serve its own trade area. Most stories, therefore, are primarily of local or regional interest. The community its economy, geography, history, traditions, and ethnic composition plays a large role in determining what constitutes news. For example, a story from Cuba presumably is more important to people in nearby Miami than it would be to Kansans. And a story from Oslo or Stockholm will attract more readers in Minneapolis with that city's large population of Scandinavian descent, than it would in Houston, New Orleans, or Santa Fe. Similarly, a change in the price of gold automatically is top priority news in Lead, South Dakota, whose only industry is the Homestake Gold Mine. And the price of corn means more in Iowa than in California.

No community, of course, is an entirely homogeneous group of people. Instead, it consists of many small publics within the general public. Each of these special groups is united by a common bond of interest. And to build and hold mass circulation, newspapers must recognize the particular interests of each group-blue-collar workers, fans, youth, housewives, parents of school children, the family and friends of the bride. Reporters soon learn to write for numerous publics with interests they may not share.

Interests Shared by All

Regardless of their different interests, all our readers and listeners are human beings, and they are alike in all ways that one human being is like another. No study of the reporter's audience is complete, therefore, without some examination of what writers call "the human condition."

Lawrence Durrell wrote four novels, known collectively as The Alexandria Quartel, in which he attempted to demonstrate that in the final analysis all things will be shown to be true of all people. Perhaps Durrell's is an overstatement, but psychologists agree that all humans are much alike, that they are both rational and emotional, that they live in a constant state of conflict between self and society, that they are always struggling to reduce the tension of this conflict. Humans are basically selfish, yearning for freedom yet realizing that without social order no individual can be free. They know they are mortal, that someday they must die, a truth against which they constantly rebel. Since they can't attain physical immortality, their alternative goal is to live as long and as well as they can. Most people want love and affection, recognition for their achievements, and status among their peers. All want to be healthy, and most want to prosper.

To summarise, all humans want a longer, healthier, and happier life both for themselves and their children, who may be their only ticket to immortality. And, perhaps unconsciously, they expect the media to supply information that will help them attain these goals. Primarily, people want stories that will:

1. Warn of imminent physical danger-an outbreak of war or local violence, an approaching storm, an epidemic, an unsafe product, or adulterated food.

2. Report developments that promise to extend life-a pace agreement, a medical discovery, improvements in hospital facilities, a new system of keeping physically fit.

3. Expose threats to individual freedom-political oppression, economic injustice, infringements of civil rights.

4. Help them improve their economic or political position-simple informative stories about business developments

and the employment situation, or explanatory or even instructive stories about managing investments, preparing for retirement, juggling the family budget, or preparing the tax returns. A political or economic feature even may be a success story about a person the reader dreams of emulating.

5. Tell what is happening or is expected to happen to their children readers want to know what kind of world their children will live in and how educators are preparing them for it.
6. Describe improvements or deterioration in the quality of living-urban decay, the crime rate vanishing wildlife, advancements in housing and recreation, changing mores, improvements in clothing and cooking.

Reporter as Watchdog

To help protect their audience, many reporters view their role as that of a public watchdog. They stand ready to detect and report anything dangerous to the public's physical, economic, or political security-a hazardous drug, unsafe toys, business collapses, waste of public funds, political blunders, pollution of the environment, racial discrimination, violence and injustices of many kinds. They try to provide information that will "keep the establishment honest."

Because of this watchdog function, the press often is criticized as a purveyor of only bad news. Yet without this "bad" news, how would the public be warned? How could the average person acquire the information he needs to act with enlightened selfinterest? The thoughtful editor realizes that "bad" news is one of his more important commodities, that somehow he must keep the reader informed without becoming a chronic alarmist.

The first step toward balanced news judgment is to recognize that the press has a responsibility to report progress as well as threats. Arms limitations, cancer treatments, reduced taxes, and shorter work weeks are at least as important as the more depressing stories. Any event or situation that affects the reader's security in any manner, favourable or unfavourable, is top priority news.

Working Classifications

Not all stories deal with life, death, taxes, food, clothing, and shelter. And of those that do, not all are concerned with immediate action. Reporters write many "idea" stories about religion and philosophy which deal with universal interests but which are hardly "gut issues." In addition to such stories that appeal to the intellect, they write many that appeal largely to the readers' emotions-their vanity (they like to see their names in print), their curiosity about neighbours, their desire for a thrill, a shudder, or a laugh.

How can we classify such a wealth of subject matter with so many different goals? We could, perhaps, talk of "hard" news (that which is immediately useful) versus "soft" news (That which has delayed value). Or "spot" news (highly perishable because of the time element) versus "feature" copy (usable anytime this season). Or we could departmentalize news into sports, home and family, city, state, national, and international. Or we could distinguish between the investigative story, which can require weeks of digging, and the publicity story, which can require weeks of digging, and the publicity release which arrives without any effort on the reporter's part. We could even classify stories by whether they deal with events, ideas, or situations, or by whether they are informative, explanatory, or entertaining.

Perhaps the wise course would be to avoid categorisation completely. But to understand how professionals think, let's examine a classification system often used by working journalists. This divides stories into three categories: straight news interpretation, and human interest. Like all classification, this system is arbitrary, artificial, and often difficult to apply. Indeed, it is a rare story of any length that is entirely "straight" with no interpretation or human interest. Nevertheless, these three categories are used so commonly that the beginner at least should be aware of them.

This often deals only with events. Straight news results from simple surveillance. Most routine stories obituaries, meeting notices, traffic accidents, crime reports, and weather roundups-fall into this category. When city editors tells reporters to "play it straight," they mean to confine the story strictly to the facts and avoid any attempt to determine motivation or long-range consequences or arouse any emotional response in the reader. On most simple stories, reporters encounter no problem; they play it straight automatically. But on some sensitive developments, editors may have to warn them against interpretation because motivation or consequence can't be determined immediately or because of the danger of arousing violent public response.

Interpretation

This is an effort to tell what the facts mean in terms of causes and effects. Even the world "interpretive" is enough to start a controversy in some newsrooms, where editors may argue long and inconclusively over the definition of objectivity. For this reason, many working journalists never speak of "Interpretive" pieces. They call them "backgrounders," "situationers" or "depth reports," if only to avoid arguments.

Interpretation, by whatever name it goes, deals more often with situations and ideas than with isolated events. It is explanatory writing, usually arising from analytical coverage of government, the economy, education, or social problems. It requires expect knowledge of the subject and an imposing array of facts, plus the ability to put a complex situation or idea into simple, understandable language. Reporters try to tell what the facts mean without resorting to speculation. Occasionally, when the meaning isn't clear, reporters may be forced to quote the speculation of other observers. If so, they must know the subject well enough to pick sources who can speculate with some authority.

Because the line between interpretation and editorializing is so fine, editors often discourage beginners from any attempt to "interpret." They prefer to assign interpretive stories to reporters who already have demonstrated the necessary knowledge, judgement, and skill to present interpretation fairly and clearly.

Human Interest

In this kind of news, which usually focuses on an individual rather than a group, the actual subject is a feeling or an emotion. Writers however, don't editorialize or express subjective reaction. They achieve their effect best by "putting the reader there," by showing the event or situation that arouses emotions or a sense of humor. This is sensory writing, close kin to fiction, and reporters often use narrative organization and other literary devices. They round out the story with colour, description, anecdote, dramatic quotes, or dialogue; but as in any other reporting, they never go beyond the provable facts.

A story of this sort, if it had been written without names, probably would have been rejected. Newsreporters tend to be extremely skeptical about " eat human interest" stories. They more they sound like good fiction, the more likely they are to be fiction.

Featurising and the Feature Article

Every reporter likes to write the story that is thoroughing, and interesting from beginning to end the story that will still be usable next week or ever next month because it has a semitimeless quality. Stories of this sort, which must rely on something other than immediacy for their appeal, are known as feature articles. The subject may be anything-a person, an idea, a situation, a hobby, a process, or a historic anniversary. The purpose may be to inform, to explain, to instruct, or only to entertain. The only qualities that set the feature apart from other stories are its lack of immediacy and its depth treatment of an interesting or provocative subject. For good examples, see the inside pages of your Sunday newspaper.

A feature should have a 'news peg', that is, it should be related to a topic recently in the news. Sometimes the news peg is implicit; sometimes it is expressed clearly near the beginning. The "peg" is the writer's way of telling readers why the article is being published why they should bother reading it.

The rest of the story quotes businessmen, a banker, a lawyer, and several women on the divorcee's plight. At no point does it cite the date of any specific action. It appears, therefore, that it could have been written several weeks before publication.

Although human interest is not an absolute requirement, most effective features contain a considerable amount. The reason is simple: human interest, expressed in colour, description, anecdote, and dialogue, is a proven means of keeping the reader's attention throughout a long story. This aspect of most features has caused some confusion in terminology. When editors tell reporters to "featurise" a spot news story, they usually mean to play up the human interest, to focus on whatever is amusing, odd, or unusual. They seldom mean to turn it into a genuine depth article.

Classic Yardsticks

All news judgments are relative. Whenever editors say "This is news," they mean "for this newspaper in this community today." Tomorrow the story may be dead because it has lost its timeliness. Or it may be crowded out of the paper stories of greater significance. We can never judge a news story except in relation to other stories at the same moment. Even then, the evaluation of news is a highly subjective process.

One editor may view the events of the day in the broad context of world history while another news to the old-fashioned notion that "a dog fight on Main Street is worth more than a revolution in Latin America." The first accuses the other of provincialism; the second retorts that the first is guilty of Afghanistanism. Editors are no more agreed, on news value than are readers.

Still, no matter how they apply them, all editors measure news values by the same yardsticks. These are:

Significance—whether the event promises or threatens to change the course of history. An event's significance is determined by how many persons it will affect, to what extent, and for how long. The reporter asks what will be the consequences.

Magnitude—how much, how much, how many, how big, how fast. Everything else being equal, a million is bigger news than a thousand. A plane crash that kills 120 is bigger news than one that kills five and a hurricane with 200-mile-an-hour winds is bigger news than one that barely qualifies. The reporter asks how many are dead and how much will it cost.

Timeliness—the reader wants information that's new. The reporter asks when did it happen, and ordinarily tries to work the day into the first sentence to let the reader know that it's new. Priority usually goes to the latest action, but even an action that happened long ago may still be spot news if it is only now being disclosed. For example, any new information about Noah's Ark would be news.

Proximity—a two-dollar word for the local angle. If all else is equal, here is greater than there. Readers are interested most in those events closest to them. The reporter asks where.

Prominence—names make news. These are generally names of persons or institutions that already have aroused public interest. The name might be that of the president or a senator, a celebrity in sports or show business, or an institution such as Harvard, the U.S. Marine Corps, or the Central Intelligence Agency. The reporter asks who.

Human Interest—a quality that every reader can relate to personal experience or recognize as a universal aspect of life. Does the story hit home? Here the reporter can examine only his or her own reaction.

INGREDIENTS OF THE NEWS

You have discovered some elements which make the news. Now, in this Unit, we shall closely look at all these elements and try to understand them comprehensively. The following are some of the important ingredients of the news. We shall learn about them systematically.

Timeliness. News must be timely and new. It will not arouse interest if it is already known, or brought to notice long after its occurrence.

Nearness or Proximity. People are more interested in what happens under their nose in their village, town, country rather than in distant places. Similarly, they are more concerned in the occurrence of an immediate impact on them. The news that the price of rice may rise, will make them sit up more than a report that government subsidy for fertilizers has been abolished.

Conflict. People gather in a street if and when there is a fight. Conflicts of all kinds are part of life and make good copy.

Government Action. The passing of a law or other orders concerning general people, cabinet meetings, parliament and assembly sessions, notifications about new rules and regulations are news worthy. However, you should begin with the impact of such events such as "Motorists can make one time payment of road tax from Jan. 1. The Motor Vehicles Act was amended by parliament today to this effect."

Prominence. What happens to important people makes news. The value of the news increases with the prominence of the person involved. Former Indian Prime Minister Rajiv Gandhi's assassination made the world headlines, but the murder of a village head may be carried only in a local daily. What the prominent people say, is also grist for a reporter's mill, particularly if they make some announcements which have an impact on the common people.

Development Projects and Issues. This is not news about government action activities, though sometimes it will also qualify to be covered.. The invention of a high yield variety rice and its success in changing the life-style of a community will be of interest to people who will financially benefit from it;

Human Interest. If a woman gives birth to quadruplets in a village, it will make news in every household. That should make news every where else too. People are interested in what is happening to other people. In addition, oddities, humour, tragedy, triumph over handicap, stories involving kinds, animals all make for good human interest stories.

Weather and Sports. Both the weather and the sports have great news value. Arrival of monsoon or cyclones is a front-page news. An entire page is devoted to sports in many newspapers.

Follow-up. The news item become very interesting for the general public when the issues are followed and updated. It is extremely important to remember that follow-up of news events will keep the interest of the readers alive. A good news story does not end at the first reference.

New values differ from community to community, country to country. What is common practice to one community may appear to be an oddity for a city-bred audience. While reporting such events, you should be careful not to appear to be derogatory in tone or in content. Similarly, news values are different for developing and developed countries. For the industrialised and individualised societies of developed countries, communally provocative speeches and incidents may be reported word for word, blow by blow. But the same treatment would be suicidal and would be lighting a powder keg in a communally sensitive, illiterate, developing country. You should take all possible care in reporting such developments keeping in mind the volatile nature of the audience and the reach of your publication.

You must also follow some journalistic ethics; and at times impose & some selfcensorship. Freedom of the press is not a licence to damage or destroy anyone's reputation. You should strictly adhere to the following guidelines, among others to ensure that journalism is constructive and not destructive.

Accuracy is basic to any news item. When you fail in accuracy, you lose credibility. Cross check your facts and information. Check figures, names and facts. Check how names are spelled. Did you get the first name correct? People are greatly offended by misspelled names. If you are paraphrasing a speech from a text given to you, make sure you do not change the meaning or quote statements out of context. Exclude rumours or gossips from your report. To be balanced in reporting, is as important as being accurate. If you are writing about a controversy, give both sides of the story. When reporting a strike, for instance, give the claim of the authorities and also that of the workers on how far it is successful. If it is a 'hartal,' or tends to give too much of foreign news which has little relevance to your readers. You should not mix your opinion in the story. Report only facts and other people's opinions. You should be a disinterested observer, reporting events without taking sides. A story may be best in verbiage. Your introductory sentence should be short and in active voice to the maximum extent possible. The ideal length of each para may be 3-4 lines containing one two-three small sentences to facilitate easy comprehension. The original news item has statistics and many technical terms which may easily confuse the ordinary readers.

Whenever you do a news report, consider the impact your story should have. Will it induce some changes somewhere for the better? If you write about a dilapidated, overused bridge in time to move the authorities to take up repairs, you may help avert a tragedy. Develop a "nose for news", particularly news that will make an impact.

A reporter, to be successful, should have a variety of reliable and highly placed contacts. They are some of the useful "sources" for his information. Among the news sources, some are available to all reporters, such as Public meetings, monitoring of radio and television programmes, press conferences, news briefings, seminars and other functions. But the contacts are sources of exclusive information for the reporter. They may be in the government, public or private sector business or just anywhere. Sometimes a valuable tip-off may come from an ordinary person such as the driver of a minister's personal car.

Some of the contacts may like to be quoted for the story as it gives them publicity. In case of a critical story, they may not risk their neck. In that case, the story may have to be distributed to 'sources' only. It is the responsibility of a reporter to ensure the truthfulness of a report. In such cases, it will be advisable to keep some documents (copies) or and audio tape to prove your story.

In the business of collecting the news, particularly of critical and investigative nature confrontation with the government is inevitable. A politician seeks to shape the world towards the ends he considers worthy, A journalist chronicles daily events, places facts before the public, and tries to communicate that he considers truth. This may not suit, the politician all the time, hence confrontation may occur. In case, confrontation becomes inevitable, a reporter should face it.

He should also treat his sources as "sacred". There may be pressure on the journalist from the government and the judiciary at times to disclose the sources. Protecting one's source is a cardinal principle of journalism.

You have to be cautious of advice of unattributable information by the government.

An editorial in the Washington Post on Dec. 17, 1971 by Executive Editor, Bejamin Bradley is still relevant today.

"Over the last five years, the reporters and editors of this newspaper have become increasingly concerned about the use and abuse of the unattributable information by the government at background briefings. In theory, un attributed information given to the press by the governmental background briefings enables the press to do a better job of reporting. In practice, this is less and less true. Background briefings have become the vehicles for the government to give its versions of the news, to use the press as a vehicle for its policy announcements and its political advantage without taking responsibility for what it is saying. This practice has been true of every administration. The Washington Post, newspaper has long been a party to this practice. The public has suffered from this collusion between the government and the press.

We are now convinced that we have engaged in this deception and done this disservice to the readers long enough. Therefore, it is now the policy of the Washington Post in its coverage of government news briefings, to insist on public accountability for the public business. We instructed our reporters to insist through every means available to them that material offered at these briefings should be on record and fully attributable. If ground rules are imposed providing for anything less than full attribution on the record, Washington Post reports will immediately say that attribution be made direct on the record.

If that request is refused, the reporter will seek attribution specific enough so that no reader can reasonably be confused.

If this request is refused, the Washington. Post has instructed its reporters to inform the agency or official that the newspaper's handling of the material will public we believe that responsibility cannot be transferred by us to any public Official or circumscribed by government edict. The Washington Post believes that while certain circumstances may make full on-the-record attribution impractical, the public interest is not served permitting statements of policy to be made by government officials who are unwilling to be held accountable for their own words.

The decision whether to remain voluntarily in the briefing is one for the reporter's discretion, under normal conditions, he would remain and report under these guidelines.

Nothing in this policy concerns contacts with government officials and other news sources, initiated by reporters of Washington. Post. In these instances, the contacts will continue on an independent, individual basis, under terms understood and accepted by the reporter and the news source.

FUNCTIONS OF NEWSPAPER DEPARTMENT

The FUNCTIONS of a newspaper can be set out under three main headings: *(i)* to inform, *(ii)* to instruct and *(iii)* to entertain.

Information

The first is obviously the most important function but the other two must be paid equal attention if a newspaper is to make a lasting appeal to the public. The first channel of instruction is the leading article or, what is called, the editorial which is the best medium at the newspaper's disposal for the interpretation of the news of the moment. The leader writer today may not have quite the same influence on the reader that he had when there were few newspapers but, nonetheless, a popular newspaper even today guides the public opinion by interpreting the news and elaborating the opinions for creating an impact on the readers.

Instruction

Modern newspapers cannot afford to make their leading article dry as dust. In fact, the short snappy leading article has become one of the most striking features of modern jounialism. It can fairly be said that if the reader studies the leading article in his favourite newspaper every day, he can obtain a very good picture of international, national and local affairs. While a reader may not accept the views of the leader as the gospel, all the same it enables him to adjust his ideas and encourage him to think for himself. Instruction is also to be gained from many of the articles on specialised subjects.

Entertainment

Modem newspapers tend to carry many light materials including articles written in light vein. These features not only indirectly influence the opinions of the readers but also fulfil the third function—entertainment.

Every paper by a process of trial and error must discover what form of entertainment pleases most of its readers for the greater part of the time. The tastes of the readers: of different journals vary considerably. Even serious newspapers and magazines nowdays are expected to carry strip cartoons or topical ecomics here and there. It is one thing on which most of the newspapers seem to be agreed as it makes for the continuing popularity of short stories, film reviews, social comments, etc. The pictures, perhaps more than anything else, combine the three functions of the newspaper. The decision on the part of some of the more serious-minded papers to introduce a picture page receives welcome letters. Newspapers have many ways of entertaining the, reader. Articles on every conceivable kind of sport, on bridge, on gardening, on chess on cookery and even on the latest fashions achieve the same aim of giving the readers, for a few moments at any rate, a welcome change from the cares and anxieties of every day life. In the same way, cartoon is always welcome.

The reader may complain that there is so much in his newspaper that he cannot read it at all, but the aim of the editor must surely be to provide something which will interest, instruct and entertain every reader in every issue of the paper or journal.

ATTITUDE OF A NEWSPAPER TOWARDS READERS

A newspaper is primarily dependent on its readers for its very existence. Circulation is fundamental. It is not upon advertising but upon circulation that the life and prosperity of a newspaper depends. If it has readers it is in a favourable position to get advertising; but it has to get readers first and to keep them. In earlier years of Indian journalism, the circulation brought more revenue into most newspaper tills than advertising. However, in a period of business expansion, advertising has had an extensive growth. In the case of some newspapers it provides two-thirds of the incomc.

However, there are many newspapers, specially the smaller ones published from State capitals, instead of metropolitan cities, who receive a large revenue from circulation as from advertisement; some receive more. But quite apart from this matter of proportional income, it has always been and always must be a fundamental fact that newspaper publication is founded on readership and that the social, economic and political functions of a newspaper are performed primarily for the benefit of the readers.

This puts a great deal of power over a newspaper into the hands of its readers. They can make or break it. It cannot be said too often that the people as a whole can have very much a kind of newspaper they want. Even in a city with a monopoly newspaper situation, editors and publishers are very sensitive to a situation when readers begin to turn to the radio or out-of-town papers for their news. They know they are never secure. Hence, they do not dare to let circulation slip. They know that the paper's prosperity depends upon readers' aceptance. This power of their newspapers cannot exist in a dictatorship in which news as well as editorial policies are controlled by government. Nor is there need in such a state for the people to exercise any control over news policies, since they have ao political powers which true information by newspapers would implement.

But in a democracy, the benefits which the people derive from their power over the newspapers are balanced, of course, by responsibilities. This is a privilege which readers enjoy of being informed about events and situations at home and abroad.

No wonder, newspapers depend on their ability to gear up information system to satisfy their reader. Some of the newspapers carry out systematic surveys about their readership. They invite comments, suggestions and even criticism from their readers—firstly to satisfy the ego of the readers; secondly, to make their newspapers more responsive to the readers' opinion.

A large part of our newspaper reading is done in situations of relaxation. Father comes home from work tired. He washes up, has a good dinner with his family, feels better. In the living room, the children have turned on the radio, or perhaps the television set. Father settles into his easy chair, takes off his shoes, lights up his pipe picks up his paper. Who can begrudge him enjoyment of his paper? He needs enjoyment, relaxation, escape- from his day-long worries. That is what comics, sports and amusing features are for; that is why picture pages, comics, and sports pages (in that order) rank next to front pages in reader-taste surveys.

But good reading. of newspapers does not stop with such diverting matters. A mind which is awake to the crucial problems on which the fate of the world depends today wants far more than the answers to such questions as 'What has the Shah Commission heard about the emergency excesses today?' or 'How Bishen Singh Bedi has fared in India's test match with Australia?' A lively minded reader looks over the latest dispatches from European and African capitals; he reads the correspondence from Washington; he must gather the views of the columnists and editorial writers, In other words, a hardheaded reader will always spend a considerable amount of time oil 'hard' news, leaving concentration on 'soft' news to soft heads.

The serious reader will also want enough of a given story to get his teeth into. If the Prime Minister or a retired General of the Army,or a Nobel Prize winner makes a major pronouncement, he will read, if not the whole of it, at least a sizable portion. The news paper serves all classes of readers and must always be a highly composite miscellany, with thousands of brevities; but a good reader wants significant' events, situations and pronouncements set forth with fullness and detail, and he is wilting to give time and effort to reading and studying such stories.

In these days when there is more leisure than ever before, there should be more me for serious reading. If our people will not read seriously, they will not deserve a mature press and radio.

Colleges can do something about it. College courses on current events which emphasise techniques of newspaper reading and radio-news listening (and now television viewing) are now part of the curricula of all good moder colleges. In colleges and universities, specialised training of this kind, outside schools of journalism, is likely to be neglected on the theory that the student will keep abreast of the news anyway—perhaps in connection with courses in the social science . But neither the colleges nor the universities should dare to neglect this essential training.

Colleges may help, and the press and radio may do much toward the end of the proper reception and appreciation of the news-an important patriotic duty—but we must remember that, after all, the final verdict on good reading and therefore on a good news system rests with us, the people—the readers, hearers, and viewers themselves.

GENERAL AND ADMINISTRATIVE FUNCTIONS

A newspaper is of all modern private institutions, most comprehensive in function and complicated in principle. Although the existence of a newspaper is subject to economic problems right from the first issue until it comes have a very large circulation, primarily it is a vehicle for the satisfaction' of human wants. It performs this function in three ways: firstly, the newspaper is a collector and distributor of news and in this function it beats every possible rival except perhaps the radio and' the T.V. Secondly, it is a vehicle of opinion and in virtue of this capacity, it often becomes the victim of the mighty or of the long purse, although occasionally, it enjoys the capacity for resistance to outside pressure—a factor which guarantees to it more independence than sometime appears on the surface. Thirdly, a newspaper serves as the great introducer of business from one trader to another.

In modern businesses, the annual amount spent on advertising in general, and newspapers in particular, runs into millions of rupees. It is only recently that Radio and T.V. commercials have started sharing a good part of this amount. It is the existence of this colossal revenue which makes possible the costly task of collecting and transmitting the news of the world from all places to all other places at once. It is common place that the small amount paid by each reader for the purchase of his newspaper, journal or periodical whatever it may be, would be very far from defraying the expenses of providing him with all that he finds in it.

The most important and exacting function of the newspaper is the provision of a daily or periodical supply of news—and all the news. The distinction between supply of enough news and all the news is of immense practical importance for a newspaper, because it trebles the difficulty imposed on the producers of the newspaper. The reader as a general rule, consults only a small part of the reading matter of interest to him—sometimes this may be very little in any issue. The reader therefore commonly receives the impression of a large amount of space regularly wasted, but very few readers are aware of the simple truth—what may be called pure news matter that almost every issue has had much more 'copy provided for it and fejected' as appears in the paper.

The practical task of the editors and sub-editors in making up their daily issues consists not just scrapping together material for the printer but rejecting most of it. This particularly applies to all the evening newspapers wherein many a report or 'story' appearing in the early morning is cut down or 'killed' before nightfall. However, a newspaper is expected to fulfil its responsibility to provide all news, everything printable that has happened and not kept secret by governments or private parties. There is only one excuse for leaving out an item of news, that is, that more important news has claimed precedence over it and crowded it out.

It is evident, therefore, that the collection of news is, strictly speaking, extra-editorial or, to be more precise, it is under the general but not the immediate direction of the editor. It is an elaborate and almost automatic system consisting partly of a few world-wide organisations or news agencies functioning for general news which supply the news for the common 'benefit of a large number of newspapers, and partly of a team of special correspondents attached to each individual newspaper.

Special correspondents of a newspaper have the function of securing exclusive news for their own newspaper and to emphasise and pay particular attention to that class of news which their paper would consider its strong point. This may involve, to some extent, duplication or overlapping of news systems but it is a matter of importance for each newspaper to provide special services to the reader which car have access to exclusive 'stories' other than those distributed by national or world news agencies. The stories received from the special correspondents are also a means of directly or indirectly influencing public opinion in favour of the policies to which the newspaper may be wedded, or it may help the editorial viewpoint of a newspaper.

If each and every newspaper in a country were required to limit the publication of news subscribed by world-wide agencies or national news agencies, all the newspapers would become stereotyped and there will be no point in having several of them. It is only in totalitarian regimes like Russia and China that national newspapers bring out millions of copy each morning under government auspices and control, and the dissemination of news and views is thoroughly controlled.

NEWSPAPER DEPARTMENTS

Bruce Westley divides newspaper work into three basic categories. Each of these departments is distinctly different yet each is wholly dependent on the smooth functioning of the others. These areas of responsibility are usually referred to as "business" "mechanical" and "editorial". Working newsmen are more likely to call them, in order, "the front office", "the back shop" and "the newsroom".

Newspaper editing is actually only one operation among several in 'the newsroom" but the editors, particularly, must know how other branches of the total newspaper operate in order to do their job with maximum efficiency. The copy desk is essentially the "crossroads" between the editorial and mechanical branches of the business. The copy editor must know the mechanical phase pretty thoroughly in order to perform his editorial function.

Business Administration. The business office is the "counting house" of the newspaper profession. It has an obvious duty to keep the organization afloat financially (It could even be argued that the 'newspaper has a duty to its readers to keep solvent).

The newspaper business office operates pretty much like any other business office. Ordinarily, it has major divisions: an advertising department (which might be broken down into two autonomous departments, classified and display advertising); a circulation department, a promotion department, and an accounting or auditing department. Each of these branches is typically headed by a major officer of the business staff. Usually the entire operation is directed by a "business manager," to whom each of these department heads is responsible. The business manager function often is handled by the publisher himself, especially in the case of smaller dailies.

Advertisement Department. The advertising department, headed by an advertising manager, ordinarily has four divisions:

(a) The local or retail division consists of a staff of specialists who solicit, lay out, correct, and sometimes "merchandise" local advertising accounts. This can be expected to be the largest of the advertising department subdivisions and offers the most creative employment in newspaper, advertising for journalism graduates with advertising training.

(b) Another group of specialists concerns itself with obtaining and handling "foreign", or "national' advertising accounts. This division deals, directly with advertising agencies which handle the "accounts of the big advertisers, usually with the help of an advertising representative in metropolitan cities, a service which intercedes for the newspaper directly with the agencies.

(c) Another concern of the advertising manager is "classified", although this may be a separate department. Classified ads have gained steadily in recent years as a source of newspaper revenue and hence are receiving increasing attention by newapaper executives.

(d) A fourth division of an advertising department is the "merchandising" or "service" division. Its purpose is to assist the advertiser in getting the maximum return on his advertising budget. This is the most recent and rapidly growing phase of newspaper advertising and ranges from a part-time trouble-shooter to a complex research organisation ready to provide a potential advertiser with detailed information on the buying habits of the newspaper's readers with reference to his particular product.

The advertising manager coordinates all these activities and is the person ordinarily responsible directly to the business manager, and so metimes directly to the publisher, for their successful operation.

Circulation Department. Circulation is another major division of the business office and is usually headed by a major executive, tht! circulation manager, since the newspaper ultimately stands or falls on the basis of the number of steady readers that can be enrolled.

The circulation manager may have any or all of the following subdivisions under his supervision:

(i) **City Circulation.** It involves the maintenance of circulation records for the city of publication; the recruitment supervision and reimbursement of carrier boys; the supervision of district men who oversee circulation by subdivisions of the city, taking responsibility for moving papers to the news-stands, relations with news-stand operators, etc.

(ii) **Area Circulation.** Responsibilities here include getting papers destined for the surrounding area into the mail and operation of a fleet of tempos/taxis to carry the papers into surrounding are as where mail service is not rapid enough.

The circulation manager is also in charge of moving the papers into the appropriate distribution channels as they move into the mailing room from the press room.

(iii) **Sales Promotion.** It involves the direction of an office staff to keep records, notifying subscribers when their subscriptions need renewing, the handling of complaints, new subscriptions and renewals over the counter, by mail, etc.

Promotion is essentially the "public relations" department of the newspaper. Where a separate promotion department exists, it usually is responsible for initiating promotion policies, subject to the approval of the publisher, and usually coordinates the promotional activities of other departments.

Mechanical Department. The entire mechanical operation is usually under the supervision of plant superintendent who is directly responsible to the publisher. In a typical situation, he will have five departments under his control; the composing room, the stereotype department, the press room, the engraving department, and the proof desk.

The basic functions of each are:

(i) Composing Room. This is the point of chief contact between the editorial side and the mechanical side. It is. in this department that "copy" is set into type and the type is assembled into newspaper pages. The type is "set" by automatic typesetting machines such as the Linotype. "Straight matter" or body type is set according to instructions on news copy sent from the newsroom, headlines are set from similar directions, ads are first set into type and then assembled on the basis of instructions on advertising copy from the advertising department. All of these materials are then assembled into newspaper pages, following the instructions on page "dummies," which show where each element is to go.

The composing room is often subdivided, especially in the larger plants, to permit the greater efficiency that specialization makes possible. Hence there may be an "ad alley" where ads are made up before they are put into newspaper pages.

(ii) Press Room. Rotary presses can turn out newspapers at phenomenal speeds. They not only print but cut, fold, and trim the papers and deliver them directly to the mailing room.

(iii) Stereotype Department. Here newspaper pages are run through a series of steps which prepare them to be clamped as curved plates of metal onto today's high-speed rotary presses.

Some small daily papers still use "flatbed" or "cylinder" presses and others use "Duplex" presses. In both cases the papers are printed directly from type and hence there is no need for a fullscale stereotype department as described here. The vast majority of dailies use rotary web perfecting presses, which means that the newspaper is printed on paper which feeds from huge rolls and the impression is applied from curved plates which rotate at high speed. This requires that the pages be converted from the flat form in which they are originally made up to the curved plate from which they are actually printed.

The stereotype department has two major operations; first, to roll out a reverse impression of the newspaper page onto a papiermache "mat"; then to "cast" into a curve by pouring molten metal against the curved surface of the mat. After the cast has cooled and been trimmed, it is ready to be clamped onto the press.

(iv) Engraving Department. Many smaller newspapers have insufficient need for "art" to operate an engraving department, having the work done commercially instead. However, most large newspapers find it economical to do their own work.

Photoengraving reduces news pictures and other newspaper art to a form in which they can be printed. In the case of a photograph, the job is to "screen" the picture in such a way that an etched metal plate is produced with a surface of dots. The dots vary in size to produce shadings of black and white that can be impressed on paper.

(v) Proof Desk. In a sense, proof desk lies by the side of the mechanical, editorial and advertising departments but is usually responsible to the mechanical superintendent. Its object is to correct all typographical errors. A "proof" is taken of all material set in the composing room, including ads and editorial matter, by inking the type and taking an impression of it on a rather simple "proof press". These proofs are then compared with the "copy" to make sure that the two conform. Proof reading is hence a more or less mechanical operation, unlike copy reading.

Editorial Department. The primary concern of the copy editor in the organizational chart of his newspaper is, of course, the editorial department. Here the description is not so easy, since very marked differences are discernible from one newspaper to another. However, a typical organizational scheme would go something like-this:

The editorial department actually has two sides, and usually these are separately responsible to the publisher. They are "news" and "editorial". The news side is usually under the supervision of a managing or executive editor. The editorial page crew consists of editorial writers and is directed by a "chief editorial writer," and "editor", or "editor-in-chief", or sometimes an "editorial page editor".

(i) **The News Desk.** All stories destined for the newspaper, whether they come from the typewriters of reporters and rewrite men or from the several wire services, teleprinters. and other sources-require editing. This, duty falls chiefly on the copyreader who sits on the horseshoe shape table called the desk. The city editor and other editors read all the copy.

In the old days there was what was called the universal desk system under which the desk editor handled everything that came in. Nowdays, even in small dailies, the work is usually divided between the city desk and the teleprinter's desk. Between them they edit the copy and write headlines for all spot news—everything except sports and financial coverage.

The independent or separate desk system in operation on a large scale allocates the news of different readers, each of whom has his own team of copyreaders. The editors with a crew of men edit the news designated as cable, teleprinter, city beats, society, business, finance, sports and reserve news. In larger newspapers there is a separate desk for international news.

Where the system is the universal desk or separate desk, the process of editing runs along similar lines, in which case the story goes to a 'slot man' who sits at the head but on the inside rim of the horseshoe desk. This editor, called the news editor, glances through the copy quickly, gauges its relative importance, determines the space it should occupy-200 words or a half or three-quarters of a column and decides the type on the copy and passes it on to one of his copyreaders who sits on the rim of the horseshoe.

This copyreader, also called the desk man, rim man or 'mechanic' of the editorial room, is the anonymous and frequently unappreciated collaborator of the writer. News men or correspondents who see his blue pencil flay their cherished prose, have no words of praise for him. Neil MacNeil in his book "Without Fear or Favour" indicates the newsman's true worth. He says that the reputation of many a still reporter rests partly on the work done by rim man in the green eye side who combs out the reporter's cliches and trims them to pieces.

Only where the copyreader happens to be a former reporter, driven to the horseshoe desk by the dint of seniority, does the correspondent feel encouraged.

Copyreaders are generally paid higher than reporters. The work holds out attractions for men with editorial ability. The chances for advancement are good as the copy desk is recruiting ground for office executives. The work is mainly two-fold: the editing of the story and the construction of a suitable headline for it. The amount, of this work varies with each paper and even at different timings on each day. On a big desk the copyreader may edit from 10 to 15 columns. His editorial function is to bring each news that comes to him up to par. As he picks up the copy and reads; he forms general conclusions about the story in hand.

Has it news value? If it hasn't, then it is not worth printing.

Is it accurate and fair? Inaccurate and uncertain items are not wanted by a good newspaper. If at all he selects anything which is dubious or doubtful, he takes the responsibility for published inaccuracies.

Is it libellous? An item that contains words or implications that may get the paper into legal difficulties has to have the danger spots eliminated.

Is it complete? Is the treatment fragmentary and partial? Will it lead the reader up in the air? If so, its details must be rounded, with or without the help of background materials.

If the item meets these qualifications, the copyreader starts his editing to fit his paper's requirements. These requirements may vary but, as a general rule, we take it that the paper requires:

(i) **Clearness.** The reader must have no difficulty in finding out what the story means.

(ii) **Condensation.** The copyreader must cut and condense each story to the length assigned to it. Condensation applies to words and not to ideas. Verbal frills may go but the meaning must remain. Condensation is done by substituting short words for long ones—even smaller words for bigger ones; for example, 'try' in place of ' endeavour'.

(iii) **Arrangement.** The copyreader's notion of arrangement differs from that of the literary man. It is based on the convention of the 'lead' which puts the important parts first and the least important parts last. It also makes for the sequence of ideas.

(iv) **Style.** The copyreader's style has nothing to do with literary quality. It refers to particular rules which his paper has laid down for spelling, punctuation, capitalisation, abbreviation, use of numerals and the like.

The copyreader edits his copy along the foregoing principles by means of a set of standardised copy reading symbols, which tell the typesetter what section to omit, when to transpose, when to spell a word out and when to contract. He then proceeds to check the copy paragraphs and if the story has sufficient length, supplies subheads. The subhead is a line to be printed in a type which differs from the body of the story/article and is used to break up the too solid look of a long column. The best rule is to paragraph for ideas and not for mechanical reasons. Copyreaders try to avoid being mechanical when it comes to the subhead. The look of the column demands a sub head every two sticks or a stick and a half at least, or say about every 300 or 350 words.

The copyreader aims to have his subheads make divisions in the subject, each division meant for something new, and not merely for repeating what has been already told.

The copyreader usually faces three problems: *(i)* to tighten up the story and thereby speed up the action; *(ii)* to cut out the excess matter and bromides; and *(iii)* to reduce the story so that a telegraphic editor could splash it in a page-one box if he chose to handle it that way.

❐

5

Traits of a Reporter

QUALIFICATIONS OF A REPORTER

(1) A young reporter must have good memory for faces. He must cultivate the sixth sense and grow particular brain cells assiduously if he is to make full use of his opportunities. Once he is out to achieve this, he will find plenty of people in his circle who are valuable to him as news supply source. He must know them and develop this foible even though its mainspring be vanity.

The occasional task of a young reporter is to find a well known man or woman upon an incoming aircraft at the airport or a liner at the seaport. Very occasionally his task is easy enough because an outstanding personality can be easily known and approached at the right moment. Moreover, if the reporter is associated with a good newspaper, the personality may himself/herself be interested in being accessible. He or she may be bursting with ideas and opinions in search of a right outlet. The journalist is the right person to avail the opportunity.

(2) A successful reporter must have good memory for pictured faces. He must also take out information about the personality he wishes to approach for interviews or news, A good memory for pictures is of tremendous utility to a journalist in a strange environment. Every journalist has the expenence of going from pillar to post for information or confirmation when minutes and seconds keep flying past. He may be sometimes held up by the official folk unnecessarily. What he should do is to care for every precious moment if he wishes to be the first to get the news through. But he has got to do everything so diplomatically that he does not lose any friend who can be of use as a source of news.

No journalist expects that requests preferred to Secretaries and Ministers of Departments will always be met but he must move on the right track. As a result of the common experience of the current generation, a studied courtesy and in many cases a measure of personal friendship with high-ups would be of great value. Journalists can make use of the gift of remembering faces if they wish to avoid and embarrassing situations in their social career.

(3) It is important for the reporting journalist to make right type of friendships with his sources of information or news. He will find his source of knowledge widened or restricted, according to the way in which he can cultivate the friendships. Sometimes it is alleged that journalists are too busy to keep a social life. In actual fact, the case is the reverse. A journalist touches more of the social circles than any man. He remains on the fringe of them all and can turn them to his own professional use if he has the necessary capability.

A journalist is inevitably in many respects a public figure. He sees the world, the both saint and the devil at close quarters and must on occasions hobnob with people for whom truth is no terror. The only temptation to which a journalist should not fall is superficiality. a shallow outlook and, perhaps a certain amount of cynicism. He should have the sense to discriminate between what is superficial and what is real. He should not be easily bought over by vested interests by temptations of cheap entertainment or the offer of wine and women. Once he falls the prey to these temptations he will be ignoring his duty and not doing the right type of roporting which he is expected to do as an unbiased reporter. He must maintain a worthy utlook, keep up his standards steady and judgments firm. A Journalist has the advantage in forming his judgments of men and things as he sees the inside aspects of movements which often present a different side for the public view. While the man in the street sees the superficial, the journalist has gone into details and witnessed events from the deepest quarters.

(4) A journalist cannot afford to be stale in his ideas, concepts or pursuits. He has to be on his mental toes all the time. He must do a lot of reading and writing, be honest to himself. Find out more

quickly than others the precious little knowledge he is in search. His writings must emit the bright sparks with every new contact. His every new story must be an improvement over the earlier one.

(5) An ideal reporter, however brilliant and imaginative, must maintain a sense of responsibility. He must adjust his balance of things in such a way that he can keep to the interests of his organisation without sacrificing the public good. His over-enthusiasm should not land him into a situation where he may be called responsible: He must realise that he holds in his hand one of the reins by which mass movements are forged and that he must use it purposefully and with care.

(6) An ideal reporter must respond to the urge and thrill of the news. News getting is not a matter of routine. He must be dynamic in his approach so that he can get preference to the routine journalists from the news agencies or other newspaper that may compete with him to find access to the source of news. Unless he has a thrill for news, he cannot prove to be a more efficient news-gatherer and interpreter of the movements of which he is an observer and from which he has to build the background for future coverage. The competitive aspect of modern journalism adds to the thrill rather than subtracts. The lust for a new fact in competition with others must have the effect of throwing a heightened light upon it and of getting it out of focus in relation to its setting.

THE REPORTER'S CHARACTERISTICS

The gathering of news is as old as humanity. But now the arena has been expanding fast and today it is world-wide. Today one must step out armed with knowledge and the tools of the crafts as the news writer is no more just a scribe but is an arti in more than one sense. As the art of collecting and writing news is becoming more specialized, one must equip himself or herself properly to function as a good and successful reporter.

One may experience many set-backs and disappointments but it should be remembered that such trends are inevitable in the writing profession. Frustrations should be used as incentives to finer and better work. It is imperative, however, that the aspirant should necessarily continue to work hard. Changing styles should be followed and it should be the policy to ensure that the work turned over is up to the standard.

The job of a reporter is not so very bonny as many wrongly construe it to be. In fact the occupation of a newspaper reporter is tiresome. He has to be present at odd places and at odd hours. It is not a routine job where specific timings like 10 A.M. to 5 P.M. can be adhered to strictly. It is a job wherein one must be ever ready to step out and evince the needed interest with least frown or minimum of consternation. Best meetings or worst meetings, school's Kabbaddi play or eagerly awaited cricket test- match, scavangers' strike rally or convocation of the university, he has to attend with a hope that something will turn up so that he will catch the headlines. However effective or communicative the story may be, it does not appear in the name of the reporter. It is mostly anonymous. Reporting is a thankless job also in this regard. But the reporter must be selfless in his work and should not hanker after by-lines to earn publicity. Publication of his name with the news item should never be the sole aim of a reporter. He must pay attention to his job with the mind that every appreciation of the news reported is in fact a silent tribute to his interest and genius. His rage must be to narrate a news story so that it may be highly appreciated by the readers.

The master of storycraft, Robert Louis Stevenson, has stated that "Narrative is the typical mood in literature." Telling the news is simple, but making a story out of it makes it picturesque. Stilling Fleet has summed up the rules of a good news story in the following words for the benefit of young journalists: "A story should, to please, at least seem true, be apropos, well told, concise and new; and whenever it deviates from these rules, the wise will sleep and leave the applause to fools." Everybody admires a good news story and will not sleep through it. Nobody likes a hard-and-fast sermon, however good it may be. If a journalist wants to convey a message to the readers, he must weave a story which seems highly plausible.

Asking question of public interest is a reporter's job. Hence his objective should be a good story and not a bold credit. Nowadays, however, some of our best known daily newspapers publish the names of the reporters, particularly when some reporting job is splendidly done. This is a real stimulus to budding newsmen.

A reporter, to achieve success, would be courteous, kind and considerate to all at all times, and should have a pleasant and cheerful face on all occasions and with all people. What are all the requisites of successfull reporter? He must develop the news-sense so that he can recognize forthwith the press value or what we may call the news value of the simplest things, *i.e.* split-second discrimination between the necessary and the unnecessary from the news angle. Patience and perseverance are required. Whatever obstacles are put in the way, the job of the reporter is to get the story. A pleasant and confident manner helps even when there are weak spots in the barriers. Amiability in disposition is bound to clear the impediments. An assured manner would smooth the path, removing all hindrances.

Journalism is now a highly organized activity with a technique that demands the closest attention to details. It moves with the times and indeed is often the initiating factor in many of the developments of which we may be proud. A journalistic vocation calls for sincere and continuous work. There are many failures of expectations but this is a profession where there is a feeling all the time that the work is one which is well worth doing. It is a calling which exercises a magnetic fascination over people who are ambitious and possess a flair for writing and anxiety for adventure. Other careers may offer more valuable prizes in life, more security, and more ease; but none can successfully compete in charm with the career of a journalist.

Capacity for infinite work, a gift of imagination, power of conveying news and views to the public in clear and concise language are necessary. As the newspaper reporter is an observer of human activity, he must be a specialist in quick gathering of news. He has to know something about every subject and everything of some subject. He should have a well-stored mine of general knowledge and a thorough knowledge of at least one particular subject, say agriculture, commerce, economics, geography, international relations, law, music, political science, sociology, sports or the United Nations.

The qualities that makes for success in journalism are precisely the qualities that make for success in any other profession—brain power, foresight, enterprise, and industry chiefly. Possession of a "heart" is also deemed one of the primary qualifications of the reporter. He must be sympathetic and always avoid cynicism. The first duty of a journalist is to touch life at as many points as he can. So, he must be "alive", and he who does not feel does not live. Time is everything for the journalist and an understanding of "time value" is of utmost necessity. One must first know things and where to find things. Another quality must be inherent in the reporter: "instinct or intuition; flair, a keen scent both for news and other objects."

He must know what the public will want to read about next day. These delicacies of perception are feminine, but require to be controlled by masculine judgement.

To the aspirant, T.P. O'Connor says: "First of all, be certain that you possess a distinct gift for writing." In journalism a high standard of serious endeavour can only be maintained by the motivepower of intense devotion. Love of work is the extra-special qualification anticipated of an ambitious journalist. "There are no doubt other professions where mental activity is more sustained and intense, but for endless variety and contact with everyday affairs of life modern journalism has a charm one finds it extremely difficult to define."

"To report the news accurately and fairly without prejudice or personal opinion is the No. 1 obligation of the reporter." And to fulfil he duty anticipated one must have the basic competence. To become a proficient reporter one must be honestly concerned in the cause. He must have training for it either at a college of journalism or a newspaper office, and stick to reporting until he succeeds.

Departments of journalism, schools of communications in colleges and universities are providing the best kind of vocational as well as professional training for newspaper work. Students who have obtained degrees or diplomas have real opportunities for a flying start. First class newspaper offices are excellent training grounds for aspiring young journalists but they are not institutes for apprentices. They are eagerly looking, however, for energetic and resourceful men who do more than they are asked to do—and a little better than expected. The departments of journalism of Indian universities as in the U.S.A. and other progressive countries—can be responsible for filling the jobs in newspapers. They also can channel these students into allied fields. like radio, general and specialized magazines, information officers, public relations wings of industrial firms, and advertising agencies. For reporting is a skill which is useful not only in a newspaper office but also in many other spheres of activity in life.

To say it more emphatically, the ideal reporter is one who knows everything about. He should study the literature of the language of the paper he represents until he learns to use the noble tongue to express to the best advantages and in the fewest words whatever he has to say. High character of expressiveness and economy of words should be his watchwords. He should know the people, the plain, everyday average man, the "man-in-the- street", his rank, his requirements, his inclinations and his thoughts.

"Reporting is a profession, trade, science, art, craft and sometimes a game." And for one who wishes to embrace this multangular manual art the following list also of pre-requisite qualifications must be of interest and concern:

(i) Good eye-sight and hearing;

(ii) Strong pair of legs;

(iii) Ability to use a typewriter;

(iv) Knowledge of spelling, grammar;

(v) Love for accuracy and perfection;

(vi) Capacity to grasp complex events;

(vii) Possessed of a broad background of studies;

(viii) In commands of at least one foreign language; and

(ix) Mastery over current affairs.

With stress it should be said that he should have the invigorating curiosity to know more and more about past, present, and future. A craze for particularised details is one of the assets of a competent reporter. He must plunge into the problems and find out the truth hidden therein, using his skill, intelligence, discretion, and common sense.

Objectivity is one more concentration facet of virtuous reporting. Despite the apprehension that it is rather arduous for a reporter to write dispassionately or extrinsically about the multifarious activities of persons or institutions, because his writing is in the danger of being influenced by prejudice, the reporter has necessarily to aim to relate matter impersonally and unobtrusively. It is the sacred duty of a conscientious reporter to stick as far as humanly possible to the basic truth in submitting his news stories for publication.

A reporter must possess some of the fundamental qualities discussed above. Noteworthy among them are a sense of trust about his duty towards people, an understanding of the complexity of the recent affairs, and a solid and growing fund of information especially about the history, economics and politics of his own country. If the newsman has these elementary qualities, he is in a position to acquire automatically the other requisite attributes of a reporter.

A reporter, to sum up: must be a good reader, a good listener and a good writer. Above all he must be a sociable gentleman. The more he knows of men and events the more successful his career ultimately becomes.

Above all these, there is one more which is vitally important. An aspirant of journalism must know typewriting and ,shorthand. Without equipping oneself with these twin essential crafts, one should not take to reporting. Ignorant of typing, when the reporter is at work, his contributions to the newspaper office must be in handwritten manuscript. Few sub-editors take the exertion of reading badly written sheets, unless of course the matter is manifestly important or is deemed extraordinarily interesting. A knowledge of shorthand the art of taking brisk and correct notes—is an added asset as it assists the reporter to jot down information with maximum accuracy. Speeches made at a high speed can be coherently taken for annotation. Verbatim versions are possible only when the reporter uses shorthand. That is why in well-known offices a certificate of proficiency in shorthand writing is insisted upon.

People depend heavily upon newspapers for their knowledge, intelligence and generally for words and their spelling and use. Hence a journalist should give special attention to accuracy of statements of facts, to grammar, and to perfection of punctuation. To a greater extent, the newspaper writer is the teacher of the particular language for much of the population. Obviously the press is fundamental institution of society, fulfilling a role that grows in importance as men are thrown more closely together and have an increasing need to communicate with each other. Reporting of the news is the basic function of the newspaper. It means gathering of information of interest to other people and presenting it to them tersely in a way which makes them understand and remember it.

Reporting, when we delve deep, is not only the gathering of news in the strictest sense. It also includes reporting and writing news and feature stories and snapping of news and feature photographs. Hence, newspaper work is an adventure—full of fresh experiences and excitement. Historically the journalist has been identified by society as carrying out two main function: reporting the news and offering interpretation and opinion based on news.

RESPONSIBILITIES OF A REPORTER

It is said that a reporter is both eyes and ears of a news organization. It is not possible to strictly prescribe qualifications which a good reporter must posses. However, novice reporters must train themselves informally for the job so that they would be able to discharge their responsibilities with confidence, courage and competence. In order to qualify the role of a reporter you must prepare yourself in many ways.

It helps to be well-read, and you can do full justice to your reporting beat. You must equip yourself adequately with all aspects of your beat. If you are covering the civic body proceedings, you must be fully knowledgeable about several laws and rules under which the proceedings are regulated. In addition, you must know its various functions, areas of operations and jurisdiction. You should cultivate wide contacts with all kinds of sources in your beat, some times even outside your area of activity. As a reporter, you should be able to find out information; you should have a bent of mind for research. You should be a perfect talker, you should possess in inexhaustible patience and the ability to get along with any kind of people in difficult situations. To be a successful reporter and to accomplish your job competently, you must be able to perceive, calculate, predict and plan your action appropriately in anticipation of a news event.

The sole aim of good news reporting should be writing with a certain amount of responsibility to oneself, to an organization, to society and to humanity at large. You must use your pen consciously, carefully and should bear full credit (or discredit) for what you say: "Just as an unclaimed torrent of water submerges the whole countryside and devastates crops, even so, an uncontrolled pen serves but to destroy."

Besides, as you must write everyday, you should write to build your own image, as well as the image of your institution. You have a responsibility towards your city, state, region, country, even the world at large. Echoing this, the noted editor M. V. Kamath once said: "A newspaper's sense of purpose and integrity, rather than its circulation, would determine its influence." And it is the reporter who is a builder of a newspaper's sense of purpose and integrity.

Let it be said here that a reporter is neither a social worker nora preacher nor a reformer. Reporters are duty bound to keep a finger on a sore point in society. For it is only then, that the attention of all those concerned is drawn to the disease that ails the society. Unless cub reporters are imbued with a total sense of responsibility towards the profession and the news organization, they will not be able to rise to the expectations reposed in them by the news organisation and the society.

It is essential for a news reporter to be alertminded and curious. In addition, one should be in excellent health and should have inexhaustible stamina to chase difficult assignments. Most of all, a reporter should be a sociable person.

ESSENTIAL QUALITIES OF A REPORTER

It is true that one must posses the right attitude toward the vocation. This would include intelligence, initiative, industry, general competence, objectivity and accuracy.

There are several other features of one's personality and character which can contribute befittingly to one's profession as a journalist. In this section, we shall elaborate the salient qualities.

The reporter is the most important functionary of a newspaper, as far as news operations are concerned. So one must know what constitutes news in order to be able to gather news.

A reporter's job of discovering the news has been simplified in one way and rendered difficult in another sense, in this age of information. While there are the usual press notes on which news reports can be based, there are other sources of information on a variety of news event. The range of sources stretches from official spokespersons and press conferences to unidentified members of the public and the regular sources which one meets on the beat.

But quite often, most of the material before a news reporter may just be publicity matter or advertisements in disguise. Therefore, as a reporter; you must check the material and squeeze the news that would interest your reader. When you are overwhelmed by an ocean of facts, you can always rely on the readers' interest for guidance. Here is where your ability (to-select the right information and present it to the reader comes to your help. Besides, most of the time you will cover routine matters such as press conferences and press notes that are hardly exciting. At least you may have to begin at quite a low level like covering local matter. Later you may be given the opportunity to cover major national issues.

For the most part you may find yourself reporting the speeches, declarations and announcements by V.I.P.s, persons in authority, politicians and political parties. Occasionally, you may get an exciting newsbreak. But your routine reporting should not prevent you from looking for something unusual that may lurk under the ordinary occurrence. You have to be a keen observer so as to discover unusual and exciting material even in routine stuff. A sharp sense of observation may also help you to gather amusing sidelights of interest to your readers. Your alertness will help you to discover contradictions and problems while you are on your daily beat. This can be the basis for an exciting news story even where apparently there was none.

Outgoing Nature

Professional journalists are never armchair writers. Introverts normally make poor reporters. Reporters have to move about meeting people, making their acquaintance and winning their confidence. This would help them to establish contacts, which in turn helps in writing well-investigated reports. This is the era of investigative reporting and readers are keenly interested to know what is going on behind the scenes. To get that kind of stories, you have no alternative but to be outgoing. You have to develop an affable temperament and an easy-going nature.

Ability to Establish Contacts and Develop sources

An outgoing nature is the basic quality to establish contact and develop sources. During the course of your duty, you may meet several people who may help you in gathering information. You must have the ability to win the confidence and respect of those who may be potential sources of news. During the course of your regular duties, people may voluntarily offer you information. Alternately, this might not be the case when you are working on an investigative story. People may hesitate to talk on sensitive matters. They may like to reveal yet are afraid to in case it were to affect them adversely. Such people may be government officials whom you may meet while investigating matters ranging from inefficiency to corruption. They could be informers of the underworld, if you are doing an in depth crime investigation. What may be at stake for them could be their jobs or their lives. It may be quite difficult to win their trust. In such situations, you must be able to assure your sources that they will remain protected and their identities kept secret if they so desire.

While you are establishing contact, there may be some among them who may want to plant information on you to serve their vested interests. Such information may consist of half-truths and even lies. So, you must have other independent contacts through whom you can verify the information.

Remember, even the most ordinary source at times can become very valuable, providing important leads and a wealth of information. A couple of years ago a newspaper carried a story about a footpath hawker who once was a wrestler of international repute, thus throwing light on the neglect of the sportsmen in the country. You must make it a point, therefore, to pay attention to your sources howsoever 'ordinary' they may seem by appearance.

Remember, the classic case of the Watergate scandal. The scandal that shook the United States and the Nixon presidency was not exposed by any ace newsperson, but by ordinary local reporters acting on a tip from an ordinary source.

What matters is the alertness and ability to pursue your sources to get the—right lead. Take the case of the securities scam. The entire expose began wth a source contacting Ms. Sucheta Dalal of the Times of India, Bombay, with an unconfirmed report about some activities in the State Bank of India. Ms. Dalal, Assistant Business Editor of the paper, followed the lead provided by the source and got the story confirmed from reliable contacts bringing to light the stock scam concerning stock broker Harshad Mehta and others involving a staggering Rs. 6,000 crores.

Ability to be an Unprejudiced Observer

The reporter must be an unprejudiced observer of events, one who presents the facts to the reader in a balanced, objective manner. Now, objectivity is a much debated topic. It has been said that reporters mix comment with fact and so their reports are quite subjective. While reporters may have their own views on the subject of coverage, they should not allow personal opinions at any place in the copy. One must be able to throw light on unclear aspects if any, of the news event. At the same time, the news reporter must endeavour to write a report which is only a statement of facts. An observation or viewpoint, might occasionally creep in and one must be alert to such strips in straight news items.

How do you maintain balance and objectivity in your coverage? The first and foremost thing to do is to source your copy properly to assure the reader that what you are passing on as news, is not your opinion or some publicity matter in disguise. The sources must be quoted except when they want to remain anonymous. Even when you are not able to quote the sources, you must ensure that the story is balanced, by giving adequate coverage to all the sides of the subject. You should always ensure that the information you are presenting is true. You can do this by counter checking.

Remember, what may appear fair to one group will amount to bias for another. So, Always ensure that you give both sides of the picture.

But, remaining an unprejudiced observer does not mean adopting what is known in American journalistic parlance as "man from the Mars" stance, *i.e.*, seeing each event afresh, unconnected to any previous expectations or future possibilities and passing them on untouched by interpretation.

In an increasingly con;tplex world, this would not amount to objectivity or fairness. In many cases, it would simply mean an irresponsible attitude, a refusal to make the reader understand the event in its proper context and realise its significance.

In many cases, you not only report the events but interpret them for the reader. But, remember, interpretation does not mean backdoor editorialising. It is not an excuse for colouring the story with your personal opinions.

Clarity of Expression

As a reporter, you may cover several complex and specialised subjects, such as science and technology, law and economics. Your command over the language must be such that you can explain even the most complicated issues in single terms to any general reader. In addition to specialised subjects such as science and technology, even government press notes are written in complicated language, burying the news point. You must be able to simplify it and bring ut the news point.

Team Spirit

Except for routine coverages which can be handled by one person, many investigative stories have to be handled by a team. The Bofors investigative stories in the Indian Express and other papers were based on reports from Geneva and Stockholm, besides New Delhi. The securities scam investigations by the Times of India involved, besides Sucheta Dalal, one more correspondent, R. Srinivasan, who posed as an investor and went to the State Bank officers in Bombay to get confirmation about the goings on in the bank.

If you see investigative stories in the Statesman, you will find that they are always attributed to "The Statesman Insight Team." You must be able to work as a member of such a team. Here, you must pool your talents, sources and contacts into the team and work under a leader. In the course of time, you may rise to head such a team. Working under a team discipline will certainly be of help to you later.

Ability to Cope with Inside and Outside

With investigative journalism seeking to bring out scandals and exposures, there is bound to be pressure on journalists to keep someone's wrong doings hidden from public view. This 'someone' is usually a person with considerable clout. The 'pressure' on journalists is exerted in the hope of preventing exposure. The concerned journalist may also be bribed with attractive favours in return for silence on the matter.

As a newsperson you may provide helpful or harmful exposure to persons holding important positions in your beat. Since many of them need publicity to perform their functions, they seek you out to provide them with the required exposure.. They are on the lookout for a minimum of harmful and the maximum of helpful publicity. If they consider it necessary, they may use their power and influence to pressurise you for this.

The pressure could be used to make you change the news or "kill" a story. This constitutes censorship. Pressure could also be applied with the hope of inducing journalists to volunteer the change or omission which is then equal to self-censorship.

While groups like the government and the advertisers could indirectly pressurise you through your news organisation, direct pressure could also come from the government and political parties. In case you are doing stories on something which could lead to harmful exposure for someone, they could take recourse to a range of legal and illegal options, including legal action, threats and violence to pressurise you.

There are three ways of coping with pressure: fighting it, giving in, and anticipating the pressure and taking preventive measures. The first one is the most noble of the three options and history is full of shining examples of this category. During the British rule in India, many papers decided to close down, rather than submit to censorship and government pressure. The father of the Nation, Mahatama Gandhi, exemplified this spirit when he wrote during the Quit India Movement: "It is better not to issue newspaper than to issue them under a feeling of suppression. " Even during the 1975-77 internal emergency, journals like Mainstream closed down rather than submit to government censorship. But the heroic option is not always feasible.

Remember, running a newspaper is a business, apart from being a service. Thousands depend on it for a living. You are in it as a professional, seeking to earn your daily bread. So few expect you to be a hero or amissionary. If you give in to pressure which you cannot fight on your own and if your news organisation does not back you, the consequences could be disastrous for you as a professional journalist. The reporters who generally brave powerful pressures are those who have the full support of their organisations or their professional colleagues backing them unitedly. But, still, you must have the strength of character to fight pressures that come in the form of inducements like lavish gifts, favours, etc. to influence your reporting.

Preventive measures to fight pressure could be legal steps, like seeking a court stay on any law or ordinance that could affect the freedom of the press. In case you feel threatened by some physical violence, you can always seek security from law and order authorities. The journalists of the "Punjab Kesari" group of newspapers, who have taken a courageous antiterrorist stand in Punjab, work under extremely tight security. The group has lost two of its owners to terrorist bullets, but has not given in to pressures.

❐

6

Interview—Technique

The work of the newspaper reporter is, in a sense, one long interview, for he obtains the majority of his information by asking people questions and noting the answers, but the published interview in which a writer gave word-for-word answer and described even the actions of the interviewee is no longer in fashion. This technique is employed only in reporting press interviews of film stars or cultural dignitaries.

Interviewing is one branch of journalism that a junior can practise early in his career for in every locality there is at least one person who can provide a good story, which may not be actually topical, but can still make pleasant reading. Perhaps it is simply a man who has succeeded in curing his own to baccohabit, or the woman who has gained renown for her noble social work, but they are the sort of interview to which a young man can first try with comparative safety during his apprenticeship period.

When detailed to interview a personality, it is necessary to try and find out something about him before making any visit. Obtain as much information as you can, particularly about personal idiosyn cracies. In most newspaper offices, particularly dailies, there is a 'mortuary' (a filing system where biographies of local personalites/ celebrites are stored against the possibility of having to 'write them up' quickly) and it is sometimes useful to refer to this material. An interview begins at the moment you send in your card, or knock on the door; but the success or failure of it wiIl depend entirely on the impression you make on your entrance. It is at times like this that the affinity between the press and the public personalites becomes really close, for the journalist must often be something of an attraction for the publicity hungary person.

To begin with, so much depends on how you pass the time of day. Have you ever noticed, even in general life, what effect your 'good morning' or 'good afternoon', can have upon people? With the next three or four acquaintances you meet, try greeting them in various ways as an experiment, and notice the different reactions. The responses obtained will be interesting, and for the junior who cares to observe them, they hold important lessons. There are, indeed, several ways in which a 'good morning' can be said. The surly, grumpy person spits but the words as if getting rid of an unpleasant taste; the preoccupied says it automatically and in a monotone; the alert will utter the words in three tones; he will say 'good' as if he really means it, 'morn' on a slightly lower pitch, and the 'ing' on an upward inflection so that it finishes a tone above the 'good'. And when it is said in that fashion, and with a smile, notice the reaction. Almost right away the person spoken seems to brighten up, and he gives a more ready response than if the word 'morning' was spoken as if it came from the bottom of a deep pit. He says to himself: "Now here is someone who isn't merely saying 'good morning' because it is customary. He means what he is saying; he obviously enjoys his 'good morning' and the fact that he is wishing me one is a compliment !" Immediately he is in a receptive mood, and even if he intended to refuse an interview, the chances are that he will give up to you after all, if you play the rest of your cards correctly.

Start off with the Brasstack

The opening gambit of any action or interview is always important, and a person's reaction to what has gone before can have an effect on your own personal efforts. Reporters have been known to return from unsuccessful attempts to get an interview and confess that they thought that they 'started off on the wrong foot', whereas the fault had probably been that they failed to get a favourable reaction to their introduction, and not that they said any wrong things. Many things may have happened earlier that served to put the person being interviewed in a bad humour; therefore, a well spoken 'good morning' or 'good afternoon' can do much towards bringing about a useful response.

In most cases, the man or woman you are visiting will be quite prepared to grant an interview, but whatever the immediate response, your first sentence should always state the purpose of the visit. You are not to know whether the person being interviewed is tremendously busy or whether he is merely idling away his time; and it is wise to assume the former. If he is not busy, he will take it as a compliment. In any case, frame your opening sentence carefully; treat it in the same way as you would an introduction to a new story and decide before you arrive what that first sentence shall be. Do not waste time on trivialities at the outset, although they may well be useful at a later stage, should you need to gain a few moments before putting your next question. Say your name clearly, so that you can be addressed as Mr. X or as Mr. Y; give the name of your paper, and say why you have called on. Never make an apologetic opening, for it makes a bad impression. To commence with 'I'm sorry to trouble you, but would you tell me..., betokens inexperience and it is more than likely that your effort to gain the man's confidence will end in your receiving only his pity. The same applies to negative questions which begin; 'I don't suppose you could tell me if or "I don't know whether you could say". The man will immediately say to himself, 'What does this fellow take me for? An ignoramus? If he doesn't know whether I can say this, that, or the other, why is he asking me? Why has he come here presuming I don't know? He is wasting my time.'

Give the Lead and Then Listen

It is a good and wise plan to decide not only on your opening, but also on the first three or four points you wish to raise. Much depends on the nature of the interview. It it is to obtain views on something that has happened and the person being questioned has had no time to consider the situation, try and give him a lead. In order to give him a few moments, tell him, as sincerely as you can, that you have asked him for his views because they may be of assistance to others. Stress the usefulness to the public generally of knowing his views. Do not make this piece of flattery too obvious, but say it in a way that will convey sincerity. Throughout the interview, do no more talking than is absolutely necessary. It is not unknown for reporters, especially when a little self-conscious, to dominate the interview almost to the point of boredom, instead of giving the other man his tongue and only making a comment now and again. The best reporter is he who can listen.

The Notebook

Every interview has a common problem; how is it to be recorded? The sight of a notebook on the knee of a reporter sometimes has a paralysing and tongue-tying effect on the person whose views are being sought, unless such happenings are a common occurrence for him and he is perfectly used to them. The best way is to make your entrance apparently devoid of all the tools of your trade and to listen intently for a minute or two. Then you can quietly produce your pen and a piece of folded paper and make a few notes, if possible, while still watching the speaker. Never look away from him for longer than you can help; make him feel that he, and not your note-taking, has your attention.

Another way is to wait until the speaker has made a point or half given a string of figures, Then, producing your paper and pencil, ask: 'May I quote that?' and as you make your note, allow him to prompt you on the words to be used, if he wishes. Then look up at him again, put a question, or allow him to continue talking. Later you can make another note or two, perhaps with increasing frequency as the sight of your slip of paper becomes familiar, but watch him as much as you can and appear interested.

Don't Yawn

Once, a reporter from the opposition newspaper and his colleague arrived to interview a man at the same time. The speaker went on and on for a while and then the reporter's colleague was guilty of failing to conceal a mighty yawn. The effect on the man was startling. A look of astonishment spread over his features, his words trailed off, and the interview ended rather abruptly. The ice did not even thaw whell the reporter paused on the way out to admire an of painting although it had been painted by the man himself. When the door closed behind, the man probably thought: 'What a rude person. Coming to ask my opinions and then when I give them, he yawns!" It would be quite understandable if, on a future occasion, he adopted the same attitude if the reporter went for the interview again. The reporter on such occasions should not feel the loss of the interview and should go to other sources for his information.

MANNER OF CLOSING

It is advisable, before departing, to spend a minute or two discussing common-place matters. A quickly-ended interview in which the reporter puts away his paper, stands up and bids good-day creates a bad impression. It leaves the person interviewed with a feeling that, having pricked his brains, you have no further use for him. Your last words should be. 'Well, goodbye—and thank you', and say 'thank you' sincerely, for you have been granted a favour.

The written interview, where a person writes answers to a series of questions sent to him, is now seldom employed. Perhaps this is as well, for it is never wholly satisfactory. For one thing, a 'follow up' question can never be asked, and it may so happen that a written answer almost demands further questions in order to elucidate a point. In addition, it lacks the personal touch that is so essential. Avoid it as much as you can.

The Telephonic Interview

In recent years many papers have adopted the technique of the telephone interview : a method which has the great advantage of saving time for the reporter; but that is all. It is a selfish way of doing about things, for not only is the personal touch again lacking, but it assumes that the paper is more important than the person being interviewed—and that is a thing the person being interviewed should never be allowed to feel. It is possible, too, that he may' unnecessarily be on his guard, for anyone with an ulterior motive could ring him up and profess to be a newspaper representative; on the other hand, he, may for some reason dislike using a telephone, which immediately places you at a disadvantage.

It is willingly conceded that on evening papers especially a telephone interview is sometimes necessary, but in general, it is a lazy and bad-mannered way, particularly with a strange. With someone to whom you happen to be well-known the telephone may occasionally be a useful way of obtaining you information, but taken by and large, it should only be used in cases of emergency it is always; better to call in person.

The telephone interview has been found a useful way of getting: the views of local people when you are very near press time, which perhaps accounts for the extension in its use. For instance, suppose some restriction on a commodity was suddenly lifted, and you were told' to get interviews for a local-angle story: you would need to contact the President or Secretary of the association concerned, one or two leading people and a house-wife. From them you should obtain a pretty good variety of views some of them welcoming it, others fearing. that the sudden lifting of the regulations would cause such a run on it that the commodity would be virtually unobtainable, and so on.

Before ringing up these people, try and put yourself in their position: if you were contacted by the ringing of a bell and asked for your views, would you have able to give them on the spur of the moment? Even if you could, would you be prepared to do so, knowing that whatever you said would be made public in the four corners of your locality? Would you not prefer to have a few minutes in which to give a little thought to the matter? These are points. which the thoughtful reporter will bear in mind, and it may well be, as a result, that he will first ring up his people and ask them if they would give their views when he rings up again in ten minutes time. Many people are only too willing to assist, but they like to have a brief period for reflection before committing themselves and they appreciate the friendly tip that you want them to do so.

What has been said above applies to all reporting work and not merely to interviewing; put yourself in the other fellow's place try and understand his position. By doing this you will be helping yourself immeasurably; you will be cultivating a completely detached and unbiased outlook. Thus you will be better able to appreciate that there is another side to every question, and because of that you will gain variety of approach when hunting for news. Many young reporters today take so much for granted that they become their own worst enemies, simply because they either refuse to appreciate, or are incapable of appreciating, that there are more points of view than their own.

Specialised Interview

In the case of important individual interviews only a senior reporter is generally given the assignment well in advance. He spends a few days in studying the career of the great personality to be interviewed and frames the questions to which he wants an answer. If the interview is to deal with a specific subject and is not intended to be a general survey of the world or of the locality in which the news paper is published, the reporter must make certain that he has at least a redimentary ideas of the matters which he wishes his personality to talk about. It is no good being ushered into the great man's presence and then waiting for something to turn up.

The reporter would be well advised to utilise the resourcefulness of the office librarian, who can generally provide a host of ideas and cuttings, when he is told the name of the man to be interviewed.

The reporter is sometimes asked by the personality to submit the receipt of the interview report and if time permits, he should comply with the request and make the stipulation that when it is returned the words 'O.K.' should appear on every sheet. There can then be no post-mortem either on the interview or the reporter. But it most be made clear that the general sense of the interview must not be altered and that in agreeing to the request for a script the desite is that the interview should be rounded off and that occasional words should be altered if they do not entirely convey the intended meaning.

There are a few 'Do's' and 'Don'ts which journalists should keep in mind while they are functioning as reporters:

Do's:

(i) As far as you can, thoroughly study your man and the subjects about which you wish him to talk.

(ii) Show interest in the job and try to get on easy terms with your man quickly.

(iii) Go on the job well-dressed but not over-dressed.

(iv) Get an understanding at the outset that you are at liberty to publish any of his remarks unless he asks for special points to be regarded as confidential and as 'off the record'.

(v) Always remember that there is such a thing as the law of libel and that the indiscreet journalist personal remark may cause a great deal of trouble.

(vi) Submit a copy of your interview to the person interviewed if time permits and see that when he returns it, he 'O.K.s' every page.

Don'ts

(i) Don't think that you know more about the subject than the man you are interviewing, because you definitely do not.

(ii) Don't adopt a servile attitude, but at the same time, show that you respect your man for what he has done.

(iii) Don't outstay your welcome. When you feel that you have got all you require do not hang about talking of crops or cricket. Remember that he may have another appointment even if you have not.

(iv) Don't feel that it is necessary to argue with your man if you do not agre with some of the views he expresses, because after all the interview is not at all a debate.

(v) Don't flourish a notebook in your man's face as though it was the newspaper man's Bible.

Press Confereates

There are frequently occasions for Press Conferences at which ministers or leading figures in the world of 'industry, science. entertainment or sport wish to inform the newspapers of latest developments. In such cases, the Editor gives instructions to the Public Relations Officer to get the journalists together' and hear the pronouncements if any. It is generally left for the PRO or the News Editor to decide whether he will make it a 'free for all' 'conference or a gathering limited the specialists live the Parliamentary, or other correspondents. Generally, a Minister prefers to meet a party of experts because he realizes that knowledgeable and sensible questions will be put to him after his pronouncement. There are sometimes Press Conferences and interviews 'which are simply a waste of time, where the information could have been issued by the Public Relations Officer of the Ministry concerned in the form of a 'handout.'

The Editor should watch most carefully when 'interviews are arranged by the Public Relations Officers of the Government departments representing special interests to make certain that an attempt is not being made to issue material which should really find place in the advertisement columns. This of course, applies only to the mass production type of interview and not to those cases where at the request of an individual journalist the Public Relations Officer or Press Officer arranges for a meeting with his chief. There is always a controversy where newspapermen are gathered together as to whether the Public Relations Officer is a help or a hindrance to them in their work. The general feeling seems to be that if he knows his job thoroughly he can be a very real asset provided that he does not erect a barrier between the reporters and the heads of departments. The ideal P.R.O. is the one who, when be receives a request for information knows exactly the man within the organisation who can provide it and if neccessary, is ready to bring into direct touch the inquirer and the person with the knowledge he wants. The ramifications of Government departments have grown so considerably in recent years that some kind of central office, such as the 'Public Relations Department provided is recognised to be vital, provided always that it does not stifle the zeal of the individual journalist who wants to dig out his own story.

One type of interview prevalent in a democratic country like India or the United States is that with the President or the Prime Minister or a foreign head of State visiting the country. The procedure here is that written questions are submitted in advance to the PRO of the authority concernd, and when the dignitary replies to them, he would indicate whether he could be quoted for the information he was imparting or whether he is not to be quoted as the source of the news, or whether he is speking entirely off he record. If the has a particularly important statement to make, he will generally issues copies of it at the close of the conference.

ART OF GOOD WRITING

* Good writing, particularly for the mass media, is clear, concise, to-the-point. It transmits information, ideas and feelings to the reader clearly but without overstatement. It is writing that outlines pictures of ideas which the reader fills in with his or her own imagination.

* It uses the minimum number of words to make its point. It is precise. As well-written piece uses words for their exact meaning. It does not throw words around carelessly or without cause.

* Good writing is modest. It does not draw attention to itself. Good writing does not try to show off the intelligence, or lack of it, of the writer. It lets the content speak for itself and it allows readers to receive message directly. Remember, people who like to read enjoy the ideas and information they get from reading.

And for this you have to know the tools of the trade: know your subject and learn to write it down and then learn to rewrite. Wait till you come to these subjects one by one I will explain to you the basics of all these but it would be you who would have to take up the cudgel and get in to the act—that is writing. Here, I have a small suggestion. After you have finished this lesson, read Henry Fowler's Modern English Usage.

NEWS STORY REVISITED

Most of you would be expressing your creativity through the mass media. We are taking up this subject once again, to tell you how news story forms the basis of all writing.

The ability to write well requires that the writer should have a thorough knowledge and understanding of the news event. In addition, you must understand the basic structure of the news story and the conventions or customs of news writing just not in order to complete the process of news writing but also to lead you to the path of creative writing. You must have read in the previous units of this course about basics of journalism. Here, we will recollect this very briefly so that you can understand how the same principles can be applied to virtually any kind of writing and not just for a mere news report.

The focus of this chapter is on writing a story, the cliche used for any matter to be published by a newspaper or magazine, as if it would appear on the pages of a newspaper. Any student of mass media has to learn this form, even if he never plans to work for a newspaper. We are stressing on this as we believe that mastering the news story is the first step on the road to mastering the mass media.

Are you feeling a bit confused? Let us explain to you what news in reality is. We are not taking up news as something that appears in a newspaper or television. Can you think of another word for news? Think for a while and may be you could? get close to it. It is simple "information". Yes, it is as simple as that. If you are reading a newspaper or watching a news bulletin, you are doing this so as to enrich yourself with some information.

A newsman, as a journalist is often called, looks for information in conversation, not only with top people but even with commoner while travelling in a bus or train, or in company news-letters or employees' magazines or any other such innocuous document, not necessarily the bulky files marked 'secret' or 'confidential'. At times, even, advertisements can be a vital source of information.

To be a good writer, particularly for the mass media—and if you are discerning you would notice that even books of eminent writers can be included in this category—you have to have two important tools. First, is to gather information and then in the second stage it is necessary for you to know how to transform this information in an appropriate form.

Once you know what this form is, you have virtually overcome the very first requirement to becoming a writer. A news story requires simple, straight forward prose, clear thinking and a complete understanding of the subject on the part of the writer as well as conciseness and precision in the use of the language. All forms of writing for the mass media require adherence to this rule.

We would like to tell you about some of the criteria that editors insist upon for selecting a story. The criteria briefly can be named as impact, timeliness, prominence, proximity, conflict bizarre or unusual and currency.

Impact is the consequence a story has on the people. Some events may not have many people behind it but its impact can affect the psyche of a large number of people. The budget or any tax proposal, affects almost all persons in the country, and so, if you can select any particular aspect to write on, it will generally be accepted for its impact value. For example, if you can write about how the income-tax rate is irrational for the salaried class, in comparison to the scheme that is in force for the shop-keepers, it is likely to be accepted by most editors for the logic that you would use for it. Timeliness is an important factor for any event. If you had some material about arms dropping in some other land and could relate it to Purulia arms dropping, it would have been a worthwhile exercise soon after the incident had been reported.

Prominence is a factor that largely revolves around prominent people. Even their trivial actions are read with great interest. It may relate to the Prime Minister, a top official, Lady Diana or Madhuri Dikshit and M.F. Hussain.

Proximity is how close the event has taken place. Any event at home, your town, state or nation is more catchy than a happening taking place 1,000 miles away. That is why when five persons die in a road accident near your town, it gets front page treatment, but 1,000 persons dying in South Africa in a train disaster get dumped in some corner of the paper.

Conflict is always read. It is not just two nations being at it. If people are fighting in Congress, it is news. If they are exchanging fistcuffs in Gujarat Bharatiya Janata Party, it is news. If Janata Dal leader RK. Hegde disagrees with the appointment of Laloo Prasad Yadav, it is news. Conflict is one of the journalists' favourite news values because it generally ensures that there is an interesting story to write. In fact, there can be many such stories if you can talk to different people.

In fact, if there is a fighting between two groups of traders or any other influential people in you neighbourhood, it can make a good copy for your local paper or magazine. That is why journalists who go out on election tour scan small newspapers to get the lead to a juicy story.

Bizarre or unusual incidents always attract readers. This is an old fact of journalism. 'If a dog bites a man, it is not news, but if a man bites a dog, it is news'. Normal hospitalisation is not news, but when recently a newlywed Arab Sheikh reached hospital due to exahustion after a marathon honeymoon, newspapers all over the world gave it a prominent display.

Currency has a somewhat similar appeal like timeliness. These are ongoing events but having a continuity. Take the issues of reservation, for instance, or the recent court judgments on hawala or Hindutva, or take any ecological event or discussion. Issues that have the value of currency come and go, but there are always several such issues being discussed by the people. In the late 1960s food shortage and long queues at fair price shops was such an issue. In early 1970s, it was the green revolution, family programmes during emergency, aforestation and failing ecology in 1980s and the hawala now-a-days are some such issues.

Individually or collectively all these can give you opportunities to write a good story. You, however, should know how to structure the story so that the most important and interesting information gets to the reader in the most efficient manner.

You must recall the 5 Ws and 1 H — the six basic questions of a reader. These are Who, What, When, Where, Why and How. I hope you know these but incase you cannot recall them, I would briefly again tell you that:

Who—denotes the people related to the story.

What—is the major action or event of the story.

When—the readers should have a clear idea of when the story or the event takes place.

Where—the location of the event should be clearly written. Nobody can assume the place of occurrence nor can you leave it to the reader's imagination.

Why and How—the reader deserves an explanation about events. If a story is about something bizarre or unusual, the writer must offer some explanation, so that the questions that are raised in the minds of readers are answered.

THE INVERTED PYRAMID

Once you have gone through the stage of information gathering, you have to decide on the structure of the story. A proper structure is necessary to bet information to the reader and allow the reader to move through your piece easily. This is the most crucial aspect, though it may look very simple, for your story. As I have told you earlier, it is on the basis of this crucial factor that an editor or sub-editor–the first reader in the literal sense—will be accepting your piece from among a number of competing pieces.

The most common structure for writing your story would be the same inverted pyramid, which you were told to use to write a report. In this structure, the first paragraph, also called 'intra' or introduction, gives the most important information of the story.

The second and third paragraphs follow up on the information by expanding on the lead and adding information that is of lesser importance.

As the story continues, more information is added, but it is of lesser importance and serves to support the information given at the beginning of the story or 'intra'.

The inverted pyramid structure allows the readers to get as much information as possible, in the shortest possible time. The better the inversion, the better the interest of the reader would be, to proceed through the story. In a novel or fiction, very often what happens is that near the end of the story the most important or interesting thing is presented to the reader. However an inverted pyramid structure is somewhat similar to the 'flash back' style in a movie. By showing a shot of the event that happens at the end, the cinematographer keeps the viewer glued to his seat to tell him how that particular scene (read event) took place. This is exactly what an inverted pyramid does. Readers are not accustomed to wading through a lot of less important or less interesting information to get to the end of the story. So a news story is any piece for a mass medium which begins at the end and then goes on to the beginning. In short, that is what an inverted pyramid is.

Points to Remember

While you write, you must remember a good write-up uses short sentences and short paragraphs. To convey your points more forcefully the usage of simple words are more useful. Better use more common words than what are known as bombastic words. I remember when in the beginning of my career, I used the word 'counterpart', my editor M. Chelapathi Rau asked me, "Why have you written so long a word?" And he suggested that it is better to tell what a counter part is, than use such vague words that tease the reader. He may have to go back to understand what you mean.

Paragraph lengths should be limited to 100 words or so, or say about four to five lines of a printed column of a newspaper. The aim is to convey the information to the reader. Another reason is that the width of a column of a newspaper is so narrow that a long paragraph is difficult and daunting for a reader.

For both these styles, you should read My Experiments with Truth by Mahatma Gandhi. this is one of the few books that elucidate how simple style can be effective as well as attractive.

Write your stories in the third person. A writer should not be seen in story and he mnst not use first person pronouns (unless they are part of a direct quotation from one of the story sources).

Similarly, avoid addressing the reader by second person pronoun 'you'.

While writing, you also have to learn how not to pontificate. You must not give your personal opinions in your stories. Your job is to write what you see and hear. The reader is not usually interested in how you feel about it. Your feeling is known as your bias. The more you put your feeling into it, the more the story would be considered to be biased. Such writings are not considered good writing either by the journalist community or by the reader who wants unadulterated information. You should present the information and let the readers make up their own minds about it.

Also practice, not to twist the facts. The more simple your presentation of information, the better will be your copy. A lively copy is nothing but a vivid presentation of facts in the minimum possible words.

STORY A

Offensive Against Rao Put on Hold
BJP Finds Itself in a Jam

NEW DELHI, Jan 31 : The BJP has decided to continue with its "wait and watch" policy on the hawala issue, thereby staving off for the moment, the crisis threatening it as it fumbles along in coming to terms with the CBI charges against its president Mr.L.K. Advani.

After demanding the Prime Minister's resignation last night in the wake of the Supreme Court's directive to the CBI, the party put its offensive against Mr. Narasimha Rao on hold today and confined itself to demanding that the investigating agency "do its job honestly now."

The consensus seems to be to wait for the outcome of the next hearing in the special court, slated for February 12, before planning the next move against the Prime Minister on the hawala issue.

The decision has also temporarily stopped the turmoil in the party that erupted following reports that the CBI had collected damaging evidence against Mr. Advani in the Jain hawala case.

Although murmurs of discontent continue, the official line has prevailed—that until CBI produces documents to back the charges in court, their will be no discussion on the matter.

Senior leaders in the party are keeping their fingers crossed on whether the CBI will find it impossible to link hawala money with Mr Advani's personal assets.

Yesterday, the BJP president had stated to a group of correspondents that all his assets were listed in his income tax returns and they had never been questioned.

The fact that the CBI failed to produce anything at the hearing on January 29 has given the party hope that nothing will come of the present speculation on Mr. Advani's supposed wealth.

The leadership is also optimistic that the Supreme Court's observations on the CBI's handling of the hawala investigations will strengthen their stand that the case against Mr. Advani is politically motivated. A senior party leader pointed out that so far, the Court has not had a chance to apply its mind to the validity of the chargesheet filed by the CBI.

The BJP is hoping that should the CBI fail to come up with the promised addition evidence, when the case does come up for hearing on February 12, the Court will throw out the charges against Mr Advani.

Notwithstanding the optimism in the party after the developments of the past two days, the hawala issue, however, weights heavily on the collective consciousness of party.

Given the divisions that have appeared within the party over the past few days, the February 12 hearing will be crucial in deciding to what extent the BJP will identify itself with the case against Mr Advani.

The surprisingly low-key briefing by the BJP today on the hawala issue seems to be the result of the decision to await the next move by the courts.

Should things go in their favour, the party will mount an all out offensive on the streets against the Prime Minister. Till then, it will restrict itself to keeping up the pressure and abstain from an head-on attack.

Today, the spokesperson, Mrs Sushma Swaraj, demanded that the CBI proceed against Chandraswami and Union Ministers, Mr. Satish Sharma and Mr. R. K. Dhawan, who, she alleged, were "conduits for bribes to the Prime Minister."

She observed that the Supreme Court order ensures that even the Prime Minister was not above the law and the CBI was under obligation to obey the law and not the Prime Minister when it comes to charges of corruption against him.

She also took Information and Broadcasting Minister Mr. P. A. Sangma and Doordarshan to task for blanking out the Prime Minister's name in yesterday's News Tonight programme on the hawala case.

"This is censorship," she declared, adding the Doordarshan officials should take note of the Supreme Court order asking government agencies to function independently.

STORY B

BJP Plans to Go on Offensive Against Rao

NEW DELHI, Jan. 31 The Bharatiya Janata Party, in a decidedly upbeat mood after the Supreme Court's directive to the CBI yesterday to probe every accusation in the hawala case, has tentatively planned to go on a major propaganda offensive against the Prime Minister and the CBI in a fortnight's time.

The party is ostensibly waiting to cross the Feb. 15 "hurdle". That is the next date of hearing in the designated court, when the CBI is slated to file additional documents with regard to the chargesheets filed against BJP president L.K. Advani and nine other politicians.

"We are fairly certain that the CBI will not be able to come up with anything of consequence against Mr. Advani yet, we will prepare to wait until Feb. 15," senior vice-president S.S. Bhandari said during an informal chat with a group of newsmen here today. He expressed the view that the chargesheet itself is too weak to stand scrutiny. The Supreme Court's order of yesterday has evidently given the BJP a talking point. Having levelled serious allegations against the Prime Minister, the BJP has greeted the apex court's directive to the CBI to probe every accusation made in the case with a sense of vindication of its stand.

"The party, which has been irked by the CBI's disinformation campaign" against Mr. Advani, has already begun to train its guns on the investigating agency. Party spokesperson Sushma Swaraj gave enough indication of the BJP's unfolding strategy in this context.

"We hope the CBI will now do its job honestly and fearlessly and proceed against Godman Chandraswamy, Mr. Satish Sharma and Mr. R.K. Dhawan," she said referring to S.K. Jain's purported statement that they had acted as "conduits" with regard to payments meant for the Prime Minister.

The Supreme Court order, she said, also "ensures that even the Prime Minister is not above the law and that the CBI is under obligation to obey the law and not the Prime Minister when it comes to serious charges of corruption against him." She went on to say that with their "biased track record," the CBI officers right from the director downwards "need to read this order again and again to correct their approach in the investigation of cases."

DD 'CENSORSHIP'. The BJP spokesperson remarked that another man who needed to read the SC order was Information and Broadcasting Minister P.A. Sangma, along with his band of officials in Doordarshan, "We think his transmission tower is leaning towards Race Course Road", she remarked and came up with an allegation of "censorship" during last night's transmission of the "News Tonight" programme on the Metro channel.

When anchorperson Prannoy Roy referred to the Jain's statement on alleged payments to the Prime Minister, the word Prime Minister was blanked out, Mrs Swaraj alleged. "Mr. Prannoy Roy temporarily lost his voice the moment he was to utter the word Prime Minister," she remarked.

GOOD FEATURE AND MAGAZINE WRITING

It is difficult to differentiate feature writing from news stories. Both have a great deal in common. They differ only in emphasis. Our aim is not to tell you in great detail about this method, as you have already learnt about it in a detailed lesson on this subject.

A feature is a departure from the way a news story is approached. A feature mostly contains more details and description. It is also the way to breath life into a publication. It is a way of humanising the news.

A feature or a magazine article need not necessarily follow the inverted pyramid structure. But you can do this only when you have learnt about this most important aspect of writing. As a feature or a magazine article writer you have greater freedom to choose the structure.

An article lead will grab the reader, but not necessarily with all the important facts. The reader of an article will have to go through the whole story to understand the writer's goal. Significant information appears all through the article and not just at the top. In fact, the most important part of an article is its body or the middle section in which the central ideas are developed. An article is different from a feature. But some one who has mastered the art of news and feature writing, normally comes out with a better written articles.

To imbibe the habits of good writing, it is necessary to note how intertwined all these forms are and even then these have very different structural presentations.

A feature can be anecdotal, suspended interest feature or question and answer (interview), but an article is the dissemination as well as the analysis of information. If you are still not sure look for an article on the top of the editional page of a newspaper and for a feature sift the weekly magazine pages.

In fact there is a lot that is common in a feature and an article. A feature as I have told you, is to put ideas in an interesting manner. As in an anecdotal feature, it can be started with an anecdote or quote and then facts can be weaved in and out of one another throughout the story—sustaining the reader's interests.

In the suspended interest feature, a special effect is produced. In either case, the style requires the writer to lead readers through a series of ambiguous paragraphs while at the same time keeping them puzzled and interested in solving the problem. The story is finally solved in an unexpected way.

Similarly, there are a number of effective article leads that grab the reader and bring him or her into the story. You can give an overview—the 5 Ws and 1 H — in a summary lead. The catch point, like in a feature, may be a startling statement that arouses curiosity. Your expression can be unique, unusual paradoxical, novel with a strong, crisp style.

A fiction-like tone is characteristic of a narrative lead. You can use dialogues, personal experience and adventure writings, using strong incidents, examples and interesting events.

The question lead is another way to raise the curiosity of the reader. There may be a single question or a number of them put to the reader in direct address.

A descriptive lead can also be used. The appeal has to be to the senses and the emotions. Detailed facts can be used in the body but not in this kind of lead. The language used should be the one that creates high impact. Quotes as well as direct address, or second person leads, can also be used in articles where you want to personally speak to the reader. In the beginning of this unit, we have discussed this style. Finally, an article may open with two or more of these leads in combination. An entertaining article or feature may use humour, suspense, adventure, romance or pathos to keep the reader's attention. Illustrations and photographers can make the subject come alive for the reader. Your language has to be crisp, imaginative, clever, colourful and if possible fast-paced.

Here, let me briefly tell you what makes a good magazine article.

* You have to choose a subject of compelling interest to the magazine's particular audience. If you know the market and the readers, selection of interesting topics will not be difficult.
* You must establish a strong reader identity, so that your reader is involved with the article or feature.
* You should plan to use colourful or entertaining material examples, anecdotes and facts to, what in journalistic jargon is called "spice it".
* Your writing should be clear, absorbing and to the point.
* The article should contain a strong element of appeal. Some subjects have more appeal than others. Once again, it would not be out of place to recall that the rules that are good for news writing are also good for articles. They are proximity, prominence, timeliness, conflict, bizarre and currency. Other elements are glamour, sex, success, human interest and competition.

TECHNIQUES FOR GOOD WRITING

So far we have told you about various forms of writing. This is an essential requirement on your way to becoming a writer. We have also told you the basics for a good write-up. Now, we are coming to the specifics. Writing is not simply an inherent talent that some of you may be having and some other won't be. There are steps that all of us can take, to improve our writing skills.

Writing is a process. We are only suggesting the rules, techniques and norms to you, but these have to be mixed with your own individual style, thoughts and methods, and with the subject and form of the writing. To produce a good write-up, you have to learn to combine all these.

Also remember, that writing is hard work. Most people give up writing as soon as they can, because it is such hard work. It is physically, mentally and emotionally demanding. Good writing does not happen all of a sudden. The writing process is often slow, at times tedious and even frustrating. This is not to frighten you. We just want to tell you about a phenomenon that most writers pass through so that when you come across such a situation, you do not give up writing. Remember, good writing does not happen all at once. It is the result of sweat and blood—in a literal sense.

We are again giving you some suggestions for improving your writing. We want to apprise you with its technique. Yes, it is a technique. Not all of these suggestions fit every piece of writing and should not be considered as set of rules. These can be considered a guideline for ensuring that what your writing comes of standard.

(a) **Write Simply.** We have been telling you repeatedly about this aspect. Simplicity is the best way to achieve clarity. Gifted writers take to this method to convey their message. A student, a beginner in the profession of wrtting, will also find it easy to write in a simple manner.

(b) **Use Simple Words.** Many people think big or complicated words will impress the reader. In fact it has the opposite effect. "To write clearly, not only the most expressive but the plainest words should be chosen", Benjamin Franklin once wrote. It is better to write ease instead of facilitate, many instead of numerous and use instead of utilise.

(c) **Economise on Words.** Mostly writers use too many words in their drafts. A careful editor deletes these at the time of editing. (This sentence itself can be written in simpler way.)—"A careful editor edits this out". There is no substitute for simple, straight forward prose. You should not try to use one word more than neccessary. Be on the look out for phrases, words and sentences that do not add substantially to the content of what you are writing. You should also guard against those fancy phrases which draw attention to the writing and the writer—and take away the content. Do not boast while writing.

(d) **Use Simple Sentences.** It is easier to write five simple sentence than one complex or compound sentence. So why not write simple sentences? Long winding sentences only distract the reader.

(e) **Do not use Jargon.** Each group of people has a technical language of their own. This is called jargon. You may be using certain abbreviations or names in your schools, sports field or in an office. Scientists do so in their labs. These are jargons. They are understood only by the select group. As a writer, you should not use these. You should rather explain the jargon if you have to use it. Your aim should be to make your message clear to the people who have no direct relationship to such groups. Your writings should not cut people off from receiving your ideas by a language that they cannot understand.

Avoid using overused words or phrases. These are called cliches. A write-up with cliches is not considered good writing. Cliches are so overused that they become trite, tiresome and bereft of any meaning. Some columnists have a tendency to use such cliches and that is why you call their writing boring.

(f) **Tie Together—Avoid Jolts.** Quite often you might have heard that writing must be well knit. Please do not wonder how to achieve this. You knit not the words alone but the thoughts as well. Readers should be able to read through a piece of writing without stops and surprises. While introducing a new idea or piece of information, do not do so without tying it to other parts of a story. Springing up with sudden thoughts jolts a reader, and like a sudden jerk on a smooth road, he is thrown off balance.

Connect any new information in a story to information already introduced. You have to develop a mental discipline and read your copy with discerning eyes. Expect your reader to condemn you for any folly you make in the copy. For a reader, your name is immaterial. For him, you are either a good or bad writer.

(g) **Avoid Adjectives.** Adjectives and adverbs are often superfluous. You should build up your sentences around nouns and verbs. Usage of adjectives often weaken your message. We would suggest that you write two simple sentences than use an adjective, which more often is unnecessary if your descriptions are clear and vivid. You should select good active verbs to enliven your copy. A good verb denotes action and a better verb denotes action and description. So choose your verb carefully. It will reverberate and rejuvenate your copy. Remember, adverbs and adjectives modify (limit) and verbs expand your thoughts and thus the writing.

(h) **Be Specific.** Brevity is the soul of wit. Just as you try to avoid someone who talks too much, so do readers about writings, which-have too many superfluous or high-sounding words or pilings of phrases or long-winding sentences that have run out of thoughts. Eliminate all that which you have said once. You have to have accuracy and clarity- But never try to sacrifice these for the sake of brevity. As I have told you earlier, if some facts need explanation do not economise on sentences. Instead of one long sentence, it is better to explain it in five sentences.

To be specific, get to the point, sometimes, it is certainly a difficult task. What I am suggesting is to decide on the theme of the write-up and weave your story around it. Once you have done it both writing and editing would be easier.

(i) **Cut Out Unnecessary Words.** I have told you earlier to avoid adjectives and adverbs. As you write, such words often creep in. Be alert to weed these words out. Quite often you write 'really', 'actually', 'very', 'in fact' and similar others. These words do not tell much to the readers. Rather they tell nothing. So cut these out. This will also help you in keeping your story trim and fit it into the limited space of a magazine or newspaper.

(j) **Avoid Repetition and Redundencies.** Both these traits show lack of discipline on the part of the Writer. Sometimes facts need to be repeated but that is not the case very often.

❑

7

Presentation and Newscasting

To sit in a chair and talk to a few people in a room is something most of us can do without too much trouble. But ask us to do exactly the same thing via a television camera, and we go to pieces. Only a handful of people can do it really well, and it is interesting to speculate about why this should be so. What is going on when one talks to a television camera?

Every new boy in front of camera is told that he is merely speaking to two or three people in a room, and this is true in a sense—that is the average size of the television audience at anyone place; but he is also speaking to many thousands or millions at any one time. This is a curious and unique circumstance of broadcasting. There is another one: they can see him, while he cannot see them. They are in their various homes at their case, while he is in a studio earning his bread. If he were present in the flesh, both he and the audience would behave quite differently: In the first place, they would not stare at him as they do at the image on the screen: it would be reckoned bad manners. If he could see and hear them, he would modify his manner according to how they reacted to him, and they in turn would respond to his reaction.

An actor can deal with this situation in. a fairly simple way: he retreates into the play and the character he is playing's, and ignores the cameras and the audience they represent (except for purely technical matters like moves and positions). He may miss the response of the audience, especially in a comedy, but it is not essential to his performance. A stand-up comedian on the other hand is lost without a live audience. He must be able to sense their reaction before he can work, and he is usually given a studio audience for that reason. The presenter or newscaster has neither of these methods open to him, and must find another, usually devising it for himself in a pragmatic, instinctive fashion, since there is precious little theory on the subject.

A few natural extroverts find it easy to talk to a camera. They are the kind of people who respond happily and spontaneously to others without selfconsciousness, who see no problem in talking to a duke or a dustman, a professor or a prostitute. They are television's naturals, although they often lack the imagination or the drive to go right to the top of their trade. Other performers in this curious field assume a particular persona in front of the camera although they may be complex and even neurotic off stage. They have learned to act out convincingly a particular facet of their personality that they have found to be generally acceptable to the rest of the world. It is not necessarily a mask; more a kind of make-up. Both these categories of presenter need to learn technique—not just the mechanics of the studio and the minor tricks of the trade, but the fundamental self-preparation for a performance It has much in common with that of an actor, although actors themselves are rarely much good at presenting television programmers: they need a character to play; asked to play themselves they are usually at a loss. Presenters in factual programmes shy away—quiet rightly from any identification with the world of map—believe, but they can profit from some of the techniques and exercises of the drama school.

The first and most important quality is relaxation. A man who is frightened or physically tense and tries not to show it is likely to have a harsh voice, an awkward posture, strained facial muscles and a mind off balance. He looks graceless and unhappily and it makes an audience feel ill at ease. The only remedy is preparation. It begins with thorough mastery of the material. No presenter should think of going on the air without a complete understanding of every though in his script ad of the programme as a whole. As far as most viewers are concerned, he is the man who is introducing the programme as a whole. As far as most viewers are concerned, he is the man who is introducing the programme, and his is therefore responsible for it. This may not be strictly true, but a presenter is entitle to demand that it should be taken seriously. Unless he has this involvement and identification with the programme, his performance on screen is likely to suffer. It is the presenter's equivalent of an actor's immersion in character and situation. Rehearsal is another stage in the preparation that builds confidence and relaxation. In news and current affairs, it may be fragmentary, but the presenter should be sure that he is getting the full benefit of whatever rehearsal is going. Director and technicians can sometimes become so involved with other problems that they take the man in front of camera too much for granted.

Relaxation is the key, too, to voice control. Any tension in the body tends to hawthorn up the chest and abdomen, making it impossible to use the diaphragm properly. The diaphragm is a large, muscular membrane that seals off the bottom of the chest and, as any actor or singer knows, you cannot use the full range of your voice without controlling the diaphragm. Most people not only do not control it—They hardly use it at all. They breathe in shallow gasps at the top of their lungs, talk in a monotone, and run out of breath in the middle of their sentences. Tension also constricts their voice-boxes and throats and the resultant sound varies from the unpleasant to the hideous. It is not obtrusive in ordinary daily speech.

Clarity of Diction

Diction is another lesson to be learned from the actor again not the exaggerated articulation necessary in the theatre, but the clarity of a good film or television actor, who uses mouth, lips and tongue to sound the whole of a word clearly. Words and phrases that blur and slur into one another are no help to understanding.

"Pry minstruff rance," is just that bit more difficult to grasp than "Prime Minister of France"

But even more important is the pattern of emphasis and inflection in a sentences. This can sometimes change the whole meaning.

Then the captain ordered a *change of course.*

Then the captain ordered a change of *course.*

Then the captain ordered a *change* of course.

Then the *captain* ordered a change of course.

The permutations and implications are legion. But even a completely unambiguous sentence can be difficult to assimilate if it is not spoken in the right war:

"John Smith, the scientist, whose comments on English cooking raised protest from the British catering trade last week, arrived back in London today after a trip round the world". For maximum intelligibility and euphony that sentence needs a wide range of vocal inflection and punctuation. Try it and try removing the second comma for a start.

Scene speakers like to analyse their script and mark the sentence with their own notation to indicate rises and falls of voice, emphasis and pauses. Others just master the sense of it in detail, and leave it to instinct on performance.

For the newscaster particularly, finding the right mood is a recurring problem. A lively up-tempo delivery is obviously appropriate for most news, but it can seem insensitive on stores involving disaster and suffering; artificial lugubriousness can be even worse. The change must be more than superficial, and to get it right newscaster needs to be sure of his own role. It is not for him to share in the sorrows of the world, or to display his own personal feelings. He is a professional reporting the news, and he must report it with detachment and a basic seriousness. When a story comes along that is highly charged with emotion, it is usually wise to stay on the side of detachment. The restrain itself counterpoints the emotion. A pause of a second or so helps the actual "gear change". In a normally fast-moving news programme it will seem two or three times as long as it actually is. :Funnies can be even more difficult. Gag humour is usually best avoided, and laughing with is more acceptable than laughing at; but intuition is the only guide.

Modes of Address

Even with all this analysis of philosophy and technique, one is still no nearer discovering to whom one is relaxing when talking to camera. Some—presenters begin by imagining their wife or friends behind the lens; some have a vague picture of an average family; one man at least addresses his words-doubtless for Freudian reasons to his father. Any surrogate is probably convenient to begin with and probably tends to wither away in time as the camera itself becomes a familiar.

Apart from these personal and subjective techniques, the presenter also needs to master the tricks of the studio and the camera. The first question a beginner asks is, "Where do I look?" The answer is into the lens, but it is not a complete answer because no one can stare fixedly at a camera with any degree to naturalness. In the private life we do not stare fix edit at a camera with any degree of naturalness. In the private life we do not state at the person addressed, but we do have frequent eye-to-eye contact, and we avoid looking at anything else in particular unless it is relevant to the conversation or we are frankly bored. On television, any definite look away from the lens can give the impression that the speaker is interested in something the viewer cannot see, and this is irritating. Vague flickerings of the eyes to and from the lens market the speaker seem nervous or shifty. The presenter must discipline himself into a compromise between what feels natural and what looks natural. Looking down is acceptable to the viewer because he knows that a newscaster is likely to have a script or notes, and, even it he hasn't, a look downwards is neutral—he is fairly obviously not looking at anything special. A glance upwards is tolerable for similar reasons, a particularly if the speaker seems to be recalling a fact or seeking a phrase. Looks to right or left without clear motivation are wrong.

If—like a newscaster—one is expected to refer to a script, the difficulty is less. It is natural to glance down at the beginning of a story, as though to check the subject, then up at the lens to say the important first sentence. One can then ago on looking at the camera, and return to the script for facets, figures and quotations thirteen could not be expected to memorize in detail. It is positively preferable to read this kind of thing openly, but straight narrative must be told, not to read. In fact, the newscaster nearly always has a teleprompter that unrolls his words either in front of the lens, or just above it or below it. The presenter of programmes other than daily news looks better without a script, but it would be a great burden to him to have to learn everything word for word, and he too will use a teleprompte; supplemented perhaps by cue cards that can be held easily in one hand.

The technique of using a teleprompter is not to become fixated on it. To read from it word for word gives one a glassy-eyed look. One should take in a whole phrase at a glance, and say it into the lens. If the content of the script has been properly studied this shouldn't be difficult, with practice. There are other useful tricks that help one round the problem of eye lines in presenting a current affairs programme. The presenter can sit or so that his body is angled a little off camera, and his head is turned toward it. He can has a natural and acceptable motive for looking away occasionally, and can imply with his glances that he is looking toward the source of the next item he is introducing. He can walk in shot while talking, and need only glance at the lens occasionally, because it is obvious that he must watch where he is going.

The nearer the camera, the more important it is that the presenter should look into the lens itself. A look directed only an inch or two off camera shows up at short range far more than at long range, no matter how close the actual short range far more than at long range, no matter how close the actual shot that the camera is framing. With zoom lenses, however, the camera cannot usually focus at less than ten feet, so that provided one looks at it generally the eyes will seem to the looking directly at the viewer.

Throughout the whole business of talking to camera, the viewer is staring at the presenter, probably on close up and observes more of him and his manner in a few seconds than none normally does in several minutes of listening to someone in the flesh. It is important therefore to have as few tension and insecurity, for which the cure has already been suggested-relaxation. Without it, nothing will look or sound right.

Seaking Film Commentary

Speaking commentary to film demands even more technical control over voice, diction and inflation. Face and gesture cannot be seen so the voice must work harder; but at the same time it must key itself to the image and action on the screen. The film is dominant, and the words must support and supplement it. The informal almost conversational pattern of speech to camera must become much more exaggerated in expression, with words and phrases pointed and emphasized in a way that would seem artificial away from the film. There need to be a greater range of tones; from high to low, from head to chest. Where the voice might naturally rise a little-say at a comma-it must be more; where it drops at the end of a sentence it musts drop more definitely. At the same time, diction musti be crystal clear, with all consonants sounded, particularly at the ends of words. The viewer has a lot to take in through eyes and ears, and the effort to follow a badly spoken commentary is a serious distraction.

Timing is vital. A well-written film commentary is calculated to fit the film by the careful counting of words and footage, but it is up the commentator himself to inflect and I place the words with precision. A mistiming of less than a second can sometimes ruin an effect. When a commentary is' recorded in advance, it is usually possible to cut the track into position before the final dub, but it is always better get it right on the original recording, and of course no amount of editing can force ten seconds of speech into eight seconds of screen time.

During a recording session, the film commentators its in a dubbing theatre or sound-proof box, and watches the film projected along with a footage or seconds counter. The start of each paragraph of commentary has a footage cue, and the voice must come in at the precise moment. Usually, someone is there to cue, the commentator with a tap on the shoulder, but once he has begun to speak only he can match the words and the picture. He needs to see the film once or twice, and rehearse the words with it to understand the total effect that producer and writer are aiming at. Film and commentary should ideally seem to blend into one rather than be two separate activities going on at the same time. The picture should become part of the sentence, as it were, and the sentence an integral part of the film. Often the words will not make complete sense unless they are heard with the picture and the two are absorbed simultaneously.

Commenting on Outside Broadcasts

Doing a commentary for an outside broadcast involves totally different techniques. The pictures are the slave of the event, and must follow it as it happens, including the inevitable periods when the action is slow and the cameras are not able to get the best shots because of their lack of mobility. The events themselves may be unpredictale, and the commentator must make sense of things as they happen.

At a big set piece event, hc has a predetermined position and a monitor screen to key his commentary to; on a news assignment, he may have to manage as best he can with a microphone on the fringe of the action. In either situation, there can be no set script, and any attempt to write one is likely to do more harm than good. What the commentator needs is a ready likely to do more harm than good. What the commentator needs is a ready supply of information to cover any situation that might arise. A lot of it has to be memorised. Sporting commentators do an immense amount of homework before a match or a race to ensure that they will recognise a player or a horse instantly and confidently. Some have racing colours painted on cards, and practice recognition by shuffling and dealing to themselves in random order. Whatever the method or the occasion, it is essential for the commentator to immerse himself in deep and intensive research.

As with film commentary, there are two extremes of error to be avoided: one must not describe what the viewer can see perfectly well for himself, and one must not talk about something unrelated to the picture. Whatever is said, must be additional and complementary:

an identification, a curious sidelight, a comparison, a phrase that puts an incident into a new perspective. The viewer must be told first what he needs to know to understand the picture, secondly anything he might be curious about, and thirdly anything interesting and amusing; but there is no necessity to talk all the time: when the picture is telling the story, let it. Memory, of course, is fallible and limited, and most commentators have their own system of supplementing it with notes. It is worth spending a good deal of time in organising them for rapid reference. A useful system is a card index with the cards mounted on flaps in a folder. Each card projects slightly from under the next, and is identified by a word or phrase. When the First Battalion. The Grenadier Guards appears in shot, one can then flip over the cards to reveal the notes about them; or when an election result is announced, one can compare the voting figures immediately with the last election.

An OB can rarely present pictures as vivid and selective as those of a film camera; its great strength is the sense it gives the viewer that he is there with a ringside seat on the event as it happens. A good commentator reflects the mood of the occasion he is reporting, but he identifies with the viewer. He sees himself not as the spokesman of the event, addressing the television audience, but as the knowledgeable friend at the viewer's elbow. Like the presenter, the announcer, the reporter, he is the vital human link between the television machine and its audience.

❐

8

Broadcast News Writing

WRITING FOR THE EAR

You may find radio and television news writing a refreshing change from newspaper style. Broadcast copy not only permits but requires the form of expression which is probably most natural for you—namely that of speech. We learn to speak before we learn to write, and we talk a lot more than we write in everyday communication. The naturalness of the spoken word is too often lost when the writer thinks in terms of narrow columns of type and rules of journals left over from another era. As a broadcast writer, think instead of how words and their combinations sound. Talk the news as you write it.

We don't go around talking in awkward newspaperisms like the dangling attribution.

> Out-of-state students are vital to the University of Wisconsin, Gov. Patrick J. Lucey said today.

You might say:

> Governor Lucey said today that out-of-state students are vital to the University of Wisconsin.

or:

> Governor Lucey says out-of-state students are vital to the University of Wisconsin.

Read the three versions to someone and you'll see the difference. The last two — in broadcast news style — read easier for you and come across better for the listener. Those are the objectives toward which most guidelines for broadcast news writing are directed. The copy should be *(1)* easy for the newscaster to read and *(2)* easy for the listener to understand.

Since newspaper copy is often difficult when read aloud, should you do as one manual suggests and "forget cverything you have learned about newspaper writing"? Certainly not. Most of the fundamentals of effective news writing apply across the media. For example, the story must be accurate and clear. The word used should be precise, the grammar correct, the sentence construction easy to follow, and the story organization logical. The lead should draw attention to the main element of the news story. Thought units placed together should indeed fit together.Modifiers should be close to what they modify. Long phrases or clauses should not separate the subject and the verb. And a clear writer must be a clear thinker. Such elements underlie all effective verbal communication and are basic to good writing in all media.

Any sloppiness in thinking or writing which makes a newspaper story hard to follow is even worse in broadcast news. Readers may be able to go back and re-read until they figure a newspaper story out. But listeners normally cannot call back the newscaster to run through it a second time. In broadcast news, a story must be perfectly clear and easy to understand the first — and only — time it's heard.

It may also help to remember that the person on the other end may be only half listening. His or her attention may be divided between the news programme and rush-hour traffic, homework, the morning paper, conversation, or a combination of such distrations. Much as newspaper readers scan headlines to decide which stories they want to read, listeners may be catching only key words which alert them to those stories they care to pay attention to. This means that if the lead does not clearly cue listeners as to the nature of the story, they may not start paying attention until most of it has been missed.

With these general considerations in mind, let's go to some specific guidelines to make the news easier to read aloud and easier to listen to.

Focusing the Story

The shotgun appraoch of reporting every fact in sight won't work for broadcast news. There's no time for it. For example, when commercial time has been deducted from a 5 minute newscast, seldom is time left for more than 50 lines of copy. (The average newscaster reads 15-16 lines a minute.) And you may want to get 8-10 stories into those 50 lines. This means that you must exercise news judgement and report only the most important element of those stories.

More than your newspaper colleagues, you must be selective. You must focus clearly on the most important part of a story and not bog down in secondary details. Listeners can effectively take in only a limited number of different bits of information in a given period of time. So don't try to cram too many facts into a story. Its better to do justice to one or two main points than to try to communicate a telescoped digest of six or eight points which overload the listener and may actually communicate nothing.

At the same time, avoid the kind of headline treatment that leaves listeners wondering what a story was all about. Some background or elaboration is often needed, even if it crowds out some new information. Again, you serve listeners better with one report that says something than with two reports which are so sketchy that neither makes much sense.

Writing from Wire Copy and Newspapers

Never parrot a story from a news wire or a newspaper. Get into it with your own approach and tell it in your own words, using the source copy only as raw material. Too many so-called rewriters are in fact little more than re-typed excerpts. Although such is discouraged by the wire service, their broadcast stories often consist of the first two or three paragraphs of a newspaper wire story with a word or two changed here and there. Many of them read well enough and may be appropriate for the wire service, but this is not broadcast news writing.

Especially if the original reads well, as it often does, you may find it hard to break away from its wording. The trick here for most people is to lay the source copy aside and write from memory, referring to the wire or newspaper story only for exact quotes, names, and such. This forces you to put the news into your own words.

Learn to scan the source copy, looking over it quickly and dwelling only the highlights. If you read all of it carefully, you may find no time is left for writing newscasts. To be a competent news writer or editor, you won't have time to get that backgrounding from the present day's file, and it's not available on the radio wire anyway.

So prepare yourself by reading newspapers, magazines and other materials to keep you up to date on everything of importance in the world about you. Journalists who know only what they read on the radio wire (a service that prints out headlines and little nutshells all day long) are only superficially informed and not really up to writing or editing a newscast.

If you don't understand a story, there's a good chance that many listeners may share your bewilderment. The lazy writer will copy an explanatory clause or phrase from the wire without knowing what it means. The good writer will figure it out and express it in a way that's perfectly clear.

What of writing from a newspaper without permission? It's done in hundreds of broadcast newsrooms every day. It need not constitute a copyright violation, though it often does, and may stations get by with it. News- information about events- is not copyrightable, but authorship the wording of the original - is. When the broadcast writer uses the newspaper story only as a source of information and then turns away and writes a story in his or her own words, that's all right in most cases. But when the wording is the same, or even substantially the same, as that of the newspaper, the station is guilty of copyright violation or a similar transgression. And now and then, it's pleasing to note, one of them gets caught.

Telling it Clearly

There's no substitute for the direct style of sentence and story construction. When you have the story in mind, tell it in a straightforward way. Avoid putting participial phrases or dependent clauses at the beginning of sentences. If the main element is qualified by some "ifs" or, "buts," present the main element first and then get into the qualifications.

The lead should call attention to the main element of the story and should not be crowded with too many facts. Don't try to cram all five Ws and the H (Who, What, Where, When, Why and How) into the lead. You'll lose the listener through overload.

The first words of the story should clearly cue the listener to what it's all about. A fragmentary sentence may make a good scene setter. For example:

> Labour trouble in New York tonight. The city's transit workers voted to strike unless....etc.

But use this approach sparingly. It can get montonous and also consumes time unnecessarily. A sentence is the best lead for most stories. Example:

> Transit workers in New York City voted tonight to strike unless....etc.

Avoid leading with direct quotes or questions. A direct quote may make the listener wonder for a moment or two whether the words are those of the newscaster or someone else. The question lead sounds too much like a soap commercial or game show.

Make your points one at a time. Wrap up one aspect of a story before going to the next. For example, tell what the President said about Vietnam, then what he said about taxes, then his comments on politics in California, etc. Don't jump back and forth from one to another. This forces too many reorientations on the listener.

The general usually requires fewer words and is easier to grasp than the specific. So when specific identifications, figures, and such are not essential to the story, skip them. In the New York labor story, we could give the exact name of the union local, but most listeners couldn't care less. "Transit workers" conveys the meaningful information.

The indicative tense, when appropriate, usually carries more impact than the subjunctive.

Heard on a radio station:

> The Board of Regents decided that course-credit would be withheld for any student who refused to be photographed for and I-D card.

Better:

> The Board of Regents decided that course-credit will be withheld for any student who refuses to be...etc.

Avoid long, involved sentences. Flesch says they should average about 17 words. Actually, sentence length *per se* is less important than a logical sequence of thought units that flow easily from start to finish of the story. But unless you're a real master with words, chances are that your copy will start bogging down when the sentences start getting long.

A troublesome sentence can often be improved by breaking it into two or more thoughts, or sentences.

Bad:

> Senator Gaylord Nelson, speaking before a meeting of University of Wisconsin Young Democrats in Madison yesterday, said the United States should stop the bombing of North Vietnam

Better:

> Senator Nelson says the United States should stop the bombing of North Vietnam. Nelson spoke at a meeting of Young Democrats from the University of Wisconsin in Madison yesterday.

Because small mouthfuls are usually easier to handle, a prepositional phrase after a word often comes across better as a modifier than an adjective preceding it. "Members of the United Nations" reads better than "United Nations members."

Clauses tend to be more forceful than verb-form phrases.

Awkward. Weekend reports of China's Mao Tse-Tung having suffered a stroke...

Better. Weekend reports that China's Mao Tse-Tung had suffered a stroke....

As limIted as we are for time in radio and TV, a certain amount of repetition or redundancy can help the listener. Repeating a key name or other important element in a later sentence is a service to the listener who starts paying attention late. It can also make the story clearer, even for the attentive ones. Be sure the antecedent or a pronoun is clear, and if in doubt, repeat the name. Never use "the latter" or "the former" — the listener cannot look back to see which came first and which last. As for "respectively," forget there's such a word.

The "ing" verb forms are overused by some broadcast writers. Direct verb forms often do the job better.

Head (re plane crash):

...landing 20 feet off the runway and settling in the mud.

Nothing wrong with that, but more direct is:

It landed 20 feet off the runaway and settled in the mud.

Forsome on-the-air reporters, the "ed" sound comes across easier, stronger, and more effectively than "ing".

Names and Identifications

Don't lead with unfamiliar names. They're too easy to miss. Set the listener up for them by leading with identifying information about the person.

It's all right to lead with a familiar name like President Carter, Senator Proxmire, or Governor Lucey. For that matter, such public officials usually carry a title before the name, so it's still a matter of going from identification to name.

Middle initials of most newsmakers are omitted for broadcast. Indeed, if a person is very well known—like Carter, Proxmire, and Lucey (in Wisconsin) - first name is usually skipped. If you're sure most members of the audience know the first name, omit it. Otherwise, include it. The middle initial should be included if it appears needed for exact identification, as with an accident victim or a suspect in a crime.

The newspaper form for ages - John Jones, 30 - should usually be avoided. The standard broadcast approach for years has been 30-year old John Jones. If-in doubt, use this style. But now and then it's good to hear someone break the monotony of the standard treatment of ages. For example, with a separate sentence — Jones is 30. Or, in a series, the newspaper form may be the most practical: He has three children—John, 6...Edward; 4...and Susan, 2. When is one form more appropriate than another? When that's how you would say it in talking with someone.

Attribution and Quotes

Attribution should be made clear and should be placed before what the person said. This is part of direct oral expression: who—said—what. As noted at the start, the dangling attributions so common in newspaper stories make for unnatural speech patterns. Do not use them.

Use Quotes Sparingly. The paraphrase or indirect quotes is, usually preferable. You can often say it more concisely than the news source, and the exact words are seldom so important that you gain by presenting them as such. If a dairy spokesman tells you that "the price of milk is going up" and those are the words you use in the story, the fact that they happen to be exactly the ones the spokesman used is too trivial to justify making them stand out as a direct quote. Such quotes only clutter your copy.

Direct quotes are usually taken from a larger context and may not be as clear as paraphrase.

Bad:

> Democratic Chairman Lawrence O 'Brien said in Washington today, "A year and a half of attention directed to the Southern Strategy has not worked for this administration.

Clearer:

> Democratic Chairman Lawrence O 'Brien said in Washington today that the Nixon administration has directed a year and a-half of attention to the Southern strategy and it hasn't worked.

If the exact words, are so colorful, m-eaningful, or controversial that you feel you should make them stand out as a direct quote—do just that. Remember that the listener cannot see the quotation marks on the copy. If the newscaster is proficient in oral interpretation, the handling of direct quotes is not much of a problem. But for safety, in case he or she is just reading words, make the quote stand out as such by the way you write the copy.

The method used in the early days of radio—quote...unquote"—has fallen out of favor in most newsrooms, probably because few people talk that way. Some acceptable methods now in use include:

...What the senator called "gross deception"..

The senator put it in this way: "A nation divided..."

The President said—and these are his words—"That's the ugliest thing I ever saw."

Said the governor: "We'll win by a landside."

Other approaches may corne to mind as you write a story. Use the one that fits the particular situation best.

Time and Tense

Listeners expect broadcast news to be up to date. Without misleading, your writing can make it sound fresh and current even if it's getting a little older than you'd like at times—as in the early morning when most of the file is what happened yesterday. For example, the morning paper says:

President Carter yesterday began a study of .....

Continuing tense can freshen it:

President Carter is studying....

So can present perfect:

President Carter has begun a study of....

Ask yourself what the current situation is and use the most appropriate tense, which may well be different from the past tense rigidly used by newspapers. Using present and continuing tense helps you avoid constantly repeating the words "yesterday" and "today" in the many items which make up a newscast. For the matter' 'yesterday" is implied for many stories in the early morning newscast - congress, speeches, news conferences, etc. And on a late afternoon or evening newscast, "today" maybe assumed for must most of them. So the ' 'Yesterday" or' 'today does not have to be repeated in every story. The tricky time—when there's likely to be a mixture of today and yesterday stories—is between and mid-morning and mid-afternoon. When there's danger of having the listener think a yesterday story happened today, include the time element.

Never use a story that has been out more than 24 hours. It's no longer news. You waste the time of listeners or viewers when your 10 p.m. newscast includes stories they read several hours earlier in the morning paper. This happens quite often where some of the newspersons apparently don't bother to read the morning paper. The wire-sevice rewrites the story from the morning paper and sends it over in present perfect tense. Since all these writers or editors know is what they read on the radio wire, they assume that it is fresh news.

Never assume that a wire story written in present perfect tense (..."has done" such and such) is a today story. Unless you are absolutely sure, don't change it to past tense with the time element (... "did" such and such "today") Among other journalistic traversities inflicted upon listeners and viewers are yesterday's stories reported as having happened today.

When "Yesterday" is used, it is sometimes effectively delayed until the second sentence. Example:

> President Carter has appealed to members of the United Nations to help in working for peace in the Middle East. He told the General Assembly yesterday....

Do not use both present perfect tense and the time element in the lead sentence. Write either "has said," "said today," or just "said", but not "has said today."

It's yesterday, today, and tomorrow—not Monday, Tuesday, and Wednesday.

Never use such time redundancies as 10:30 a.m. this morning or tonight at 7 p.m. Omit the p.m. or a.m. in these cases.

Choosing the Best Word

Contractions judiciously used are an asset in broadcast writing. They're much used in speech and our "ear" copy tends to sound stilted without some of them. Walter Cronkite does not normally sign off with: "And that is the way it is, Tuesday, etc. " That's just not the way it's usually said.

But don't overdo contractions. Often, for ephasis or clarity, "not" should be used instead of a contracted form. Unless emphasis of "not" is wanted. "won't" is fine. But you're safer in getting across with "cannot" and "would not" than with "can't" and "wouldn't". The nasal "n't" is easy to lose in enunciation or transmission. Keep that sort of thing in mind or in ear—as you write.

Avoid cumbersome words when simple ones are available. Why say "approximately one million dollars" when "about one million dollars" does the job as well? There's nothing wrong with "about" used as an adverb. As other examples, simplicity recommends "begin" over"commence," "try" over "endeavor, ""buy" over "purchase" and "Says" over such often strained and even incorrect synonyms as "declalres, " "states", "asserts," and "announces." Of course if the source does indeed make an announcement or issue a statement, then "announced" or "stated" or "stated" are appropriate.

When should" that" introduce a clause? A good ear is the best guide. "Announced" and "reported" will be followed by "that" more often than will "says" or "said."

In general, when two acceptable form of a word are available, use the simpler one: "toward" (NOT "towards")... "inregard to" (NOT "in regards to ") and in enumerating "first", "second", and "third" (NOT "firstly", "secondly", and "thirdly".

Television is a medium—NOT a media (plural)

Don't confuse robbing and stealing. A robber takes by force or threat of force. A thief steals - by stealth. DO NOT say that a robber stole 5-thousand dollars from a bank or that thief robbed a woman of her purse while whe was not looking. A robber only robs or takes. A thief only steals.

Watch out for sibilants in successison—the "hiss." Try this one from a UPI stylebook: "Since Senator Sam Simpson has seen

Secretary of State Sawyer, he says " Or the old one Phil Harris used to do: "Six tall slim, slick sycamore saplings..."

Don 'tabbreviate, except for Mr., Mrs., Ms. and Dr. Spell out: Captain Johnson, Professor Jones, State Street, November 15th, 10 dollars, 15 per cent, etc.

Most stations use Mr. only for members of the clergy. A few use it for the President of the United States.

When you want initials read as such, use hyphens: N-A-A-C-P-R-O-T-C, C-B-S, and U-S. When treating them as word, omit the hyphens: NATO.

When it's opinion rather than established fact, don't use "pointed out", "noted," or "stressed that." Example:

The assesmblyman said (NOT noted) that out-of-state students are the worst trouble-makers.

Avoid sterotypcs, cliches and fad expressions. Such stereotypes as "hippies", "hardhats," "hawks" and "doves" are gross oversimplifications which often do a disservice to the great variety of individuals in the real world. Cliches such as "mounting tension, "massive attacks," and "mute evidence" fairly inocucous, but you can add class to your writing by avoiding them. And most writers do well not to use or (as likely) misuse such "in" (and soon "out") expressions as right on" or "lost his cool.."

Include pronouncers for difficult words which may be familiar to the newscaster. He or she should know Saigon, Haiphong, and Hanoi by now, but could well be misled by Patna (PUTT -nuh), India. And foreign cities to the contrary, as Cairo (KAY-roe), Illinois, and Versailles (verSALES), Kentucky.

Numbers

Treat numbers in the way they'll be most easily and accurately read by the newscaster. Some stations spell out almost all numbers, thus providing a check against typos on the relatively little used upper row of typewriter keys. But spellouts of numbers like 365 can become cumbersome, and many newscasters prefer the numerals. Policies on numbers vary from one newsroom to another and can be confusing. Only a few changes from regular newspaper style are called for.

Round off large numbers when the exact figure is not essential. For example $54, 136 can usually be treated as 54 thousand dollars. Or if you feel it should be made clear that this is not the exact figure-about 54 thousand dollars.

If the number you plan to use ends in two or more ciphers, spell out what the ciphers stand for. For example: 5-hundred, not 500; 8-thousand, not 8,000; / 5-million, etc. This keeps the newscaster from having to count ciphers before reading the number. On numbers from thousands up, when something more exact is demanded, do it: 5-thousand 280 or 2-million 400-thousand.

Mechanics

Use normal capitalization. Do not use ALL CAPS in copy the newscaster is to read. They shoule be reversed for pronouncers and technical cues such as: CART #3 or TAKE FILM.

Use normal punctuation in most cases. Be sure to put commas on both sides of elements in opposition. When you want the opposition to stand out clearly, dashes may be used Broadcast writers sometimes use three dots instead of 1 comma between parts of a compound sentence...

before 1 subordinate clause that trails off a sentence... or between the units of a series when each unit is several words long. But use dots and dashes sparingly, and if in doubt, stick to normal punctuation.

Triple-space. This leaves room for neatly typed corrections.

Don't split words between lines. This can bring at inappropriate pause in the middle of a word.

Use paragraphs logically. If a Viet Nam wrapup story has three distinct aspects, it makes sense to use three paragraphs.

Unless you have a couple of items you're absolutely sure will be used in one-two order, start each story on a separate page. This makes it easier for the editor to shuffle them around and do last-minute updating.

Never hand a newscaster messy or unedited copy. Corrections should be neatly made, preferably typed in above the corrected line. Scribbling and exotic printing art unacceptable. The linotype operator can stop for a while to decipher it, but not the newscaster. If you mess up a word, try again. When you've completed a story, blacken Xed-out portions with a copy pencil. If a page has many corrections and you possibly have time, type it over.

Voice Reports and Actualities

Voice Reports of correspondents (like Phil Jones of CBS) and actualities which let the listener hear the voices of newsmakers (like Senator McGovern) should add to - not duplicate - what the newscaster says. Especially avoid letting the last words of the newscaster be the first word of the tape.

Bad intro:

President Weaver said the proposed legislation could ruin the University of Wisconsin.

WEAVER CART (#8)...TIME -: 35

TAPE OPEN: "The proposed legislation could ruin the University of Wisconsin..."

OUT CUE: "...the regents and I will stand firm."

Better intro:

President Weaver commented on the legislation.

Keep lead-ins to voice reports general and brief. Example:

A new crisis in Jordan. That story from Bob Richards in Amman.

Avoid much redundancy between the newscaster and the correspondent. Broadcast time is too valuable for the newscaster to tell a story and then call in a correspondent to tell the same thing in different words. Sometimes this happens because the writer or editor has not listened to the tapes carefully before incorporating them into the newscast.

After the Weaver actuality and most others, find a way to work in the newsmaker's name again. This serves listeners who missed or only half -caught the name in the introduction and are now wondering who that was. It is usually best handled by telling something else the person said. Example:

President Weaver said he will talk with the governor on the matter next week.

Such tape wrap-arounds, as they are sometimes called are not necessary if the voice is a very familiar one like President Carter's or Senator Humphrey's or if the actuality is extremely brief-say 15 seconds or less. Nothing further a needed, of course, when a correspondent signs off a voice report with his or her name.

Present tense may be used to introduce a correspondents voice report—"Phil Jones reports from Washington." But past tense normally should be used for actualities—"Senator Percy explained his opposition," NOT Senator Percy explains..."—lest it mislead by sounding as if Percy is on live instead of taped.

When the correspondent is on tape (as is usually the case), don't write: "We switch... " "We go to... "or "We call in..." This gives the false impression that Phil is on live.

It is professionally dishonest, though perhaps technically correct, to imply exclusivity where it does not exist. For example, a station subscribing to the UPI Audio Service might be technically correct in introducing a UPI Audio voice report. "Pye Chamberlain reports for W—News." Yes, he's reporting for W— AND 300 other stations. Even worse, an audio service actuality may be introduced as if it had been acquired through the efforts of the local station. Stations practicing such fraud lower their credibility among the many listeners who can see through it and also invite trouble from the Federal Communications Commission.

Tapes must be clear and understandable if they are to communicate rather than serve largely as a gimmick. If one from overseas transmission is so garbled that it's hard to follow, or if the witness sounds as if she had mud in her mouth, ask yourself—is this really necessary ? You do the listeners no service by broadcasting something they cannot understand. That's not communication. And remember when judging the technial quality of a recording, it's easier to understand in the ideal acoustical setting of the station than on the freeway.

If an engineer is running the tapes, give him or her a carbon of the script with everything he or she needs to know made perfectly clear. This includes the newscaster's introduction, identification of the tape, its exact time, and the closing cue (last words on the tape). Some stations also require the opening cue. And be sure the engineer knows about how far into the newscast the tape comes.

You're also a Reporter

In most newsrooms, the news writer or editor (often the same person) is also a reporter. Much news can be gathered by phone. And if you're writing that police still are looking for a bank robber or that someone remains in critical condition, check police or the hospital shortly before airtime to be sure that such is the situation.

In handling news agency stories, be alert for angles of particular interest to your audience. The list of witnesses called before a congressional committee may include someone from your state. And in the tally of votes for and against a bill, look for how your state's delegation voted.

Although the five Wsand the H should not be crammed into the lead, they are still useful. Before wrapping up a story, ask yourself if all these questions - who? what? where? when? why? how? - pertinent to the story have been answered.

If an important question is not answered by news agency copy or other source material available in the newsroom. you may be able to get on the phone and track down the answer yourself. Such initiative separates the broadcast journalists from the mechanical writers.

Responsibility

Accuracy is highly important in broadcast news. With radio especially a correction may reach relatively few of the people who heard the newscast on which the error was made. Check out anything that's questionable. For the responsible radio or television journalist, it's more important to get it right than to get it on first.

Don't state cause-and-effect unless you're sure (and you seldom are).

Controversial matters by definition have two or more sides. Seeking out and reporting all significant points of view is your professional responsibility as a journalist and your legal obligation under the Fairness Doctrine. Because most stories are shorter for broadcast than for print, it's not always easy to include both sides. But if you can find time to report charges against a person or organization, try to find time to seek out and report a reply to them. This is only fairplay.

A note on colorful and "cute" writing. A few "whoop it up" stations have gone off the deep end with over-personalized, over-dramatized news writing. In their efforts to make a show of it, they sometimes distort the news and embarrass persons in the news. When there's doubt as to the accuracy, fairness, or good taste of something imaginative that pops into your mind, skip it. Write interestingly and perhaps on a light story a bit lightly. But for most stories, your best bet is to play it straight. Your primary job is to inform rather than to entertain.

Putting the Newscast Together

In picking a lead story, consider such factors as significance, interest, and immediacy.

Immediacy is usually given higher priority for hourly newscasts than for the longer wrapup news programmes. When you're going on with a newscast ever hour, a fresh lead story helps keep the overlap listeners from feeling they are getting the same old report hour after hour.

Significance gets higher priority in the longer, more comprehensive wrapup programs. The signoff news on local stations and the early evening network television news programmes usually lead with the top story of the day even if it broke in the morning.

If a good story is an exclusive for your station, or if you have especially good tape or film with it, the story may be give higher priority.

As editor, you can help the listener by lining up the stories so that the newscast has continuity. Some departmentalization is usually desirable. Stories may be grouped by geographic area (world, national, state, and local), by topic area (war, Congress, labour, etc.), or by a combination of the two. Few stations follow the more or less rigid departmentalization prescribed by some of the older text-books. News value and the pace of the newcast should also bc considered. Perhaps your biggest story of the day is local, there are some important world-national stories, and several relatively minor state and local items. You might appropriately organize your newscast in exactly that order.

Sometimes a change of pace is needed in a heavy file of significant but dull news. For example: Congress on the budget, defense spending, and housing legislation; anti-war demonstrations in various parts of the nation; back to Congress on consumer protection and oil depletion allowances. A simple transition from world to state news is "In Georgia news ..." A more sophisticated transition is none at all, as such. Simply let the opening words of the first state story be something like "The Georgia legislature..."

Wrapped up stories should normally be written first, leaving the time nearer the newscast for breaking stories. This can cut down on the rewriting and revising you have to do.

A Frame of Mind

The numerous other suggestions which could be included in this broadcast news writing guide would still be aimed at the same two objectives stated at the start: *(1)* making the news easy for the newscaster to read and *(2)* making it easy for the listener to understand.

Keeping in mind specific points to help you achieve these objectives can be useful, especially for the beginner. But you'll become a really effective radio or television news writer only when these things blend into a frame of mind which marks your approach to the writing - a constant awareness that this is oral communication of news. You're writing talk copy.

What goes through your mind as you write a broadcast news story? Possibly something like this. You have the facts, a full two pages of notes or 30 inches of wire copy. But you have time for only 10 lines.

First you decide what is news, what is really important, how you'll use these 10 lines. You know you can include only the essence, so askwhat's the story all about? What has happened that should interest our listeners? What information is most important to pass along to them? The list of names, those little details, some of those figures - no time for them and few listeners would catch them anyway. They would only clutter your copy, detracting from what's really news.

Having decided what's news, you simply tell the listener about it writing in much the same words and style as if you were telling the highlights to a half-interested stranger, with only 40 seconds to get your message across. The lead sentence should draw attention and let the listener know what the story is all about. Now come the specifics that develop the story, flowing logically and easily from one to the next as in effective conversation. Your story is interesting, informative, and easy to follow. You're talking the news with your typewriter.

Code of Broadcast News Ethics Radio Television News Directors Association

The following Code of Broadcast News Ethics for RTNDA was adopted January 2, 1966, and amended October 13, 1973.

The members of the Radio Television News Directors Association agree that their prime responsibility as journalists—and that of the broadcasting industry as the collective sponsor of news broadcasting is to provide to the public they serve a news service as accurate, full and prompt as human integrity and devotion can devise. To that end, they declare their acceptance of the standards of practice here setforth, and their solemn intent to honour them to the limits of their ability.

Article One

The primary purpose of broadcast journalists- to inform the public of events of importance and appropriate interest in a manner that is accurate and comprehensive—shall override all other purposes.

Article Two

Broadcast news presentations shall be designed not only to offer timely and accurate information, but also to present it in the light of relevant circumstances that give it meaning and perspective.

This standard means that news reports, when clarity demands it. will be laid against pertinent factual background; that factors such as race, creed, nationality or prior status will be reported only when they are relevant; that comment or subjective content will be properly identified; and that errors in fact will be promptly acknowledged and corrected.

Article Three

Broadcast journalists shall seek to select material for newscasts solely on their evaluation of its merits as news.

This standard means that news will be selected on the criteria of significance, community and regional relevance, appropriate human interests, service to defined audiences. It excludes sensationalism or misleading emphasis in any form; subservience to external or "interested" efforts to influence news selection and presentation, whether from within the broadcasting industry or fror without. It require's that such terms as ' 'bulletin" and' 'flash' , be used only when the character of the news justifies them; that bombastic or misleading descriptions of newsroom facilities and personnel be rejected, along with undue use of sound and visual effects; and that promotional or publicity material be sharply scrutinized before use and identified by source or otherwise when broadcast.

Article Four

Broadcast journalists shall at all times display humane respect for the dignity, privacy and the well-being of persons with whom the news deals.

Article Five

Broadcast journalists shall govern their personal lives and such nonprofessional associations as may impinge on their professional activities in a manner that will protect them from conflict of interest, real or apparent.

Article Six

Broadcast journalists shall seek actively to present all news the knowledge of which will serve the public interest, no matter what selfish, uninformed or corrupt efforts to color it withhold it or prevent its presentation (by others). They shall make constant effort to open doors closed to the reporting of public proceedings with tools appropriate to the broadcasting (including cameras and recorders), consistent with the public interests. They acknowledge the journalist's ethic of protection of confidential information and sources, and urge unswerving observation of it except in instances in which it would clearly and unmistakably defy the public interest.

Article Seven

Broadcast journalists recognize the responsibility borne by broadcasting for informed analysis, comment and editorial opinion on public events and issues. They accept the obligation of broadcasters, for the presentation of such matters by individuals whose competence, experience and judgement qualified them for it.

Article Eight

In court, broadcast journalists shall conduct themselves with dignity, whether the court is in or out of session. They shall keep broadcast equipment as unobstrusive and silent as possible. Where court facilities are inadequate, pool broadcasts should be arranged.

Article Nine

In reporting matters that are or may be litigated, the journalist shall avoid practices which would tend to interfere with the right of an individual to a fair trial.

Article Ten

Broadcast journalists shall not misrepresent the source of any broadcast news material.

Article Eleven

Broadcast journalists shall actively censure and seek to prevent violations of these standards, and shall actively encourage their observance by all journalists, whether of the Radio and Television News Directors Association or not.

❒

9

Reporting and News-gathering Tactics

Despite the enormous satisfaction it is quite possible to derive from the business of putting together complicated news stories for transmission in a very short time, there is not much doubt that the glamour image of the average newsroom journalist lags far behind that of those who appear in front of the camera. For while no viewer would be expected to name any member of the back-room team, descriptions of nationally known news performers—the 'talent' as they are quaintly described in the United trip easily off the tongue. So it is hardly surprising that, sooner or later, many a starry-eyed newcomer to television news begins itching to achieve what is believed to be the ideal-to be seen by an audience of millions through a news report made in some exotic, relatively troubled the other side of the world, enjoying what one member of the international reporting set has summed up as a front seat on history's.

That is probably a perfect example of the greener grass syndrome, for there are certainly some reporters who would dearly love to exchange their front seats for what they regard as the calmer back rows in the newsroom television reporters privately admit that, after a while, the apparent glamour and excitement of their lives begin to fall. Some learn sooner than others to detest rushing to catch planes or deadlines, living out of suitcases, eating hurried meals in unhygenic places abroad, witnessing at first hand unspeakable horrors of which the audience may ultimately see very little. All this is in addition to the real personal dangers involved in covering the stuff of modern television news: war, natural disaster, civil unrest. That professional newsmen doing their job are jut as much at risk as the combatants has been proved time- and again by events in South East Asia, the Middle East and Central America. In 1984 alone 23 journalists were killed and 81 wounded according to the International Press Institute, which has produced a survival manual for newspeople operating in dangerous situations.

Many reporters are married with family responsibilities, and live with the uneasy feeling that nay birthday party, wedding anniversary or other normal domestic occasion may be interrupted by a sudden telephone call commanding them to be on the next flight to somewhere or other. The wife of one former television news general reporter used to say that the one thing which unnerved her above all was the sight of the small suitcase containing spare shirts, underwear and shaving kit, which stood permanently in the hall as a daily reminder of the emergency assignment which might come at any time; that, and not knowing whether the news event would last a couple of days, a month, or more. Undertstandably, not all marriages endure that sort of strain.

Of course no sensible reporter pretends it is all hectic. Most will readily recall hour wasted at airports, in draughty corridors of government or other buildings, waiting for events to take place or people to turn up. Sometimes they did not. At other times, doors slammed, telephones went dead, the answer was 'no comment' or something less polite.

In contrast there are pleasant, well-ordered and interesting assignments at which the reporter is greeted with enthusiasm hospitality and a genuine invitation to call again. Do not forget the opportunities for keeping up with professional friends: Reporting television news is the only profession in which you can fly 5000 miles, drive 200 miles to a town you've never visited before, walk round the corner and meet 52 people you know.

The result of a job will done may be two or three minutes of good pictures, a visual by-line and an enhanced reputation, yet the dominating factor of it all is that the reporter cannot work alone if the assignment is to be carried out properly. For while the sole newspaperman and the radio reporter in the field area close to the office as the nearest telephone, the television news reporter has to work with a camera crew, an outside broadcast unit, or a television studio linked in some way with home base.

Even in these days of compact, mobile equipment, this is bound to put aloof on the fringe of a story in the hope of eventually being granted special dispensation by the other participants. Despite the fact that the obtrusiveness of the camera, microphone and lights makes the entire team a target for attention and occasional abuse, any reporter who is not up with the herd and sometimes in front of it does not last very long in the job.

How often it seems that the fruits of a good television interview, grabbed against all the odds, are picked up by other newsmen in the crowd and, with minimal embellishment are turned into highly acceptable accounts for their own branches of the new business. At other times during the serum it is impossible to discover who has asked the questions which are eventually heard on the sound tack, but that has not always, stopped the cracks from blaming television reporters or any bullishness or poor grammar.

In the end, though, the reporter for television news is only as effective as his last report. There is no glory to be won from the production of a brilliant piece of work which arrives too late to be edited in time for transmission. Time, effort and moneys are wasted it, at the conclusion of an extensive foreign mission, the material is confiscated, never to be seen.

Reporting As a Career

Four television reporters begin their careers as such. Most graduate from newspaper, news agencies or radio, and so back only the knowledge of television techniques to become successful. Some turn out to be competent enough without ever fully understanding how to construct the well-turned phrase which complements rather than competes with the pictures, and it is not surprising that the best exponents of the reporting art are often those who have served apprenticeships as newswriters.

Leaving aside the matter of journalistic ability, a modicum of which must be assumed, the two basic qualities every reporter must have before being let loose in front of an unsuspecting public would seem to be a reasonably personable appearance and clear diction.

In Britain, ideas have undoubtedly changed about what constitutes diction good enough for broadcasting, for the general increase in news outlets, particularly since the arrival of local radio in 1967, has allowed all manner of accents and speech impediments to become suddenly more acceptable. Whether this is interpreted as a cruel truth about television is that some expert journalists simply lack credibility in front of the camera in the studio or on location, I and that the most carefully researched, well-written material is totally lost to the nine-tenths of an audience fascinated instead by a nervous tie, bobbing Adam's apple or inability to keep the head straight. That is not thc only difficulty. What some viewers consider to be incorrect pronounciation is guaranteed to induce near apoplexy on the part of the critics, amateur and professional alike. Bernard Levin, writing in the London Times, devoted hundreds of words to reprimanding certain broadcasters, television news reporters included, for sometimes pronouncing the word 'thee' instead of 'the'. To the uncaring it may have been so much wasted printers' ink. Yet Mr. Levin was undeniably correct in his assessment of the result, that the ugly. Flat, distorted and meaningless noises made by the chief sinners are so boring that they have the inevitable use of important things we need to know.

Still, at least such misdemeanors are capable of being cured, unlike the expressionless monotones and nasal whines which apparently defy the best efforts of the voice-coachers. Little can be done, either, it seems, for those with voices so light and high-pitched as to make virtually no impact for broadcasting.

Women figure largely among the sufferers, which may account in part for what some interpreted as discrimination against female journalists in television news, although the million-dollar wooing of Barbara Walters from one American network to another and the astonishing upsurge in the recruitment of women which followed the inclusion of Angela Rippon in the BBC Nine 0' clock News team of newsreaders may help to give the lie to that notion. Another, more cynical, theory about women television journalists is that male viewers spend all their time nursing lewd thoughts about them during their screen appearances while other females among the audience either hate them on principle or wonder who does their hair. (That may cause cries of 'sexist', but there's no denying human nature.) Either way, all is lost.

For these reasons, chocolate-box good looks and speech which is too precise are considered equally off-putting, whether found in men or women. Among all except those who mourn the demise of the Hollywood glamour factories, the preference is for people who look and sound as though they lead real lives off screen.

All this merely goes to emphasize how easy it is to be critical. Given the curious chemistry at work in everybody's likes and dislike's, it is interesting to speculate on the fruits of a computer programmed to produce a picture of the reporter must likely to win universal appeal. No doubt that has already been done. But without the benefit of the computer, it must all be down to intelligent guesswork and a single, old fashioned word-style.

The novice reporter quickly discovers that there is no short cut on the tortuous route that may eventually lead to general acceptance as a competent television reporter. There is likely to be very little in the way of formal 'coaching', as the average news service cannot afford to have any operational staff missing from its line up, and expects its newcomers to pick up everything except the basics as they go along. This is sometimes euphemistically described as 'on the job training', and comes as a complete surprise to novice reporters who may be expected to be able to master the intricacies of 'filming' from their opening assignment, whether it is an interview with the distraught parents of a missing child or with the beaming winner of an angling contest.

Once some initial progress has been made, usually after a few painful lessons on the way, the new reporter may be taken aside by a more senior colleague and told gently about some of the most obvious flaws. Some of these might be avoided in the first place by attention to three factors which add to or detract from any on-screen performance: speech, mannerisms and dress.

Speech

Everyone who appears regularly in front of the camera develops a natural, personal style of delivery and emphasis, and although this individuality is to be encouraged, the aim in every case must be clarity, with delivery at an even pace. It must be neither slow enough to be irritating, nor fast enough for the word to run into each other: no audience is able to take in much of what is told by an excited reporter speaking at full gallop.

As part of a general tendency to group words and phrases in a manner which sounds odd as well as ungrammatical, one of the most frequent is the addition of non-existent full stops in the middle of sentences.

The cure could not be simpler; sentences which are too long should be broken up into shorter ones. Bluffed lines and hesitations inevitably mar otherwise fluent performances and perhaps lead to loss of confidence. The answer is for the reporter to become familiar with the contents of the scrip by rehearsing as thoroughly as possible.

When serious mistakes do occur there is no shame in asking for a second 'take', for even the most experienced performers expect to trip over their words from time to time. Where any faults persist there is no harm in seeking the advice of speech therapists, who are able to devise little training routines for the tongue which can only increase the performer's confidence.

In reporters with easy going, relaxed personalities, tiny mannerisms may become endearing to the viewer. An occasional frown, raising of the eyebrows or head movement to emphasize a point, probably comes across as genuine involvement in the story at hand. For the rest, stiff, awkward movements, facial contortions and continual passing of tongue between dry lips are among the many tell-tale signs of stage-fright. Usually this disappears once confidence comes, although not always. We know of one former reporter who, while completely at case before the microphone in the radio studio, betrayed his nerves during appearances on television by purifying almost every sentence with the word 'well', even though he knew it did not appear once in the script he had written.

Nervousness is not shared equally between recorded and live performances. In many ways the studio camera seems to magnify mannerisms which, to the consternation of studio staff, reveal themselves only under the strain of live transmission. Some reporters slouch back in their chairs, others tilt like the Leaning Tower or hunch their bodies so that one shoulder is thrust forward aggressively across the desk. Possibly worst of all is the fear which has the reporter sitting literally on the seat edge. The result is a close resemblance to a jockey on horseback, except that to the viewer the rider here seems posed to leap out of the set and land in the front room. At least twitching hands are usually hidden by the camera angle.

To all those who suffer from it, this stage-fright (no respecter of persons), can become increasingly confidence-sapping. Practice will make the biggest contribution towards overcoming it, especially if backed up by the close scrutiny of recordings of personal performances. The advice of production staff, given and accepted in the right spirit, will also help the novice to isolate and then dispose of the main problems which, if left to develop, might lead to permanent bad habits.

The medium itself imposes some restrictions on dress: the sensitive mechanism inside electronic colour cameras seems unable to digest certain striped or checked patterns which set off disturbing visual hiccups known as strobing, and some colours (notably shades of blue) create 'holes' through which studio backgrounds appear.

Aside from that, some news-type programmes have recognized how dress contributes as much as set design to the identity they wish to create.

Breakfast programmes in particular seem to like the casual look, and one ask anyone who appears, visitors included, to dress accordingly. This fits in with the general requirement for reporters to wear what is in keeping with the programmes they are working for and the stories they are covering. For example, and open-checked bush. shirt and denims would be entirely appropriate for reporting a desert war while a pin striped business suit and Homburg would not, while a formal co studio interview calls for jacket collar and tie so long as these remain convention. The important thing for any reporter of either sex is to avoid clothes and colours which the majority of viewers would consider eccentric or inappropriate. For women therefore enough smart, business-like styles available to preserve femininity without resorting to anything fussy, although almost anything they wear on television seems to be regarded affair game for criticism and comment from fashion writers and others. As for grooming, it would be unfair o expect the viewing audience to accept uncombed hair or a two-day heard where the reporters' families would not, except in those situations where such appearances are relevant to the story.

Beads, jangling bracelets or long earrings are best avoided, as their movements are inclined to create distraction at the wrong moment, especially if they fall off. Lapel badges, in particular those which use defy identification, are fraught with danger. So is the whole range of 'club' ties. The possibility here is that the viewer might miss all that is being said while concentrating hard to see whether the coloured blob three inches below the knot is of real significance or just a gravy stain.

The Reporter's Role

While local television stations may expect their reporters to find and collect many of their own stories, then supervise the detailed editing of them, in most centrally run news services the reporter's duties are more limited, with daily on-location assignments carried out on the instruction of programme editors or the semiindependent assignments staffs who control newsgathering activities.

A certain amount of briefing is usually given, even if it is limited to the approximate outline any contribution is expected to follow to enable it to take its place within the rest of the programme. Where an assignment is foreseen as representing only one segment of wider coverage of a single topic, briefing is much more detailed. Good preparation is vital at any time. Given reasonable warning of the nature of an assignment, a diligent reporter will make a virtual fetish of reading up any available background material. On foreign assignments, this may run to dossiers built up from previous visits and include a diversity of facts ranging in importance from currency exchange rates down to the names and localities of reliable laundries.

To ensure speed off the mark, those news services able to afford it provide individual reporters with office cars, complete with two-way radio telephone links, or at least contribute fuel costs towards the reporter's private transport. For those unwilling or unable to tie-up large amounts of capital in fleets of cars, reporters are expected to travel with the camera crews or simply jump in taxis, either paying as they go and recouping the money later, or as part of official arrangements with taxi companies, signing the driver's log at the end of each journey.

Some news services operate a pool transport system to ferry all operational staff to and from assignments, but this has its drawbacks. There are apocryphal tales of news teams stranded miles out of town at headquarters officially unable to move until an office car became available, while some government building went up in flames at the hands of rioters.

Once on location, technical matters are clearly the business of the camera crew, but except on those occasions where the unit is accompanied by a field producer, it is the reporter who has to shoulder the 'managerial' mantle, with overall responsibility for the shape and content of coverage.

In between lies a fascinating, ill-defined area of ground which in non-news location work would be covered by a director. For reasons chiefly of cost and mobility, it is generally accepted that television news does not need to have separate directors, the role being shared by reporter and cameraman on the spot. So it is probably here that the greatest scope exists for disagreement between members of the crew. The ideal working compromise consists of a reporter with journalistic skills an den eye for pictures sketching an outline to be filled in by a sympathetic, experienced camera crew. Detailed discussion about the best way of achieving the desired—end product is advisable before a single shot is recorded. But, in the final-analysis, it must be the cameraman who decides what is 'technically possible, depending on numerous factors including the available light and distance from the subject.

Once a general storyline has been agreed, the reporter then has to trust the crew to supply what they say they are supplying. Long arguments about the closeness of a close-up or the speed of a pan from left to right only hinder the completion of an assignment, and no professional news cameraman would tolerate a reporter's demand to look through the camera viewfinder before every shot.

Relationships are therefore important, particularly on some dangerous foreign assignments, where the degree of mutual trust between members of the team could make all the difference, literally, between life and death. Sometimes a reporter and crew will build up personal friendships and respect over a series of difficult, successfully completed assignments. Between others, the chemistry will be all wrong, and no amount of attempted peace-making will put it right. To team a lazy reporter with a go getting crew or vice-versa and still expect the screen to reflect only successful results is wishful thinking. Far better to ensure that, where possible, incompatible factions are kept well apart.

Even when prospects for co-operation are good, there is no sure recipe for success. The reporter must always remember to be considerate and tactful in the treatment of his professional colleagues, resisting any attempts by misguided outsiders to create separate categories of 'officer' (reporter) and 'other ranks' (crew). The reporter who allows himself to be swept off to the executive dining room while the crew makes do in the factory canteen deserves the inevitable opprobrium. Equally the camera crew must be patient with a nervous or out-of-sorts reporter. After a long, tiring day with very little to eat or drink, it is often tempting for the cameraman to give the thumbs-up to a reporter's performance he knows deep down to be flawed, just as the timid reporter, suspicious that something may be wrong, is prepared to accept a personal second best rather than risk offending the crew by encroaching on meal times.

Getting the story right must come first. As one experienced cameraman has put it: 'If the reporter fails, we all fail'. In addition to the constant awareness of deadlines, there also has to be recognition of the need to be economical in the use of tape or film, not so much for the sake of cost as for the reason that the greater the volume of material, the longer the time necessary for viewing and editing.

With the assignment completed and the pictures received at base, the reporter's role becomes blurred, for one of the main planks of the intake-output system is that it is the editorial staff back at the office who assume the final responsibility for shaping material for inclusion in the programme. Although the reporter's guidance may be sought, the theory is that those most closely involved in the creation of items are necessarily the best placed to make objective judgements about their value. This is apart from the possibility that all manner of developments may have taken place which downgrade the original importance of the assignment. Yet many reporters, as specialists in their subjects, quite understandably recent being told which are the 'best' bits of their interviews. Modern video 'packages' especially are so dependent on the reporter's ability to mesh the various pieces together, no producer or news-writer coming old to a project would probably be able to understand much of it anyway.

It is at this stage that the strict dichotomy of intake and output must seem an expensive luxury for the smaller, less wealthy news services. For them. the solution lies not in dealing their editorial talent into watertight compartments, but in seeking to create genuine all rounders.

Each would be an amalgam of news editor, researcher, director, script writer and reporter, well versed in the skills of overseeing picture editing and writing studio introductions for themselves to read on transmission.

Reporting Techniques

Although electronic news gathering has almost entirely superseded 16mm film as the main means of originating news material, most of the reporting techniques being used to present items in a fluent way for the television screen are just as applicable as they were 20 or more years ago, when they were first introduced. Then, as now, no reporter was considered to be competent until he or she had achieved at least partial mastery over a small range of basic skills which go beyond any proven journalistic ability.

These techniques, whether for use on videotape of any format, live on location or in the studio, are used to some extent separately or collectively in every contribution a reporter makes to a programme. Each demands its own careful study and development to a point where it can be applied smoothly and instinctively to add the same veneer of professional gloss to the news report that the experienced actor brings to the play.

Pieces To Camera

Of all the skills needed for television news reporting, the piece to camera is among the most frequently used. Although it is sometimes fashionable to consider it dated (some experienced reporters consider they have failed if they have to resort to it), the piece to camera, which is essentially a vision story told on location in the field, remains a sure means of giving the news lucidly.

It has three advantages. It immediately establishes the reporter's presence on the spot: it is extremely simple to execute, and it is fast enough to be considered a kind of contingency sample, rather like the dust scooped up by the first men on the moon in case they had to return to earth rather hurriedly.

Chiefly because of its speed and the fact that there may be on other pictures to supplement it, the piece to camera can be designed as a complete report by itself, yet it probably has greater worth as one ingredient within a comprehensive news report, being versatile enough to be slotted in at almost any point, not necessarily at the opening or closing stage. The term piece to camera is self-descriptive, being those words which the reporter speaks aloud while looking directly into the camera lens and, through it, to the viewer. The fact that the majority of them are spoken from straightforward positions gives rise to the alternative name of stand-upper.

The technique depends on an ability to write spoken language and to remember it word for word when delivering it to the camera. But in some respects what matters more is the choice of location for the operation. For example there seems little to be gained in travelling thousands of miles and then pointing the camera at reporter standing in front of some anonymous brick wall. Unless the brick wall is germane, or there are legal problems such as exist in filming within court precincts, the aim should always be to show that the reporter is actually where he says he is. To say proudly that our reporter is there is one thing. To prove it to the viewer is something else.

That does not mean going to extraordinary lengths to find a background which is visually exciting but irrelevant to the story. It should be enough to place the reporter in a spot which is appropriate, interesting, but not too distracting. Even if the welcome which greets the news team is not overwhelming, the piece to camera and sound equipment have been tested and re known to be working properly, and the reporter is ready with the words.

Most pieces to camera are recorded as the reporter stands full-face to the lens. But the effect of putting the reporter to one side of the frame rather than in the centre is that any action in the background is not completely blotted out and the figure becomes a part of the picture rather than a superimposition on it. Sensible variations are to be welcomed as long as they do not seem to be too contrived. On occasions these may be forced upon the reporter by the situation sitting in aircraft, cars or trains, crouching under fire or walking along a road. So much depends on the styles programmes establish for their reporters to follow.

Much of the apprehension felt by novices about their first pieces to camera is caused by doubts that they will be able to remember their words. Admittedly this can pose a real problem, for it is a knack achieved more easily by some than others.

Newcomers to television news reporting are haunted by the possibility that even a short, apparently simple piece will require several attempts, resulting in a waste of time, temper and a humiliating starring role on the private tape of mistakes that television technicians love to compile for showing at office Christmas parties. They can take comfort from the admission of some experienced reporters that, even under the least difficult circumstances, they are unable to remember more than a few words at a time. Others get them right at the first attempt or never. The majority have occasional off-days but generally survive the ordeal without too much trouble.

For everyone else there is no infallible formula, certainly not ad-libbing, which is inclined to come across as uncertainty rather than spontaneity. Perhaps the only answer for the beginner is to keep the length of commentary down to the maximum capable of being remembered without difficult, and not forcing more. Little is worse than watching someone totter to within the final few sentences of a piece clearly too long to memorize.

While there is no way of avoiding the problem posed by the limits of memory, and assuming no portable electronic prompting device is available, three possible escape routes suggest themselves. Two are relatively ugly to look at and are therefore strictly second-best, but, in a tight corner, are preferable to a halting performance which seems likely to grind to a full stop at any moment.

The reporter needs to ensure that the opening paragraph at least is word-perfect. The rest may then be read from a note-book or clipboard which is clearly in shot so that the viewer is not left wondering how the memory is being refreshed. Subsequent raising of the head from written script towards camera fro a sentence or two at a time may add just enough refinement to make the performance tolerable.

Even more than usual co-operation from the camera crew. Here the reporter does not attempt to speak the lines in own continuous take. Instead, the script is learned and recorded in two separate chunks of, say, 15 seconds (45 words). For the sections then to fit neatly different way to avoid an awkward jump cut in the middle. The use of this technique should give the reporter some confidence early on. Later attempts should be made to train the memory to accept longer and longer pieces so that eventually there is no need for the split.

Pre-recording the words on to an audio cassette machine small enough to conceal in a pocket and listening to the replayed tape through a tiny ear-piece while repeating the commentary to camera at the same time. It is an ingenious technique which seems to many to require more effort than that merely needed to learn the words, but practitioners say the recorders give them a confidence they would not otherwise feel, and if it improves their performance for the camera, then it is thoroughly worthwhile.

The method is not without its hazards, though, for there is enough evidence on film and tape to prove that the all-important ear-piece has a habit of popping out into sight at the wrong moment, and the cassette recorders have been known to malfunction and leave the reporter speechless.

Finally, there is no point in any piece to camera script which fails to refer even obliquely, to what is going on in the rest of the picture behind the reporter. Where the background is general rather than specific, it is essential that script and location, however fragile the real connection between the two, are tied together as firmly as possible, preferably by the opening words.

NEWS-GATHERING TACTICS

Deeply rooted in American journalism is the notion of the journalistic reporter. Reporters are trained in the journalistic method which gives them the tools and wherewithal to cover almost nay situation they may confront. Essentially journalistic training means knowing how to gather the news—how to sift through documents, do background research, interview sources, and so on and how to write it using the usual news and feature forms employed by newspapers and broqadcast outlets. In the midst of this seemingly routinised task, however "come all kinds of ethical issues (tactical decisions) including" checkbook journalism," fabrication of sources, false identification, lying. Some of these issues, being topical, come and go. But many are recurrent.

As with news-gathering methods and writing methods, competent reporters and editors are expected to handle tactical or ethical dilemmas. But do these problems require precise and differing tactics for different situations, or responses based on consistent and universal standards? While such questions are regarded as worthy of debate and discussion, most reporters believe that they have somehow internalized professional values, and competencies that will help them resolve any problems that may occur.

We come now to discuss a very real and important everyday convert of journalists: reportorial tactics, journalistic ways and means of gathering and writing stories. Should these tactics be situational and relative; should they be, as Professor Dennis will argue later, consistent and universal? we maintain that they are situational and relative; even more, we insist that they should or ought to be situational and relative. This position, of course, gets us into the realm of ethics.

Opposing my view, however, is a considerable theoretical tradition in this country, even if it fails to manifest itself in common practice. It is safe to say that an accepted truth in American journalism is that journalists should be consistent in their methods and their actions: that they should all subscribe to universal standards, and should, if they are responsible and "professional" have a profound respect for predictable an consistent practice. Consistency and predictability, we are led to believe, are foundation stones of professionalism.

Unpredictability is associated, on the other hand, with amateurism, with inconsistency and relativity, which are seen by many as deleterious to journalism, harmful to the journalist, and frustrating to the audience. We would maintain just the opposite: that consistency in journalism—the journalist always using the same tactics and dealing with the elements of the story in the same way—makes for a deadly dull journalism, keeps the individual journalist from full self-realization, and prevents the audience from being exposed to the multifaceted, rich, and diversified aspects of similar (but different) stories.

Perhaps it is more comfortable and satisfying for journalists to have hard-and-fast rules as to tactics of reporting. This proposition seems reasonable, but cannot believe that it is either in the best interest of the newsperson or the public to have the press tied to an absolute tactical system. Most printed codes of ethics fail because they present absolute and consistent rules or standards (or because they are so fuzzily written that they, in essence, say nothing meaningful). But, perhaps, the fact that they fail is paradoxically a good thing—for their failure assures that tactical situationalism and relativism will thrive in the absence of absolute ethical codes.

Ethics, of course, is very closely related to the subject of journalistic tactics. One cannot really separate them. Should I lie, either to get a story or while telling the story to my readers or listeners? Should I reveal the source of certain statements or quotes which I use in my story? Should I give my readers or listeners all of the information which I have collected and verified?

These are just a sampling of questions that are both ethical and tactical. I might rephrase them thus:

* Should I ever lie as a reporter?
* Should I always reveal my sources? (Or never reveal them?
* Should I tell the whole truth (as much of it as I have verified) to my audience?

Here we have introduced the possibility of tactical consistency of absoluteness. Such consistency has a notable appeal. If I am going to reveal the source in one case, why should I not reveal all sources? If I am going to lie in one case, why not in all? If I am going to withhold part of a story in one case, what would be wrong with withholding parts from any story?

Let me give an example of each of the two tactical positions.

1. Absolute: always identify victims of all crimes.
2. Relativistic identify victims in some crimes but not in others.

The first tactic (the absolute) does, indeed, simplify the journalist's decision making. If this tactic is accepted all that must be done is to identify all victims—juveniles, the of mentally ill, rape victims, and so on. The second tactic (the situational) is more difficult because it forces the reporter to discriminate, to think. The reporter must see of distinctions, think about consequences; is short, the reporter must decide that it is not only all right but good journalism to make exceptions—to have double standards, if you will.

The reporter who is situational recognises that there is a difference, and a very important one, between a rape victim, for example, and a murder victim. Naming a rape victim can bring mental and emotional harm to the victim: naming a murder victim cannot harm the victim at all. The thinking reporter understands that the naming of a nine-year-old boy for shooting his father is quite different (in psychological, if not in legal, terms) than the naming of a 39 year-old adult for shooting his father. The reporter believes that it is his duty to make certain editorial decisions impinging on what is and is not published. After all, he reasons, editorial decision is the nature of jour:nalism: selection is made to some degree-among facts in every story that is written.

I contend that a reporter must play this tactical game rather loosely: that he must not strive for consistency in tactics: that he must consider the specific situation or circumstance. In short, the reporter (to be effective and in many cases to be ethical, too) must specifically determine not to be absolute and consistent, but rather to be situational and relative.

Case. A reporter cannot subscribe to a tactic of always revealing his source—even if he does, indeed maintain that the people have a right to know. In some cases, to reveal sources would be counter productive as well as unethical. For example, the journalist may get information from a source who would be in great physical danger if his identity were know. The reporter not only wants to keep the source operative for another day, but also to avoid endangering his life. In other, similar cases, the reporter might want to keep his source from losing his job.

Case. A reporter is writing a rape story. He has the name of the person arrested on suspicion of committing the rape. He also has ascertained the name of the rape victim. He decides not to use the victim's name, although he does not hesitate to use the suspected rapist's name. Inconsistent? Yes. He is, in effect, withholding information from the reader. At the same time he is pr viding the name of another person connected with the case—even though this person may not have committed the rape. He feels no qualms about this procedure, even though it is inconsistent, reasoning that in this particular case it is tactically prudent to do as he has done. He justifies withholding verified information from the reader on ethical grounds—on a consideration of possible consequences to the victim.

The reporter in the above case is inconsistent. And he certainly does not subscribe to a "universal" tactic. A universal tactic in reporting would be: The reporter is obligated to report all the facts that he has, all that he has verified, and all that are pertinent to the story period. In this rape story, certainly the name of the rape victim is pertinent to the story, as we will be told by our absolutist reporter. After all, the reporter has found out who the woman is: therefore should not the name be given especially since the name of the rape suspect has been used?

Let us reply to the above question with another question: Why should the reporter use the victim's name?

The reporter is wise to subscribe to relativistic tactics, to play the story the way he wants to play it in that particular case—after consideration of possible consequences. Why should the reporter always name names? Why should the reporter subscribe to the same tactics in every story? Straightjacketing oneself does not assure better reportage by the reporter. In fact, a relativistic or situational tactical programme in reporting is what is called for. Consider the importance of the story. Consider each story. Consider consequences or implications for certain persons in the story (*e.g.*, the rape victim in the example above).

It may well be that when a reporter considers the importance to the public of a particular story, there will be a realisation that "usual tactics must be modified or changed. The reporter may decide that the story is important enough, for example, to steal files (or at least to make copies of papers and return the files). The reporter may even feel that in a particular case there is justification to pose as someone else. It may be that the reporter will decide to eavesdrop on conversations and report what he overhears, using or perhaps not using the names of those who said th things he is divulging. The reporter might decide to "bug" a room or wiretap a telephone in order to get some very important enough, for example, to steal files (or at least to make copies of papers and return the files). The reporter may even feel that in a particular case there is justification to pose as someone else. It may be that the reporter will decjde to eavesdrop on conversations and, report what he overhears, using or perhaps not using the names of those who said the things he is divulging. The reporter might decide to "bug" a room or wiretap a telephone in order to get some very important information which he believes the public should know. The reporter might decide, in order to get some much-needed information, to tell a source that he knows certain things or that he has heard certain things from someone else (which he really has not heard) in order to get a response. The reporter might decide to make up quotes and drop them into a story so as to prompt someone connected with the story-someone he wants to make a statement—to come forward to refute or to enlarge on the "speculated" or fabricated quotes.

Now we can justify these tactics by resorting to the "ends justifies the means" argument. We can say that we are thinking of the public, and the public's right to know. How can the public know unless we break through the barriers of secrecy with our situational tactics? So, journalists must report to these tactics from time to time in order to do their job to live up to their responsibilities.

We can justify relativistic or situation tactics by contending that they are more ethical; we can also justify them instrumentally or pragmatically by saying that they are needed to accomplish our ends. If we need a further rationale for inconsistency in journalistic practice, we can always fall back on press freedom in its editorial self-determinism sense. In other words, it is the right of a newspaper reporter to be inconsistent; if he wants to use a victim's name—(or any name) in one story and not in another, that is his right.

If the reporter wants to reveal the source of a quote in one story and not in another, that is his right. In fact, If the reporter wants to reveal the source of a quotation in one part of a story and make all the other quotes in the same story anonymous, that is his right. After all, why should the reporter consistent or use universal tactics? Even though there may not be any evidential basis for the belief, the reporter can contend that journalistic consistency is the "hobgoblin of little minds." Journalism, it seems to the relativistic reporter, is riddled with instances of inconsistency, most of which are considered valid journalistic practices. Here are just a few:

— Using the 5W lead in one story, but not in another.

— Using indirect quotations only in one story, and using direct quotations or a mixture of indirect and direct quotes in another.

— Giving the addresses of persons in one story, and omitting addresses in another.

— Going directly to persons for information in one story, while going to someone for second-hand information in another or using old information form the files

— Giving certain personal data (such as age, race, occupation) about some persons in some stories but not about other persons.

A list of inconsistent tactics could be extended easily. What is the alternative to these inconsistent tactics? Consistent and universal tactics, we are told. The intelligent and dedicated reporter can only scoff at such an alternative, seeing it as a definite voluntary placement of the reporter in a straightjacket with little chance to achieve a primary goal of journalism: obtaining the story.

News-gathering Tactics Should be Consistent and Universal

The preceding discussion of news-gathering tactics defends the *status quo* in American journalism. Reporters do use relative and situational methods when gathering the news. However, there are many agreed-upon general standards and practices. These practical tactics for getting information are undergrided by ethical judgments that are self-contained, based mainly on the immediate situation rather than considered against the backdrop of long experience with similar cases. There is more than a slight temptation in reinvent the wheel with each ethical dilemma that arises.

That, in our opinion, summarizes one of the most serious problems in journalistic practice today—a thoughtless, seat-of-the-pants approach to reporting that eschews planning and thinking. It is the journalism of intuition. "Do what intuition tells you; apply common sense to the situation" are accepted axiom. On the face of it this doesn't sound so bad, but consider the following:

A reporter for NBC News is asked how he knows when he has enough information to "go" with a story. "How," he was asked, "can you be sure that your information is complete, that you are not missing major sources that would turn a story completely around, maybe with a different interpretation altogether?" The reporter replied, "You just know." There is, "he added, "no answer, things just click into place an it seems right" An editor for a metropolitan daily newspaper is asked by a Harvard Law professor how far he would go to get a story. "Would you lie? Would you steal?" Would you disguise your identity?" The editor thought for a moment, then responded, "Yes, under some conditions, I'd probably do all of those things even though I might personally find some of them reprehensible." The professor wanted to know, "How do you make your decision; on what theory do you base your actions?" And the editor answered, "I have no theory, I just do what I think is right"

We would not accept this kind of thinking from other professional persons (say, doctors, lawyers, or architects) whom we expect to have standards, codes and a systematic basis for their decisions. We do accept it from journalists perhaps because we have no choice or because they convince us that news is unpredictable, a matter of timing that requires on-the-spot decisions governed solely by the facts of a particular situation. "You simply can't quantify these things," goes the incantation.

There is a prevailing myth in American journalism that planning news coverage runs counter to freedom of the press. Planning is thought to be dull and routine, not spontaneous and timely. It is further said that writers are creative persons who, if left to their own devices, will produce a better kind of journalism. And God forbid that journalists should have hypothesis. A hypothesis, which is an assumption that becomes an organizing principle, is thought to encourage bias and run counter to journalistic objectivity. There is also a prevailing view among many journalists that news really defies definition.

This kind of "every day a new beginning" theme in many newsrooms, the operational rule of the status quo, needs rethinking. While it certainly is not possible to always predict with scientific certainty what will happen on a given day, journalism is really much more routinized than most of its practitioners know or will admit. They may not know it because American journalism is insulated and parochial. Many journalists have little work-experience outside of their present assignments; few belong to national organizations where they come into contact with their journalists; few subscribe to professional publications or make any effort to keep up with the literature of their systematic research that gives us data about patterns and practices across many journalistic organisations. Individual journalists may know their own organization intimately, but they often have little knowledge about the field generally. This situation is not unusual because many professionals are so busy doing their jobs that they have little time to think about them or to make comparisons with their colleagues in other places. For a field that is supposed to demand so much creative calibration, journalism is remarkably predictable, routinized, even stodgy. Send any five reporters to cover a city council story and you can predict with almost considerably certainty what they will write. Why? Because the coverage of public affairs, in particular, has been standardized. There is much agreement about the form and format of stories, about what essential facts should be included, and about what most editors will accept. Reporters know what is expected of them and generally they do it.

Of course there are stores that are more complex than routine meetings, but even with these the traditional methods of news gathering pretty much dictate what will eventually appear. And if this were not enough, we have "rewards and punishments" built into the journalistic system to guarantee conformity. At a positive level there are prizes (such as the Pulitzers) that honor imaginative work within the framework of traditional journalism. Journalism schools help out by promoting conventional approaches to news gathering through courses and books.

There is in American journalism a serious perceptual conflict. Journalist on the one hand believe that their work is unpredictable, situational, and relative. Communications researchers say this is not true, that reporting is not nearly as uncertain as practitioners think. In a sense both are right. While there may be great similarity in work patterns and output from day to day, Journalist still think that there is little formal guidance and that there is considerable latitude for individual decision making. They say that with regard to ethics, they live in a conceptual thicket which requires instant decisions of convenience if not conviction. They tend to justify what they do without worrying whether their choices about revealing sources or lying are consistent with of that they did before. Scholars, on the other hand, because they are trained to look for patterns of organizational and individual activity, can see a method—whether haphazard or well-though-out-in journalistic work just as they do in firefighters or farmers. The way the news paper or broadcast station is organized, the selecting of personnel, their training and socialization, all have a hand in shaping the news.

Interestingly enough, it is the once-similar (and now quite different) practices of journalists and social scientist that explain some of this discrepancy As Philip Meyer, well known- for his work in precision journalism and now a professor at the University of North Carolina, has written.

Social scientist used to be more like journalist, They relied on observation and interpretation, collecting the observations from public records, from interviews, from direct- participation, and then spinning out the interpretations. Like many journalist they cheerfully accepted the American folk wisdom...that anyone with "a little common sense and a few facts can come up at once with the correct answer on any subject" .

But something changed. First with the development of inferential statistics and later with the advent of computers, social scientist no longer worked like journalist. Instead they used powerful quantitative tools to deal with unwieldy and massive data. Now, says Meyer, social scientist are doing "what we journalists like to think we are best at: finding fact, inferring causes, pointing to ways to correct social problems, and evaluating the effects of such correction". In short, he charge that journalism is being left behind because it lacks a systematic approach to news gathering.

The point of course, is that with an affective strategy for gathering information which systematically considers possible sources and mines them with care brings a far richer yield than old-fashioned., impressionistic reporting. It is now possible to determine how much information from what sources will be adequate—when enough information has been assembled and when writing can begin. This statement does not mean that journalists should be exactly like social scientist. Press people have greater time pressures and are more concerned about immediacy.

It is one thing to develop a strategy for news coverage that list the tactics to be employed, another to actually do it. No situation is ever perfect and no prearranged rules ever work in all situations. For this reason some journalist throw out the rules altogether and make expedient decisions. It is threatening to ask: Is the information complete? Have I mined all possible (and reasonable) sources? Is the evidence strong enough to warrant the conclusion actual or implied? Are various interpretations and leaps in logic justified?" If such questions could have been avoided in the past, such is no longer the case.

Systematic newsgathering tactics are not simply a theory for journalism schools to trumpet, but something being demanded by the rests of society. One of the most compelling calls comes in !he courts. Frequently in libel suits news organizations must offer evidence that the story is not marred by "knowing falsehood" or "reckless disregard" of the truth. How is this honesty of intent determined? By showing that reasonable efforts, consistent with national news-gathering standards, were employed. If they were not and the paper admits it, there is the possibility for a whopping libel judgment. Sloppy reporting is expensive. Of equal or grater importance is the fear that journalist will not have the credibility they need and deserve unless their methods are respected by the audience.

People who argue against ethical standards or moral imperatives in news-gathering tactics usually suggest that each case is so different that rules will straitjacket the reporter. They add that general guidelines are so vague that they are meaningless, I disagree. We need a—theory of journalistic ethics, a fundamental framework for reporters to base their decisions on. This framework requires general understanding about ethical behaviour, whether in reporting or everyday life. It means having a clear notion about how specific journalistic dilemmas ought to be handled. This general ethical understanding does not mean that rules cannot be modified or tempered to meet particular situations. We need a thoughtful policy that serves as a conscience for individual journalist and their organizations. Such a policy should spell out standards of conduct for information gathering. One minimal standard, we think, is that journalist should obey the law. In most instances this principle means they should not lie, steal, or cheat. They should not wiretap or break into places not otherwise open to them. In rare instances, a right-thinking reporter may want to be civilly disobedient, to deliberately break the law as a matter of principle because it will lead to a greater social good. In all instances where ethical questions arise, if there is not a clear answer, reporters should consider alternatives, not simply rush to judgment with the easiest solution. If the decision runs counter to conventional wisdom and standard ethical codes, there ought to be a dear and compelling rationale for making it.

In most instances it is regarded as ethical to reveal one's sources in a news story. This strengthens the credibility of the story and ties information to attributed sources. If revealing names will put sources in great danger or make them reluctant to talk, a different decision may be appropriate. If it is determined that a source benefit, clearly agreed upon and understood by the reporter's supervising editors is that they can defend the action later.

The problem today is that many reporters do not have solid ethical training and do not have the kind of foundation necessary of ethical decision making. Again, constancy is terribly important both for accountability to one's bosses and perhaps ultimately to the courts.

Journalists have gotten in trouble for being inconsistent in recent years with regard to fair-trial-freepress codes. The press was a signatory to such codes, which list tactical guidelines for covering criminal proceedings from initial investigations of crimes to court judgments. Reporters generally agree to withhold some information in the interest of not prejudicing a jury and assuring the defendant of a fair trail. This is a social compact between the press and the legal system. When the press violates this agreement or decides onto to abide by a particular provision of the code, there ought to be a good reason (beyond curiosity seeking or pandering) to justify its action. If not, reporters and editors may have to answer in court. This happened in 1981 in a notable case in the state of Washington where a newspaper was held accountable for violation of the fair-trail-free-press code.

As this example indicates, it is always possible to substitute a "greater social good" argument or a "humanitarian" argument to explain why an individual journalist or publication may deviate from an accepted news-Gathering Tactics rule. We believe such exceptions should be justified on the basis of devotion to the public interest, rather than petty or self-serving reasons.

Similarly it is quite appropriate to reconsider rules they are regarded as journalistic conventions or articles of faith. Printing the names of persons accused of rape has been mentioned. This practice would seem potentially unfair both to victim and accused. The press usually prints the name of the accused. But is it really necessary? The reasons for printing names has to do with keeping the courts open so the they do not become secret tribunal. Thus, we know who is being tried, for what, and why. But as long as the courts are open to the press and to spectators, why not defer printing this material until the trail is over? No great social good is done by heralding names of victims or accused persons in advance of trial with some obscure exceptions.

Some newspapers have abandoned the practice of printing names of persons in civil litigation cases where the truly important story is the effect of the decision on similar cases in the future. If one person is suing another to establish a legal principle and if revealing names would prove embarrassing, it may serve no purpose to do so. Some wise editors are changing their policy in this area.

Consistent and universal standard of reporting with necessary escape clauses for unusual or unique situations will do much to enhance journalistic practice in America. Such standards, if widely known land the press 'can virtually guarantee this with adequate coverage' will do much to strengthen public confidence in the fairness and completeness of reporting. It will also have real advantages of individual newspapers and broadcast stations in an increasingly litigious society. Haphazard, thoughtless conduct that meets no standard but blunders along willy-nilly is neither appreciated nor rewarded by the courts. One of the most effective ways to put the journalistic house in order is to establish coherent policies and consistent practices. This the essence of professionalism performance and distinguishes competent from rank amateurism.

❐

10

Different Types of News Reporting

A publisher, editor, reporter, or other person connected with or employed upon a newspaper, or by a press association or wire service, or any person who has been so connected or employed, cannot be adjudged in contempt by a judicial, legislative, administrative body, or any other body having the power to issue subpoenas, for refusing to disclose, in any proceeding the source of any information procured while so connected or employed for publication in a newspaper.

Nor can a radio or television news reporter or other person connected with or employed by a radio or television station, or any person who has been so connected or employed, be so adjudged in contempt for refusing to disclose the source of any information procured while so connected or employed for news or news commentary purposes on radio or television. (Evidence Code, Section 1010, California Code of Civil Procedure).

Although observers have considered it an absolute shield law, this law has not always proven so in 1971 in Farrvs, Superior Court, an appeals court questioned the law's constitutionality. Los Angeles Herald-Examiner reporter William Farr at the outset of the trial of the Charles Manson "family" on multiple murder charges wrote an account of a prospective witness who said the Manson gang also intended to murder show business personalities. The judge wanted to know where Farr had gotten the information. Farr simply said he had received information from two of the six attorneys in the case and from another source. However, under oath, all six attorneys denied having given this information. Experts saw Farr's case as constituting an exception to the privilege law. His refusal to divulge his sources specifically led to a contempt of court citation, and he was jailed.

In Minnesota, which has a qualified shield law, a judge can still force a disclosure of sources when all three of these conditions are met:

1. That there is probable cause to believe that the source has information clearly relevant to a specific violation of the law other than a misdemeanor.

2. That the information cannot be obtained from any alternative means or remedy less destructive of first amendment rights, and

3. That there is a compelling and overriding interest requiring the disclosure of the information where the disclosure is necessary to preserve justice.

Whether qualified privilege shield laws are really desirable is debatable. With such limitations with good reasons given, a reporter is in danger of being asked to be an arm of the law in turning over material that might be used in the defense or prosecution. Also such shield laws, some believe, define the rights of the reporter too closely, treading on the spirit of the First Amendment.

A set of "pros and cons" for shield laws appear in a booklet, The Courts and the News Media, by Albert G. Kerell and Michel Lipman. Among the arguments opponents of shield laws use, they say:

> A shield law could conceivably be a step leading to further governmental encroachment on the press. The news media should not be in a position of petitioning Congress for their rights since Congress would be placed in the role of defining who is protected by the status—or who is a newsman. The next step could be a licensing process, since the news media have asked to be

placed in the same Category as the licensed, screened professions receiving such privilege for example, attorneys, doctors and priests.

Press Releases as Sources

Announcement stories that companies or individuals send out often plague the newspaper office. As one editor put it, these announcements or press releases arrive as a giant snowstorm each day. Obviously, a newspaper can use very little information that comes into the office this way—even if is high quality—because of space limitations. But most releases that come by mail are worthless, especially for the bigger paper which cannot publish information on ever activity of a company and its personnel. While most releases are self-serving, telling the general public what the person or company wants the public to know, nevertheless, sometimes releases can provide sources and ideas for news.

Press Releases as Reference Material

However, releases are valuable for setting up a directory of potential sources. The professional release has the name and address of the PR officer and the company which can be contacts, as can the names of new heads of divisions and other personnel mentioned in releases. For example, if a scientific researcher is the subject of a release—may be he or she is just back from a trip—the information on the trip is probably not of general interest, but basic information on the person may be useful as he or she may later be able to supply information for a scientific article. An educator may be useful for an education article or a theater director for a future piece on the arts.

The reporter should not throw too much away without at least an evaluative glance.

Some small weeklies without adequate staff use releases directly. Most newspapers rewrite any releases they decide to use, for several reasons. First, an editor can never be sure of the veracity of all releases often the lowest person on the totem pole, a trainee in the company, has worded the release. Certainly many releases are incomplete, and the newspaper person must make a call to flesh out or verify information. For instance, a good writer or editor will want the reader to know where an event will take place, a point that a release may overlook. An announcement of a campus event by a university may make sense to campus readers, but the general readers will need to know the address of the lecture hall.

Most standard releases have a release date, or "embargo" line, which tells the paper when to release or print. Editors should respect these restrictions, but they do pose a problem.

Embargo comes from embargar, Spanish for' 'to arrest," 'to seize" (and Latin, in, "in" or "on," andbarra, "bar"). Incommerce, embargo has meant a restraint of ships. In journalism, embargo means that a hold or restraint is to be put on the use of information until a specified time indicated on the release. For example, a major corporation is calling a press conference which will likely say the company is expanding or going out of business, but the company is not to make the announcement until 9 a.m. on a certain day.

For the newspaper which may be on a different schedule, this is bad timing. A 9 a. m. time favors the wire services and afternoon newspapers.

A morning paper's main deadline is likely to be 5 p. m. the day before. The morning paper reporter, what do you do when the biggest industry in town says it will have an extremely important announcement the next day at 9 a.m. at a press conference in the ballroom of a local hotel? At this point, all you have is an announcement of time and place and no content. Some purists would argue that all you can do is sit back and wait. Others would tell you to get on the phone, call anyone you know or can find out about at offices in other branches of the company across the United States. With a general hint about the topic, a skilled reporter may be able to zero in on specifics.

Conventional newsrooms almost always put embargoes on stories until the time of the speech or event. For example, a national nonprofit agency had prepared grandiose plans for reorganization—

board officers had heard that much about the plans in a general meeting two days before the scheduled announcement in Detroit. Reporters from New York, Washington, and the wire services gathered for the 7 a.m. announcement breakfast. But to their amazement, the local morning paper was already on the street with a banner headline on the story. The other reporters were all very bitter toward the local reporter who had secured the story and who even developed it with reaction from other sources. The reporters argued: " You broke the embargo!"

The energetic reporter countered: "What embargo?"

"It's in your box in the press room!"

"You may be right: But I haven't been in the press room or looked in my box. I have not seen any embargo."

Of course, the energetic reporter, suspecting that there would be an embargo on the story, had avoided formal press room arrangements, sought out the document from a delegate who had a copy of the reorganization plan in his packet without any embargo restriction.

Investigative Sources

One of the best examples of the importance of reporters developing sources is the classical Watergate case back in the 1970s. How far would Carl Bernstein and Bob Woodword have gotten in the Watergate investigation without a basic source— "Deep Throat," the insider—who whetted their appetite for information and supplied enough to keep them going? They also had a myriad of other sources:

Telephone Books. They were able to make a profile of James McCord, one of the people arrested at the Watergate headquarters, who was at the Watergate complex after the break-in at Democratic headquarters—without talking to him. The reporters followed up on as Associated Press report that McCord worked with the Committee for the Re-Election of the President (CRP). In the telephone book they found the number of the private security consulting firm McCord ran. When they called, no one answered. They then checked the criss-cross telephone directories which listed phone numbers by addresses. Here they called these people, some were able to supply information, others were not. Eventually a profile of McCord emerged.

Washington Post Police Reporter. A Post police reporter had information of a Howard Hunt connection with the White House from one of his sources and passed it along. Address books of two of the men the police arrested had the same name and number: Howard E. Hunt with White House identification.

Library of Congress. Here Bernstein and Woodward were able to find a cooperative clerk who showed them everything that Hunt had read. Included was material on the Kennedy Chappaquiddick incident, when a young lady with Edward (Ted) Kennedy had drowned and which Kennedy did not report for several hours. Contacts in the White House had said that Hunt conducted an investigation of Democrat Kennedy because the White House feared a Kennedy presidential campaign.

Personal Telephone Sources. Persons provided information on calls and directed Bernstein to Miami for telephone listings subpoenaed by a district attorney. Bernstein was able to confirm a New York Times story about money being laudered through Mexico.

Post Researcher. The CRP guarded a list of the 100 people who worked at the national headquarters as if it were a classified document. The Post obtained a copy through a researcher for the paper who had a friend at CRP. From this, Bernstein and Woodward were able to make their nightly visits to people by using their addresses and knocking on doors. The most valuable information came from a bookkeeper who told about a slush fund and said that the FBI investigation had not asked the right questions and had, therefore, ignored some things.

FBI and Justice Department Sources. "...the reporters checked regularly with a half-dozen persons in the justice Department and the FBI who were sometimes willing to confirm information that had been obtained elsewhere. The sources rarely went further, often not that far."

Call from an Unknown Lawyer. The lawyer had nothings to do with the Watergate investigation. But he told Bernstein that Donald Segretti (a political trickster) had a friend, Alex Shipley, who had been approached by an Army friend about doing some "political work" for the Nixon campaign. Bernstein eventually called Shipley in Tennessee and Shipley told Bernstein about Segretti. Bernstein was given names of other Army friends and eventually tracked Segretti down.

Court Records. Bernstein called District Attorney Earl Silbert who was handling the Watergate grand jury investigation and asked him if he could have the jury roster: Silbert refused and rejected Bernstein's argument that the list was public record. Woodward asked a friend in the clerk's office about the list and the friend told him the same thing. Woodward identified himself as a reporter. The clerk said that he could look at the list but that he could not copy any names or take notes. Woodward found the Watergate grand jury list, memorized four or five names and addresses at a time, and slipped off to the washroom and wrote the information. They held back after Judge John Sirica warned against contacting grand jurors.

Federal Court House Reporter. Lawrence Meyer on the Postcame across a confidential copy of a routine legal agreement of prospectors and attorneys for the Watergate breaken defendents. Although it contained little new information, one thing stood out. A phone in te White House with the billing address of a Kathleen Chenow had been disconnected. Looking through the crisscross directory, Bernstein located a former roommate of Chenow. Through the roommate, Bernstein traced Chenow to Milwaukee where she had moved. It turned out that she had been a secretary to the secret White House group known as the "plumbers" which was investigating leaks to the medial.

Address on Envelope. When Bernstein was in District Attorney Earl Silbert's office, Bernstein saw a letter on the desk which proved to be from a company where McCord had bought the bugging equipment. Bernstein made a mental note of the address and proceeded to contact the company. He wrote a story on how much money McCord paid the company—$3,500 in thirty-five $100 bills.

Plaint Sleuthing. Most of Woodward and Bernstein's information came from digging. The reporters continued to expand a list of names which they kept checking. These included people who were working in or had worked in the White House, the Justice Department, and the FBI. By checking out every lead, the reporters found new leads which resulted in new connections.

Using Records

Transactions between people are recorded many ways. And various kind of records, although they may not always appear to be interesting, can communicate fascinating information—and proof or evidence—about what people do. Studying records can add depth and conviction to a story but you can also find many ideas for new stories by looking through records for unusual facts and matching these facts against other information. Besides police court, and sources you may want to check out follow here. (Be sure to check your state open record laws concerning access).

Birth Records. The court clerk or health department (or a bureau of vital statistics) keeps birth records. If you suspect that people are lying about their ages, checking records can help set things straight. Such research can also help in identifying who parents are—information which you may want to report in some stories.

Death Records. The country medical examiner can supply information on the location, time, and cause of death.

Marriage. The clerk in the marriage licensing bureau can tell you who has applied for licenses.

Divorce. The start of a suit is public. The name and action are available from the court clerk. You can find information about subsequent developments—except for grounds-in the prothonotary, or chief clerk's office, indexed by the party's name, alphabetically by month or year. You will usually need some idea of when the action started.

Wills. You can read the books of copies of wills as well as the original documents from a register of will kept by clerks of specific courts (in Philadelphia, the clerk of the Orphans Court) or by a prothonotary. Wills are filed by year and number.

Real Estate. The registry of deeds or the registry unit of the department of records keeps information which allows you to trace the ownership of a piece of land all the way back to the first owner. You need to know the address so that you can consult the special map which gives a plan number. You can look at the plan which pictures the address you are interested in. Such plans may have more than one file number on them because lots or tracts are sometimes realigned over the years. With these numbers in hand, you can obtain the abstracts, which are usually on microfilm. An abstract will contain the date of sale, the seller's and the buyer's names, and the size and location of the lot or parcels. A special section in a deed, called a "recital," traces the owners and means of sale , or transaction. These can include public grant (patient), foreclosure ; (sheriff sale), will, private grant (deed), or condemnation.

State tax stamps affixed to the deed can give you an indication of the sale price of the property.

Porperty Tax Records. The assessor's office has legal descriptions of land tracts and records of assessment.

Neighbours on a City Block. Crisscross phone directories (your newspaper and public library have these) list streets alphabetically, with street addresses and residents. You can use these to identify people living on each block. Also, city directories list people alphabetically and by street and telephone numbers, and include information about employment and spouses names.

Building Permits. On the surface, such permits may not appear to tell you very much, but they include information on renovations and additions and on contracting firms; they also provide you with a master plan of the property. By studying such permits, Jack Tobin identified a number of persons working with the contractors or sub contractors at Richard Nixon's house at San Clemente, Calif. By talking with these workers, Tobin learned that they were being paid with a government check from the National Park Service.

Bankruptcies. The clerk of the U.S. district court has papers on bankruptcy cases filed in that particular district. Such papers give a total look at the assets and debts of a person. In the bankruptcy procedure, the creditor may have instigated a "205A examination" in which the creditor's lawyer questions the debtor. The title of the investigation comes from the part of the bankruptcy code directing the procedure. If the clerk does not want to make additional material available, you can remind the clerk about the ruling supporting access (Winton Shirt Corp. vs. Elizabeth Truct Co., 104 Fed Reporter, 2nd Series, 777, 3rd Circuit, 1939).

Judgements. County clerks' offices keep records of persons collecting a debt through the judgement of the court. Such records reveal the debtor's credit standing.

Corporations. Businesses file incorporation papers first with these cretary of state in the state capital. Eventually these papers go in the country clerk' s office in the county where the new company is located. These files give the company's purpose, its board of directors, its address, and a record of stock issued. Moody's Industrial Manual names U.S. corporations, with staff members, history, officials, and budget.

Voter Registration. In the register of voters you can find a person's address, birth date, profession at the time of registration, voting record and physical appearance.

Auto Records. The secretary of state keeps vehicle records, including information from license applications.

Payroll Records. If the person is working for the state, the payroll record is public. Check with the civil service department.

Professional Records. Regulatory boards in a state keep public records available on the professional groups they control, such as doctors, lawyers, nurses, funeral directors, realtors, haird-ressers, and technicians.

Permits and inspections Reports. The department of licenses and inspections has public records of citations against any licensed establishment. The health department can make available weekly food inspection reports of area restaurants, schools, and other institutions. The fire department should provide you with reports of inspections at public places.

Traffic Accident Reports. In the records department of some cities, you can get a copy of an accident report for a modest fee if you provide the driver's name and the place and date of the accident.

Military Records. The Pentagon can supply you with names of men and women on active duty. The Army Register, Navy Register, and Register of Commissioned and Warrant Officers of the Navy and Marine Corps list the names of officers.

Income Tax Records. You may see the tax forms of nonprofit corporations by filing Form 990 with the Internal Revenue Service, but this can take several months. Members of religious and cult groups, for tax-free status, must fill out a form under Section 501 (c)(3) of the Internal Revenue Code.

Telephone Records. For billing purposes, the telephone company keeps lists of long distance telephone calls. Some times a personal acquaintance in the company can supply these, some government agencies with special powers can also subpoena them. In their investigative Reporting book, David Anderson and Peter Benjamin son add:

> It is also possible to obtain these records by trickey. At least one reporter we know would stoop so low as to call the telephone company business office, and, posing on the person being investigated claim that he didn't recall mailing certain long-distance calls that had been charged to him. He would then ask the phone company to check the numbers and dates of the calls and report back. The same gambit is sometimes used by reporters who wish to check on the money a person has borrowed. They simply call the credit company to "recon firm" the loan. A

> similar technique can be used to check on someone's airplane reservations. Obtaining such information from the phone company, however, works both ways. So, if an experienced investigator is intent on protecting a source's identity, he or she may call from a remote pay phone or from the paper's subscription department rather than from a home or desk phone.

A useful book for more detail on using records is John Ultman and Steve Honeymari's. Reporter's Handbook: An Investigator's Guide to Documents and Techniques, a proejct of the Investigative Reporters & Editors, Inc. (New York: St. Martin's Press, 1983). The book, for instance, includes names and address of places to write in all 50 states for birth, marriage, divorce, and death records.

Many out-of-the-way and little-known sources from groups may be very useful to you. The annual minutes of the United Methodists in one area in Illinois proved to be important information in profiling the Democratic Candidate for the presidency in 1972. A tip that candidate George McGovern had been a seminarian (a fact which he did not include in his fact sheets) led a reporter to interview his former instructors. The in turn pointed to recorded minutes that identified the candidate as a clergyman in his early years. Further sources included interviews done with people in the town where he had been the pastor, yellowed newspaper clips, and reminiscences that a reporter traced down from old-timers across the country.

At the Shreveport (La.) Times, an article series using a wide range of personal and record sources led to then resignation and indictment of the city commissioner of public safety. One of the writers of the series.

Lynn Stewarat, Recalls. "Our initial confidential Source was a high ranking police department official. Using the background information he gave us, we went to records at city hall to prove our case. Later we studied payroll records, purchase orders, telephone bills, and other internal records."

The series, which printed a ledger of the checks issued to the commissioner, began:

> Large sums of taxpayers' money are being spent by some city officials who give no public accounting of those expenditure, a Times survey of records has revealed.
>
> The funds are being obtained by officials with only a vague indications of their eventual use. In each case they are requested by a commissioner and approved without question by Finance Commissioner George Burton.
>
> They include 43 payments totalling $17,300 paid in the last 15 months' to Commissioner of Public Safety George W. D'Artois personally.
>
> Each payment was for $400, with the exception of one $500 check, and, since Jan. 1, 1975, these have been issued on an average of twice a month.
>
> The only information on file in the Finance Department to indicate what the funds are being used for are brief letters from D' Artois. In most cases, the letters state that the funds were being requested for obtaining evidence and information from informants on organized crime cases.
>
> D' Artois was asked by the Times for records concerning those expenditures. He produced only a manila folders filled with miscellaneous pieces of paper that included various copies of offense reports, tom scraps of papers and some receipts.
>
> Unlike other divisions of his department, he could produce no tabulated list reflecting date, payment, and case, and said the amount he had received during 1975 was "whatever the finance department says it is."

> An unusual turn of events occurred during the Times study when Police Chief T.P. Kelley said he did not know that D' Artois was drawing any funds for such investigations or conducting investigations requiring the use of such funds.

A second article went further back in the records and studied the pattern of the check payments:

> Monies paid to Commissioner of Public Safety George W. D' Artois personally by the City of Shreveport increased dramatically the same month that George Burton was first sworn in as Shreveport finance commissioner, a Times study has revealed.
>
> Up until December, 1971 city funds to D' Artois, other than his paycheck, averaged about $600 a year. In the portion of 1971, prior to Burton's election. D' Artois had received only $420.
>
> But in December of 1971—the month that Burton was elected and sworn in-D' Artois drew $600, bringing the total for 1971 to $1,020. His payments since then have never dropped below $5,100 a year and in 1975 they soared above $13,000....
>
> When questioned by the Times enterprise team about the increasing number of payments to Commissioner D' Artois since his election, Burton replied, "He requested funds to purchase information and I honored his request."
>
> Asked about the markedly lower payments to D' Artois in prior years, Burton answered, "I didn't bother to check. I don't have any idea of what he got before. I don't see the significance of it.

> "I don't know his sources of information. I do not have personal knowledge of his sources of information," the finance commissioner said, and, referring to informants, Burton added, "I don't want to be responsible for someone' s safety. Who is designated is not my business."
>
> During the period in which the large payments on a regular basis to D' Artois began, there was neither an experienced finance commissioner nor an auditing firm familiar with the city's past financial practices....
>
> Finance department records show that from 1963-1969, checks issued to D' Artois' averaged about four payments a year, and most were in the $100 to $200 range. There were no checks-other than paychecks—to D' Artois recorded in 1970.

Access to Public Records

The right to inspect government records does not exist by itself by any natural, moral, or common law, but is defined and limited by statutes of the state and federal government.

In many states, groups or committees—often connected with Sigma Delta Chi, Society of Professional Journalists—have published guidebooks on what is available from various branches of government and agencies and how to go about obtaining it. In Pennsylvania there is the Pennsylvania First Amendment Coalition which has put out a booklet, the Media Survival Kit. It offers the following advice on what to do when you are denied access to the records of any court, agency, board, commission, or department of the executive branch.

1. Make a written request for access to the documents. If the records were sealed by a judge, make the reqeust to that judge. If access to the documents was denied by the Prothonotary or Clerk of Court, the request should be presented to the Chief or President Judge.

2. The request should identify the documents which you seek to inspect as narrowly and with as much details as possible.

3. Do not state the reason why you want to inspect the documents.

4. There is no statute covering the right to inspect court records. You may petition the court to open the records, following the same procedure as with closed courtrooms.

5. If the written request is denied, ask that the denial be placed in writing together with a statement of reasons for the denial.

6. If you lawfully obtain access to a document which was ordered sealed by the court, you may publish it; however, the court may initiate proceedings to determine who provided you with the document.

The Medial Survival Kit outlines what records fall under the Pennsylvania Open Records Law (you will need to check your own state). In Pennsylvania the following records are available; they have been held subject to the Open Records Law:

1. Examination papers and scores of all applicants for Civil Service jobs.

2. Attendance record cards of professional employees of school district.

3. Records of retired state employees.

4. Building record side of property records maintained by county board for assessment and revision of taxes, containing information as to construction specifications.

5. Individual salary records of community college employees.

6. Accident reports prepared by accident investigation division of police department.

7. Review and refund docket of Board of Finance and Revenue.

8. List of names and addresses of kindergarten children in school district.
9. Completed reports prepared by Department of Labor and Industry pertaining to safety and health in industrial plants.
10. Police payroll records.
11. List of persons taking CPA examination given by Commissioner of Professional and Occupational Affairs.
12. List of delinquent taxpayers.
13. Address to which a school district forwarded the scholastic record of a former pupil.

The following records have been held exempt from the Open Records Law:

1. Field investigation notes made by a staff member of city planning department for purpose of a report to a city council member.
2. Departmental budget reports required to be provided to the budget secretary (held to be a statement of facts and events and not an "account," which consists of debit and credit entries).
3. Contents of teacher's personnel file maintained by school district.
4. Names, addresses, and amounts received by welfare recipients.
5. Financial disclosure statements voluntarily submitted in response to executive order requesting such statements from members of the governor's cabinet and members of certain agencies.
6. Physical fitness reports and promotional evaluation reports of police department.

7. Financial information regarding the operation of state-related university.

In Pennsylvania, if you are denied permission to inspect and copy documents of any agency, board, commission, or department of the executive branch, the Media Survival Kit also suggests that you appeal the denial of access under the "Right To Know" Act. A sample form of appeal is available trom the Coalition.

On the federal scene, the Freedom of Information Act of 1966 provide access to many documents, and almost every week you read of some disclosure trom the past revealed for the first time because an enterprising reporter decided to check on certain documents. In general, the Act provides that all records in the hands of agencies of the executive branch of the federal government can be inspected, unless the documents are covered by one of nine exceptions.

Excepted are classified national defense and foreign policy items; internal personnel matters; items prohibited from disclosure by a statue; privileged and confidential trade and commercial information obtained from an individual; information which would be privileged in a civil lawsuit; "unwarranted invasion of personal privacy," such as medical documents; investigation files where one of a half dozen special bad effects would occur; specified bank records; and oil well information.

To obtain records from a federal agency, write a letter to the agency, being specific and describing in detail the document sought. This request must be answered in 10 working days. If there is no answer, or the request is denied; you can write a letter to the head of the agency. Some suggest you include a legal reason for your appeal, although this is not necessary. Having it sent by an attorney might give it more serious consideration, but not necessarily so. Groups such as the Pennsylvania First Amendment Coalition provide sample appeal letters. This appeal must be answered in 20 working days. If denied, then the next recourse is to file a complaint in the federal district court.

Using Libraries

Time spent browsing in libraries can turn up prospective story ideas. You may find an overlooked author in your area. You will find consumer reports which you can localize. Glance through magazine articles. They deal with the relevant themes in contemporaty life, many of which you can adapt and discuss for reader in your locality. You can also pick up a few ideas from out-of-town newspapers. Libraries not only contain resources for story research, they can also be the source of new ideas, background information, and fact verification.

Libraries also have books about reference books and materials. Among them are The New York Times Guide to Reference Materials (New York: Popular Library, c. New York Times Co., 1971) and Rivers, William L., Finding Facts (Englewood Cliffs, N.J.: Prentice Hall, 1975). The Writer's Resource Guide, edited by William Brohaugh (Cincinnati, Ohio: Writer's Digest Books, 1979), has listings with addresses for various information services, including consumer topics, sports information, offices, musems, archives, embassies, community services and finance and banking.

ROLE OF REPORTER IN A NEWSPAPER

A reporter is one who observes the passing show in the widest sense of the word and pictures its detail for the benefit of the whole society. A reporter may be accurate, conscientious, a good citizen and take part in moulding the views of other people, but he cannot play his part successfully unless he keeps his eyes open and his mind attuned to the present, future as well as the past. He is a leader of men in many senses of the word. He must not express his own views in what he writes—he must know in most sets of circumstances—but everything he writes must express his mind and its condition. He holds up a mirror and how much clouded or clear it is, depends on the truth or a twist of the truth which he makes in accordance with his nature and mental equipment.

A good reporter seldom sticks to a newspaper for long. Usually he passes on to news agencies or gets promotion to look after other aspects of newspaper production like a news editor or a chief correspondent. A reporter's mind is like a sponge, paying a good deal of attention to purely mundane things but learning something every day and cleaning his mind of matters not upto the mark. He must organise his knowledge and codify it. He must understand the principles of government in general and in some details. He must know general history, particularly the history of his area. Though he can pick up these things as he goes along his duty, it is better for him to supplement his knowledge by a planned study.

DUTIES OF A REPORTER

A reporter is the gatherer of news, and as such performs an important function in a newspaper establishment. As he has to gather news, he is required to be on the move most of the time usually within the area allotted to him. He has to interview persons and attend public functions arid meetings, press conferences and law courts to investigate events of public interest, to collect news and to ascertain news on contemporary events. The nature of the job being such, an 'up-and-doing' type of person proves successful in this line. Naturally, persons who prefer fixed working hours and regular routine in daily life are unsuitable for this job.

His work changes daily; as such he should be prepared to handle any assignment and move anywhere. He should have special knack of meeting all sorts of people in all types of circumstances. A person of snobbish, uppish and patronising temperament has little or no chance of success in this line. A shy and a reserved type of young person is totally unfit to become a successful reporter. He must possess abundant self-confidence, so as not to be over-awed by the rank or position of an individual. He should be a man of initiative and should not be easily disheartend or discouraged. He should possess mental and physical perservance should be able to grasp the situation quickly and reduce It into writing in the shortest time and in a readable form. But while reporting news he must be able to judge its authenticity and then report the news so collected with absolute honesty. The narrative should be attractive so that the readers should enjoy reading it.

He should be able to record the happenings and incidents in a condensed form, as he has. to take into account the space available in the newspaper for it. Suppose, he has to write a report. on some important meeting which lasted for over two hours. In such a circumstance, he must have an eye for the important discussions decisions which are to be included in the report, omitting all other unimportant/irrelevant matter.

He must be temperamentally so framed that he does not get irrltated, even If at times he has to wait for hours to meet an important person or come across an event. When a news-worthy occasion does come he should be able to grasp it quickly, and write it out with great speed.

Many reporters specialise in reporting particular types of news such as those relating to political events, commerce or sports, theatre etc. In large newspapers, there is also a Chief Reporter responsible for allocating and coordinating work of different reporters.

MAJOR REPORTING DEPARTMENTS

The major reporting departments of a newspaper are:

(i) Local Administration and District courts

(ii) The International field

(iii) The Art Department

(iv) Sports

(v) Political Affairs including Parliament

(vi) Economic Affairs together with Trade and Commerce

(vii) Book reviews

(viii) Science and technology

(ix) Industry

(i) Local Administration and District Courts. As newspapers. have a large number of readers belonging to the district where they belong, there is need for two or three junior reporters, supertised by a senior one, to cover local news, administrative problems and important judgments of district courts. A senior reporter assigns the coverage among junior reporters who actually go into the field and bring news of local interest. There may be a fire or theft or important crime to report like a murder or dacoity. Then there may be court proceedings of a sensational nature wherein important crime cases are heard and adjudged upon. These reporters are called district reporters. Each reporter has an area assigned to him which may include one or more large towns with the addition of smaller towns and larger villages. In some cases, a district office is established in prominent towns to enable the reporters to cover the ground with a senior reporter incharge. The senior man also acts as the manager of the office, who keeps the accounts and is responsible for the advertisement and other revenue w'hich is received.

The district reporters have considerable responsibility as an important link in the chain of news collection of interest to the newspaper. The senior as well as the junior reporters keep their respective dairy of engagements and see that nothing is missed which may give the lead to other newspapers. If the district is large and a populous one, he may find himself with a full diary of routine engagements every day. If the newspaper feels necessary it may provide a scooter or motor cycle to its reporter to cover the news.

The district reporters usually are active men who have the opportunity of making a wide circle of friends. They develop influence in the local administration and can dig their news ahead of other contemporaries representing other newspapers. One important qualification of a local newspaper reporter is knowledge of law so that he does not commit any errors leading to libel or slander. He must be above board and not have extreme likes or dislikes of individuals, businessmen or influential personalities in the area.

The telephone is a very important means of receiving and collecting information about any event taking place in the area. A district reporter has his link with police officers and corporation administrators who inform him of anything important taking place around. However, it is not advisable to simply depend on one or the other individual source for making the story.

Immediately on receiving the hint of an event, he is supposed to either rush himself or send his junior, depending on the importance of the news, to cover it. If necessary, a staff photographer may also be taken along although many newspapers prefer junior reporters who can handle their own camera and have a working knowledge of photography. In the case of important news even movie cameras are sometimes maintained by newspapers to obtain T.V. films for supply to the T.V. Organisations on specific charges.

(ii) The International Field. One tremendously important field of journalism concerns the foreign field. The foreign departments of many newspapers are staffed by their own men of wide erudition and ripe judgment. Usually only senior reporters and correspondents are assigned to cover the international field. These persons must have a wide-ranging study of foreign affairs-politics, economics, science. technology, trade commerce, industry and diplomacy. They may have risen from local and international coverage or they may be specially appointed from outside to under take foreign correspondent's role. Some of the newspapers are known to have appointed specialists from universities to become their foreign correspondents, although preference is given to working journalists who may be well versed in public affairs, constitutional matters and be good interviewers. Foreign correspondents are persons who have quite often not only to deliver lectures in the country where they are sent to but also to interview public men, besides covering the diplomatic news of general importance. Usually, they are suppossd to be good writers who can undertake research about different fields of social activity of the country they are posted to-its history, politics, economics and problems.

The Foreign Correspondent. A foreign correspondent must know major languages of the world. He should have a liking for travel. He should be prepared to move to distant places at a short notice, and be capable of living away from his home for long periods, if necessary.

He should have more initiative and self-reliance than an ordinary correspondent, as he has to gather news in a foreign country, where he has to develop his contacts. He should be a master of condensation, for it is very costly to send long cables. Although he should be keenly interested in political affairs, yet he should not involve himself in the politics of the host country.

(iii) Art Department. One of the important reporters is the journalist in charge of the Arts department. He is supposed to supervise reports of his juniors about the following subjects:

(i) review of local art programmes;

(ii) reviews on new literary productions;

(iii) review of movies released in the city;

(iv) review of music and dance programmes, official and non-official, held in the city;

(v) articles on art and literature to cater to the needs of readers interested in literary topics.

(iv) Sports. The Sports correspondent of a newspaper has almost a full page at his disposal to fill the sports news and events of the day. He has to cover not only the local sports events but also receive reports from all over the country and even from abroad through special part-time correspondents of the newspaper at different places or through the news agencies both national and international. The sports correspondent is supposed to be an authority on sports affairs. He should know the rules and regulations of all the sports, be fully acquainted with sports terms and their interpretations and must have been a sportsman himself in one of the fields to have installed the sports spirit in his blood. He should be enthusiastic enough to cover all events with gusto and feel as if he is fully moved by the results. His commentary on sports events should depict his grasp of the problems facing sportsmen and their teams. He should have a knowledge of the sports habits of different countries and be aware of the good and bad points. of different players in different fields. He should be capable of iving a masterly round-up of sports events once in a while and also discuss the problems of the country and its participation in international events.

(v) Polical Correspondent. Most of the newspapers have pecial political correspondents selected from amongst the senior most and talented persons of the staff, to cover political news of national importance. This correspondent usually supervises the reporting of the parliamentary proceedings, interviews with the ministers and heads of political parties. He analyses political trends in the country and conducts opinion surveys to gauge the mind of the public. The feelers he throws carry great weight in political circles. He is also responsible for going through the reports about different ministries and their functioning before they are accepted for publication. He also helps the chief editor in the writing of editorials on political subjects.

(vi) Commercial or Economic Coverage. The commerical correspondent of a newspaper is supposed to be a competent economist and statistician. As incharge of the economic and commercial reporting departments of the newspaper, he gives the final shape to the few pages covering economic, commercial and trade news every morning. His responsibility lies in analysing economic trends, consideration of economic problems facing the country, proposing solutions and discussing with the authorities, official and non-official, proposals and projects under r view. He is also supposed to analyse the price trends both for essential commodities and stocks and shares, raw materials, the prices of gold, silver and steel and so many other items. He has to give a commentary whenever required on these trends so as to inform the readers interested in trade and commercial affairs. Such newspapers as the Financial Times, London, or the Financial Express in India are dailies specifically devoted to the informational interests of trade, industry, commerce and banking, but in al-round newspapers the space devoted to economic and commercial news is hardly a few pages. Usually pages 6 and 7 (in a newspaper of 8 pages) are evoted to trade and commerce.

It is but natural that these pages are looked after by a person or a team of persons who have specialised knowledge of trade and commerce and have a thorough grasp of the day-to-day developments in the economic field. They have at their disposal a good deal of literature concerning their field. They also maintain folders containing basic facts and figures about subjects of their interest. They are sometimes supposed to give backgrounders to economic news or official declarations of State policy on matters affecting trade and industry.

The head of the economics department of a newspaper is also expected to write articles on economic problems and give his commentaries in the light of the latest developments. His responsibility also includes to guide the trade and industry in the public and private sectors and set the trends wherever necessary.

(vii) The Book Review Correspondent. Most of the newspapers do not have any separate staff for the book review section. Usually, one of the assistant editors who has a list of the reviewers for different subjects, sends a copy of the book received for review to the authority concerned. Book reviews are usually published only in the Sunday Magazine section of the newspaper. A list of books to be reviewed is made by the assistant editor in consultation with the editor. Some of the members of the review panel write the reviews on books their field of without charging any honorarium while there are some professionals who are paid. Of course, the reviewers are entitled to keep a copy of the book reviewed by them.

Every newspaper has a panel of book reviewers, usually specialists on the subjects, to do book reviewing for their book review feature. The most important qualification of a book reviewer is knowledge on the subject and general ability to assess the utility of the book from the readers point of view. The comments about the book are conveyed by the reviewer in a readable and acceptable manner.

Not all books received in a newspaper are reviewed. A small number are selected but usually, out of courtesy, the unreviewed books are listed under the headline 'Books Received'.

A small review of a book is generally of three to five paragraphs. The review usually starts with the name of the book, the name of the publisher, the number of pages and the price.

Tips for Book, Reviewing: The following tips about book reviewing are important:

(i) a brief description of the objectives of the book;

(ii) something about the author if the work involves original research or the author has a standing and status.

(iii) a brief account of what the book tries to highlight;

(iv) a comparison of the book with other important books in the same field;

(v) an appraisal preferably indirect through description and exposition in terms of the aims and purposes of the author.

The book reviewer's function is to tell the readers succinctly and readably whether book is worth reading and if so, why. This is an expert's job and is done by an authority on the subject matter of the book. Since the review may make or mar the popularity of the book the reviewer has on him a serious responsibility to discharge with due consideration while giving his comments without fear or favour. He must take an unbiased view and guide the readers about the utility or otherwise of the book. One important task of the book reviewer is to bring out the main points of the book in a few sentences and apprise the readers of what the author has tried to say and bring out In this respect the reviewer's analysis can be a brief capsule of the book, making the review self-sufficient by way of its giving a brief summary both of the contents and arguments contained in the book.

The skill of the reviewer lies in his ability to hit off his points in a pithy, arresting opening sentence or paragraph which at once sums up the objective of the book and gives a glimpse of the nature and content of the publication. A good review is generally self-contained and takes the reaaer along on the journey through the book.

By reading the review the reader should get to know what the book is about, what is new or innovative in it, what is the quality of the writing and such other details.

John Pringle of Sydney Morning Herald says, 'When I find a good or interesting book, my chief aim is to share my pleasure with may readers and, if possible, to persuade them to read it themselves"

Francis Brown, Editor of the New York Times says, "The purpose of the best book review is to furnish the perspective, to put into place to further appreciation, sometimes to challenge the accepted".

An idea review, according to Marjorie Bitker, should convey to its readers a sense of what the book is about, its plot, characters, whether or not the author has accomplished what he intended and to give the readers some evaluation based upon the reviewer's standard of writing, taste and experience. The reviewer's task is to give the reader enough information to enable him to decide whether or not he wants to read the volume under discussion.

(viii) Science Correspondent. Some of the big newspapers have a separate correspondent to cover science and technology. Usually he is a well-groomed scientist-an M.Sc. or an experienced B.Sc. He is incharge of covering developments in science and technology in different fields and reporting interviews with scientists. He brings out important developments in the country's march in the field of application of science and technology to industry, aviation, pharmaceuticals and new experiments in medicine and medical surgery. He collects the necessary information from departments of science and technology and industrial research. He is also supposed to cover researches taking place in agriculture including hybrid varieties of seeds which are designed to boost agricultural production. All the news received from news agencies concerning science and technology are given the final shape by him. On the basis of these reports, he makes his own investigations and analyses and arranges the publication of the final story the endeavour of all good newspapers to splash exclusives. The Science correspondent is therefore required to do many of the reports-received from outside in his own language with additions of his own comments.

(ix) Industrial Correspondent. The industrial correspondent covers developments in Industry. He is to analyse the industrial policy of the government and maintain data pertaining to industrial production in different fields. He occasionally interiews industrial magnates and discusses with them the impact of official industrial policy on the country's industry as a whole and how different types of industries large scale, medium and small scale-are benefited or adversely affected. It is his responsibility to inform the readers of the newspaper about the different aspects of industrial development—ow it is moving forward the rate of growth it is maintaining and how it can be given a pick-up. He is also expected to write specialised articles on different industries and occasionally bring out special supplements to encourage advertisement revenue from the industrial organisations concerned. He is quite frequently approached by the advertisement department for help to secure advertisements from industrial organisations which are in close contact with the newspaper and are directly or indirectly availing of its publicity media. Some industrial organisations are interested in obliging the correspondent as they get the benefit of support to their cause from the newspaper.

DIFFERENT TYPES OF REPORTING

Let us now turn to different types of reporting such as objective, interpretative, investigative and crime reporting etc.

Objective Reporting

Reporting of news, unlike editorial writing, is often described as a coldly impersonal job. A reporter is essentially a story teller and he should tell the story in an objective and truthful manner, without lacing it with personal opinions or subjective comments. He should be fair and impartial and present both sides of the story.

Complete objectivity is a mere concept. The reporter is a human being, not a robot and he has certain ideas, feelings, attitudes, opinions and prejudices. However, a good reporter should try to rise above them and tell the facts as he has collected them in his search for truth.

No responsible reporter would behave like the notorious American jounalist, Janet Cooke, who won the prestigious. Pulitzer prize in 1980 for a story about drugs which was later proved to be fictional and fictitious. The journalist committed a deliberate fraud by dramatising a fake scene in which an eight year-old boy is injected with her in supplied by the lover of the boy's mother.

Nearer home, the story of "mass rape" at a students function in a Madhya Pradesh town, published in a national newspaper was found to be baseless. When the report appeared on the front page of the newspaper it caused a sensation. The editor asked a reporter to investigate. On arriving in the town the reporter first questioned the reporter of the news item, who insisted that the mass rape did take place. By way of corroboration he produced a number of eye-witnesses. However, when they were cross-examined and asked specifically to reveal only what they had seen, and not what tney had. heard the investigator soon realised that the reporter had written the story on the basis of a bazar gossip and filed it without verifying the facts. All that had happened was that during a function to celebrate the annual day of a local college, a portion of the shamiana came down, the electricity got cut off and a few students entered the women's enclosure and molested some of the girls.

There is this apocryphal story of a cub reporter, who, on his first day at work wrote a piece with a cocksureness which was misplaced. On reading the piece, the editor advised him to be cautious and a little circumspect when writing about sensitive issues. The press, the editor reminded him, must not ordinarily violate the various .laws on the statute book concerning libel, national security and parliamentary privileges.

The next day the cub reporter submitted a story which ran as follows:

> "Mrs. Gulab Paniwala, alleged wife of Mr. Rakesh Paniwala, who claims to be the mayor of Shangrila, gave a cocktail party at her house in Model Town on Monday to bid farewell to Mrs. Jyoti Jariwala, reported to be the wife of the well-known industrialist Samar Jariwala. Among those present at the party were Mrs. Romi Puriwala, said to be

> the widow of the late Hansraj Puriwala, a former cabinet minister, along with her alleged offspring, Jani Puriwala..." and so it went on.

The reporter had quite clearly gone to the other extreme in writing this report which was quickly consigned to the waste paper basket.

In reporting news, you must remember that facts are sacred. You must check and cross-check the facts from different sources until you are absolutely sure of them. Only then should you write your story. The golden rule is: tell the truth. Objective reporting is, of course, not synonymous with dullness. It means fair and impartial reporting that is free from personal bias or prejudice.

Interpretative Reporting

Interpretative reporting, as the phrase suggests, combines facts with interpretation. It delves into reasons and meanings of a development. It is the interpretative reporter's task to give the information alongwith an interpretation of its significance. In doing so, he uses his knowledge and experience to give the reader an idea of the background of an event and explain the consequences it could led to. Besides his own knowledge and research in the subject, he often has to rely on the opinions of specialists to do a good job.

In the USA, the first important inputs to interpretative reporting was provided by World War-I. Curtis D. MacDongall writes in his book Interpretation Reporting that when the First World War broke out, most Americans were taken by surprise. They were utterly unable to explain its causes. This led to changes in the style of reporting. The result was that when in 1939 the Second World War began, an overwhelming majority of the Americans expected it or at least knew it was possible.

MacDongall says that a successful journalist should be more than a thoroughly trained journeyman. With his reading of history, economics, sociology, political science and other academic subjects, an interpretative reporter is aware of the fact that a news item is not an isolated incident, but an inevitable link to a chain of important events. An interpretative reporter cannot succeed if he is hampered by prejudices and stereotyped attitudes, which would bias his preception of human affairs.

Interpretative reporting thus goes behind the news, brings out the hidden significance of an event and separates truth from falsehood.

Example-1. The biennial elections to the Rajya Sabha took place in July. The interpretative reporter would give the reader the breakup of the results and acquaint him with the impact they would have on the various political parties and on the composition of the Upper House. He would, for instance, inform the reader that the Congress Party lost its majority in the Rajya Sabha, following the elections and that the Bharatiya Janata Party emerged as the main opposition, pushing the Janata Dal to third place. He will then explain the effect it would have on the working of the Rajya Sabha and on political party affairs generally.

Example-2. The election of the new President of India took place in July. The interpretative reporter would not only convey the bare news of the victory of Dr. Shankar Dayal Sharma but analyse the reasons behind it and reflect on the consequences of his victory for the future of the Congress and opposition parties.

Investigative Reporting

It is difficult to define the term "investigative" journalism. Some newspapers scoff at the very idea of an investigative journalist. In one way, of course, "investigative" journalism is a redundant concept, since all stories require some kind of investigation on the part of the reporter. However, the investigative reporter is expected to dig deeply beyond the facts stated in the hard news. Though we may face difficulty in defining the term, we cannot ignore the concept of investigative journalism. Many journalism students have an ambition to become "investigative" reporters. An "investigative" journalist sees himself as the conscience of society, pursuing corruption in high places without fear or favour. In his book Press and Law (Vikas, New Delhi 1990), Justice A.N. Grover has quoted from the foreward of Investigative reporting by Clark R. Mollevhogg. According to the Foreword, investigative reporting has three elements:

(a) It has to be the own work of the reporter. Under no circumstance should it be of others;

(b) The subject of the reporting should be such that it is of importance for the readers to know; and

(c) There must not be any attempt made to hide the truth from the people.

Investigative reporting has made great leaps in western countries. In India, it is still in its infancy. Most Indian newspapers do not have, or do not allocate, the manpower and funds necessary for a first-rate investigative job.

Attempts at investigative reporting, to quote one eminent Indian editor, are like drilling for oil. A fair amount of wastage of effort has to be taken for granted. But when the oil is discovered and becomes marketable, the sense of achievement is usually more than in any other sector of journalistic enterprise.

The best example of investigative reporting in our times, was the Watergate story which led to the disgrace and downfall of U.S. President Richard Nixon. When the two young reporters of The Washington Post, Bob Woodward and Carl Bernstein, started investigating the arrest of four men for a burglary at Watergate, the Democratic Party's national headquarters on June 17, 1972, they had no idea that their inquiry would culminate in the resignation of the President. The remarkable thing about their investigation was that it kept to the highest standards of professional journalism. The reporters did not start gunning for Nixon from the beginning. They merely pursued the burglary attempt and only later came up with startling facts linking the White House with it. "We did not go after the President, we went after the story", they explained.

Though the Washington Post stories led to the downfall of President Nixon, the same paper, later in 1980, got involved in the most celebrated case of journalistic fraud in modern times-the case of Janet Cooke, already described in this unit. Janet Cooke's case gives a clear warning that every story whether "investigative" or not, should be handled by editors with great care and caution, otherwise, it will bring the newspaper to disrepute. Z.J. Herbert Altsehull in his book from Milton to McLuhan (Longman, New York, 1990) states how the Janet Cooke story got into the Washington Post. An internal investigation by the newspaper's Ombudsman, Bill Green, blamed "failure of a system" for not checking up thoroughly on Cook's story. The failure to check was in part, Green said, the result of the fact that Cooke was black and that white editors did not want to be seen as racist. The Cooke's story appeared in the Post on 28 September 1980 and the edition featuring 8 Green's report appeared on 19 April 1981. Cooke was fired from the Post and was forced to return the Pulitzer Prize.

Let us return to Indian situations. In India, investigative reporting started making a mark after the end of the internal emergency in 1977, particularly through the reports published in The Indian Express.

In our country, investigative reporters have brought to light a number of scandals the Bhagalpur blindings incidents by the police, Kuo oil deal, A.R. Antulay's private trusts, the securities scam involving Indian and foreign banks and stock brokers, etc. An enterprising reporter once got himself arrested so that he could give a first-hand account of life in Delhi's Tihar Jail.

With governments becoming increasingly secretive and corruption spreading its tentacles far and wide, the need for investigative reporting cannot be over emphasized. Yet we must remember that investigative reporting is not everybody's cup of tea. It requires hard and sustained work. The investigative reporter should be a combination of a crusader, super detective and blood hound and he should have the necessary time and finance to carry out his work.

In the pursuit of his quarry, the investigative reporter must draw a line between candid reporting and muck-raking, mud-slinging, character assassination or blackmail. He should base his report on incontrovertible facts, not on half-truths and lies. He should be wary of lobbies and lobbyists—political or commercial—trying to misguide him. And he should not behave like a peeping Tom or a prosecutor.

The best kind of investigative reporting is that which keeps the public interest in mind. It may highlight an injustice, expose corrupt practices or unmask dishonest politicians and bureaucrats.

Experience has been that unless an investigative reporter or a crusading reporter gets the support of the judiciary, the executive or the legislative, cannot bring his reports to logical ends. The Bhagalpur blinding report would have ended like any other report if a public interest litigation would not have been filed against the police. In the USA the watergate stories would not have produced any result if they did not get the support of the legislative which threatened the impeachment of President Richard Nixon.

SPORTS REPORTING

Sports editors and reporters are well aware of the criticism that has come their way. In Boston, there was no effort to play down or cover up a criminal investigation into a point-shaving scandal that rocked the Boston College basketball team. As a result, a youthful Boston College basketball player was convicted and sent to jail for ten years. Nor have sports editors always been complaisant about the rumors of wrong-doing in collegiate and professional sports. Years ago, Max Kase, sports editor of the New York Journal-American, won a Pulitzer Prize Special Award for turning over information to the district attorney of New York County about a looming basketball scandal. As a result, several local college players were convicted and sent to prison.

But then, New York and Boston aren't as likely to develop hometown pride in local athletes as are smaller communities. And in the big cities, there is less opportunity for booster organizations to bring pressure on the local news media not to interfere in the affairs of local colleges or universities.

Without much doubt, the emergence of television as a dominant influence in the presentation of sports to a mass public has made a difference in the public's perception of right and wrong. As George Solomon to the Washington Post has said, "TV buys events. TV puts on the event. And to make TV look good and sell all the commercials, the sport must look good."

Brent Musburger of CBS believes the charges to be overstressed. He says, "To a large extent we are in the entertainmen business, which leads me directly into what we do as networks. Yes, we have to buy events. Then we have to make a profit out of them. So we have to attract an audience. And, yes, there is a certain amount of hype that goes into it."

Still, Musburger argues, newspapers also try to present the news in as appealing a way as possible because they, too, have to maintain circulation to attract advertisers and they, too, have to make a profit to stay in business. True enough, but the difference is that the newspapers don't pay large sums of money to put on national sports broadcasts. In consequence, to quote Solomon, "A lot of editors are demanding the same standards from sports reporters and sports journalists as they do from everyone else—that is, aggressive reporting, looking behind the scenes, digging, being a true reporter."

The Cult of Privacy. In professional sports, where outstanding athletes can earn enormous sums of money in a relatively short time, sports writers are under even greater handicaps. Because there is a tendency to criticize those players who collect millions and give substandard performances, the cult of privacy has taken firm hold among many teams. Once it was taken for granted that sports reporters and TV cameras would be welcome in team locker rooms or at practice sessions. But not today. Access to athletes in locker rooms is severely restricted by most professional sports teams. Dave Anderson of the New York Times says:

> When I was covering the [New York] lets 10, 12 years ago, you could virtually walk into their locker room during the week at any time. You could go into a locker room before a game up until an hour before. You could walk on the

> practice field and stand behind the huddle in the middle of the field. Today, virtually all of that is gone. There is no way you can walk out on a practice field of any team. You can stay on the sideline During the week, may teams have situations whereby you are only allowed in the locker room, let's say, an hour or a half hour. You have to make appointments with players The coaches seem to think the more secrecy they have, the better. To me, the more secrecy they have, the worse it is.

In the major league baseball, star players of the caliber of Steve Carlton and Dave Kingman have refused for years to speak to sports reporters and have gone their own way. And some younger players have had a powerful urge to imitate them.

The problem, therefore, is to obtain access to the millionaire athletes and their colleagues, and not every sports reporter is successful. The athletes appear to divide reporters into "good guys"—that is, cheer leaders—and "bad guys"—those who try to do an honest day's work.

There are some coaches, athletes and club owners who still resent women sports writers and try, by various means, to make it difficult for them to obtain access to athletes. But few women are fainthearted enough to be put off by such phony excuses as male modesty in locker rooms. Nor have women sports writers turned out to be the problem that some of their male colleagues predicted they would be. There still aren't very many of them.

Making a Beginning

It is a long way from such major concerns among the top figures in the sports reporting field to the beginner who wants to break into sports reporting for a newspaper or broadcast organization. Yet sports is almost a common denominator among working journalists today. Many of them had their first task of journalism covering sports as stringers at the high school level. And few have forgotten their experience.

Getting a Sports. Job In a lot of American cities, high school sports have a wide following and particularly in communities without college or professional teams, are a dominant community activity. On any autumn Saturday afternoon, thousands of people turn out to watch high school football. In many places, too, basketball is a magnet that draws townspeople to high school gymnasiums. Such sports as baseball and track traditionally have lighter attendance, but all are reported on in the local papers and local broadcast media.

Beginners generally inherit stringing jobs in high school from graduating classmates. Or, if they are particularly enterprising, they may find a nearby publication of station that gives no coverage to a high school within the general circulation area and win the assignment. At any rate, the first time they report on a game, they may be told that the paper or station wants only the final score and how the victory was achieved. Then someone in the office writes a roundup including this information.

As the newcomer proves trustworthy, the assignments improve. In addition to the final score, other details are requested-the number of people attending the game, an interview with the winning coach or the player who scored the deciding points, plus a summary of the scoring by both sides. Once again, that story may be written by somebody else in the office.

It sounds so easy, to do these things. But actually, as all beginning sports reports learn, it is almost as difficult to pin down sources at the high school level as it is to gain access to the bigtime professionals. The reasons are apparent. Coaches, for the most part, don't trust the judgement of youngsters to report what they say and if they comment at all - it will usually be in pleasantries with little news value. The same is true of officials at the games and those teachers who have a special responsibility for athletics. Players, too, are often cautioned to say as little as possible on the air or for publication, to avoid making some statement that can be seized upon by a future opponent.

Working at the High School Level. From these experiences, the beginner will learn persistence if nothing else. And that will be all to the good. But there will come a day when an assistant sports editor tells the beginner to write the story and bring it to the office or, better still, to come to the office and do the piece under supervision. That is always something to be remembered, even if the copy is heavily edited and bears little resemblance to the original.

Most young and inexperienced sports writers make the same mistakes. They deal in cliches instead of writing simple, straightforward English sentences. They load their copy with expertise, or what they believe to be expert comment, all of which is usually eliminated. And, worst of all, they betray a partisanship for the home team that makes their credibility suspect to anybody who merely wants a fair account of what happened.

The process of learning to write a sports story, therefore takes time. Except in rare instances, beginners can't learn to do it well overnight. It helps to read the work ef outstanding professionals.

Daily Sports Coverage. Every year, depending on the size of the paper and the rate of turnover, a certain number of stringers are offered regular sports jobs. It is far more difficult to make a beginning as a sports broadcaster, because these jobs are even more limited. The progression is usually through the sports broadcaster, because these jobs are even more limited. The progression is usually through the sports pages of newspapers in medium-size cities. Such papers, though, rarely hire more than one youngster a year. Very small dailies do not have enough staff turnover to warrant expectation of jobs for beginners, and the big metropolitan papers prefer to take on people with experience.

For the lucky ones who come up through the system and land regular jobs, the routine of daily sports coverage can develop into a pleasant life. Newcomers generally are assigned to writing the same high school sports they covered as stringers—in easy way of breaking in. The next step in the progression is to handle college sports if there is a nearby institution of higher learning. It takes a while to graduate to professional sports coverage, particularly if professional teams are outside the papers circulation area. But when the newcomer does get a professional assignment it generally is to do either a color story on a major contest or to handle the play-by-play.

Regular beats-following a particular baseball or football team through the season—aren't practical for a small sports staff. Reporters may handle several different sports in single week and have to adapt themselves to local conditions.

Interviewing Sports Figures

Bob Matthews, sports columnist for the Rochester (New York) Times Union, has these suggestions for interviewing sports per:sonalities.

* Make sure your first question is a good one so the subject will know you have something on the ball.

* Try for specifies. Don't settle for generalities. Ask why the center fielder. dropped the ball in the last half of the ninth, enabling the opposition to score the winning run.

* Always be on a first-name basis with every player on a pro team. Sooner or later, one of them will good up and it's sports writer's job to ask him about it. Nothing turns off an athlete faster than a reporter who hasn't said hello to him all season but is quick to arrive after a costly error.

* I have one pet question I often ask athletes. "What do you think of sports writers?" They usually have definite opinions and branch off into how they've been misquoted, misrepresented, etc. It's a good way to build rapport and can lead to some good exchanges.

* Before I interview a national sports figure, I often phone a sports writer in his particular town for background and tips on how to approach the subject.

* Invariably there's a question I forget to ask or a point that needs clarification. So I always ask where the subject can be reached later in the day, just in case he's needed.

Patterns of Sports

There most of the sports public knows the final score of the game from radio of before the paper comes out. sports writing in the TV age is different in many ways from what it used to be. Dave Anderson of the New York Times says.

A lot of my colleagues really seem to resent television. I may be different, but I enjoy television for this reason. I think television creates sports readers. Any time people see an even on television, they invariably want to read about it next day. To name the beauty of television is that as soon as the game ends, they go off as soon as they go off, that's when we go to work. That to me is the great value of television on the sports business.

Other newspaper, magazine and syndicated sports writers have been pleasantly surprised by the self-evident truth that Anderson expressed. And they have adapted to the new dispensation by using many of techniques of the feature writer—the bright anecdote, the sharp quote, the interview with all concerned in a disputed play or a disputed decision, the description of a part of the contest that television down played. Relatively few editors now want the fast summary lead on the final score; instead, they ask for the way it happened and the answers to all the questions the fans will be raising that night and the next day.

Damon Runyon, Bob Considine and Jimmy Cannon—three of the old-time greats in the sports writing business would have been very much at home in today's sports pages. As the saying goes, they always played the angles and wrote the story for all it was worth.

Telling the Sports Story. Anybody who undertakes to write about sports must have an intimate knowledge of the assignment. The three greatest necessities are accuracy, restraint and decent respect for the English language.

Sports followers invariably pride themselves on being experts. They like to hear and rear about "inside" strategy, just as the literacy gossip endlessly about the famous people on whom characters in a sensational new novel are supposedly patterned. However, some games are more easy to describe than others—and that depends on the patterns of the sport.

An essentially simple game like baseball is easy reported. The game's play by—play, the result and the reasons for it can be quickly summarized, then documented with a description of the key plays. A few other details, and the account is complete enough for a postgame electronic roundup. But the written sports story must be different and it must have more detail.

Boxing and horse racing, too, have essentially simple patterns and need not be told in too complicated a fashion. What matters, particularly in television, is the detail that makes the tiny images on the small screen come alive—the blow-by—blow in a fight and the "call" in a horse race. By comparison, accounts of competitions in crew, swimming, tennis, polo and golf are handled with relative ease.

In football, however, the pattern of the game becomes, increasingly complicated and difficult, to follow. The effort of a play-by-play commentator here must be to simplify, wherever possible, and to explain to the viewer what happened and why it happened instead of prattling excitedly about the confusing technicalities. In a summary, oral as well as written, it becomes necessary to analyze the result, to select the principal plays and to give the public a sense of participation in the reporting. The writer, especially, must emphasize anecdote and detail.

The many events in track and field, each with special complications, also require a good deal of guidance from professionals who are intimately acquainted with the sport. This is particularly true during the spectacle of the Olympic Games every four years; in expert hands, such reportage may be the worst, rather than the best, of the year because some American Commentators and reporters know only the United States competitors as a rule and tend to give the results of each race as a triumph of American righteousness or a blow to the Stars and Stripes. Actually in any track meet, the reporting can be done very nicely and interestingly if the expert for the day studies the teams in advance, looks up the necessary background and records and comes to the field an hour before the meets starts to do a final checkup. To wait until the first event begins is to bog down completely in detail. But if it is known in advance that the pole vault, the mile run and the hurdles are likely to develop the most interesting contests, then the meet becomes a relatively easy matter to cover. What can never be anticipated is the unexpected event, such as the murders of Israeli athletes by Arab guerrillas that made so tragic a spectacle out of the 1972 Olympic games in Munich, the wholesale withdrawal of black African nations from the 1976 Games in Montreal and the 1980 American boycott of the Moscow Games.

As for basketball, with its seven-footers and its statistical labyrinths, this is less a job for a sports reporter than for a certified public accountant. It is hard to follow on television and even worse to describe in print, but it has such a large and devoted following that it receives major coverage.

It is clear, therefore, that the patterns of sport have much to do with the pattern of sports journalism. The big-money sports such as horse racing, boxing, baseball and football are the ones with the most public appeal in general, professional sports have the widest following. But college sports also attract millions of followers, and the TV contracts are much sought after.

New Interests. Two developments have broadened the audiences for both the sports page and sports events on the tube. One is the rise in participation for women's sports and the broader attention and funding that universities have given to them. In some parts of the nation, the excitement over women's sports, even at the high school level, has become, a matter of consequence. The second break in the traditional sports pages has been the interest in such audience participation events as stock car racing, motor boating and sailing, hunting and fishing, skating and skiing and the like. Such events are not easy for TV to cover, and therefore offer something to newspapers that can interest their readers. The boom in soccer, so long considered a "foreign" sport, benefits all the news media.

Writing Techniques. incomparable Red Smith, viewing an Army-Navy football game at' Philadelphia, began his account has follows:

> As some churlish historian of America's great undergraduate pastime wrote years ago, "it was an ideal day for football—too cold for the players". For l00,000 citizens of assorted nations, including Russia and Monaco, whose chattering teeth rattled like castanets upon the necks of bottles in Municipal Stadium yesterday, that just about sums up the match of Army and Navy.

Eventually, Smith got around to mentioning the size of the Army's victory, 22-6, which wasn't particularly important to him because everybody who read him knew it anyway. What was more important to his readers was his point of view.

> The entertainment seemed flat by comparison with Army Navy contest of the past. It was just too perishing cold. Reluctant to quit a slugging match which they had travelled many miles to watch, the customers nevertheless started making their numbed way toward the exits when the first half-ended, longing for a warm hotel room with the guy across the courtyard beating his wife....

Unlike Red Smith, most sports writers and commentators immerse themselves in technicalities to such an extent that they often forget entirely about the game itself and the people who contest it and who watch it. The electronic reporters becomes slaves to their equipment. The newspaper reporters worry about writing three separate accounts of a single event in order to cover all editions of a newspaper- a time consuming and expensive procedure that provides no advantage in these times of instant communication.

Advances and Summaries. Because the technique of doing multiple stories of one sports event is still practiced in a large section of the daily press the essentials are recorded here without assurance that they will survive many more years.

1. The Advance Story. The advance begins with a situation lead, relating that two teams are facing each other or that a field of seven horses is ready for the big race of the day. The remainder of the story merely discuses the background of the event, gives whatever detail there is on the participants and the crowd, and winds up in such a way the running account of the early part of the game can be added on. If the contest is under way before the edition closes, a brief high insert can give the early scoring. Necessarily, even in an early edition, the advance is bound to look foolish. It assumes that the public is entirely dependent on the news paper to find out what happened and will buy a later editor to get the full details. This used to happen, but it hasn't for many years.

2. The Running Story. Depending on the style of the paper, the chronological story of the game is told as B copy (or B matter) or merely slugged "Running" or "Play-By-Play." As an edition approaches, a two-paragraphs lead is written by the reporter at the scene or by an editor in the office and put on top of the opening of the chronological account. Once the event is over, a final wrapup lead is written and the details of the end of the game are put at the bottom of the piece.

3. If the Running Story is well done within reasonable space, it should stand. But frequently, sports writers have the urge to do the whole exercise over again on the dubious theory that they will produce magnificent prose the second time around. Unfortunately, it rarely turns out that way.

These are trying circumstances for any journalist. If the objective is to keep pace with radio and television, it is impossible to attain. If it is to "save space for the final story, the theory is lacking in practicality. Such saved space is always wasted space. The newsmagazines manage to do pretty well with their weekly summaries of sports and do not arouse great feeling among the sportsminded public that it is being cheated. Sooner or later, the newspapers will come around to the obvious—that the best way to do a sports story is to wait until the event is over and then give it the well-considered treatment it deserves. Few sports events are big enough to call for edition-by-edition coverage against electronic competition.

Statistics. The sports fans of the nation love statistics, and most sports pages provide them in abundance with columins of box score averages, racing detail, league standings and the like. Every reporter must learn at the outset how to keep an individual set of statistics and make sure they are accurate.

Sports Basics for Reporting

Here are some of the basics that should be remembered about sports reporting:

(a) Sports reporters are measured by the same standards as all other reporters. They have to do more than just report the score; it is their business to be aggressive to dig for the hidden story, to make sports pages mean something more than a repository for columns of agate results.

(b) One of the foremost problems today is access to athletes and locker rooms, at both the professional and the amateur levels. Reporters have to make it their business to ask the tough question—which means that they can't let themselves be turned aside by a stern locker room janitor.

(c) The three necessities for a sports writer are accuracy, restraint and a decent knowledge of and respect for the English language. Phony expertise and cliche-ridden writing are the principal faults of newcomers.

(d) Most beginners in sports get their first job stringing for a neighbourhood paper and reporting high school scores. The high school sports beat is a testing ground for the next generation of sports writers. Usually, the best of the stringers gets first crack at an opening for a high school sports reporter and the progression starts there.

(e) In a contest featured on TV, the newspaper sports writer has to emphasize something other than the score, even though the score does have to be repeated high up. This can be anecdote, a sharp quote, an interview or an explanation of some occurrence that was fuzzed up by the TV reporters.

(f) Keeping statistics is an important part of a sports reporter's work and he or she should devise a system that can be qucikly scanned and summarized at the end of the game. Too many states will spoil a story; too few will make it unusable. The point is to find the happy medium.

(g) In the thousands of contests that sports writers cover with little or no broadcast competition, the emphasis is still on writing the story straight and featuring the manner in which the game was won or lost. But even here, the feature approach always helps and- except for the brief summary story-good quotes are mandatory.

(h) Everybody in the business emphasizes sports writing styles. But mostly, this refers to the elite-the columnists and commentators who speak and write pretty much as they please. The young sports staffer is bound to the same rules that covere all reporters, however, and should not deviate from them without permission.

POLICE REPORTING

Angry, frightened woman telephoned Edna Buchanan, a police reporter for the Miami Herald late one March afternoon and told of witnessing the kidnapping of engaged couple that had ended in a gang rape. The witness identified one of the neighbourhood hoodlums who had been preying on passing cars as well as residents.

"I'm fed up, " the caller said. "What happened was outrageous."

Nothing could be done to help the young man, who had been beaten by the hoodlums or his fiancee, who had been sexually assaulted. But Buchanan made it her witness to interview other neighbourhood residents, and she didn't stopantil she identified all the suspects. They were arrested, charged with rape, robbery and misuse of a gun in the commission or a felony. The police gave the reporter credit. "Edna's sources," said Police Sergent Mike Gonzalez, "Knew who they were, they did, where they were and who played what role."

Covering Police News

The story was part of the daily—and often nightly-routine for Buchanan, who has had police news for the Herald for almost 15 years.

"Police reporting is exciting work," she says. "I get to see what people are really like—what makes some turn to crime, what makes some become cowards, and some become heroes. It's great job.

The Toughest Beat. The police beat in Miami is the toughest in the country. For some years now, the Florida metropolis has had the highest crime rate of any city in the country, in statistics reported annually by the FBI. And in addition to crime, the beat includes coverage of fires, explosions, accidents of all kinds and rescues as well as departmental Policies and charges affecting individual police officers and the activities of Cooperating federal, state and local law enforcement agencies.

Any newcomer who is assigned to a police beat—even a beat less tough than Miami's—is going to be tested for courage as well as ability. For historically, that is where city and metropolitan editors generally start their best young prospects. On the Heralad, they have the advantage of working with seasoned professionals like Buchanan. But very often they are on their own.

The Daily Routine. Here is a summary of the police beat assignment for the Herald's police reporters.

* Continual radio monitoring of all police calls and messages.
* Continual monitoring of fire calls and services.
* Hourly telephone checks of federal, state and other municipal departments.
* Close liaison with police public information offices and installation of related teletype, beeper and communications systems.
* The Herald uses wake up calls for reporters plus helicopters planes, ships and speedboats for reporters and photographers.
* Immediate communication with the office by car radio, beeper and walkie talkie.
* Examination of logs, uniform crime reports and arrest forms daily at police offices in Miami, Miami Beach and the Metro complex.
* Access to special categories in the Herald library on all forms of crime and crime statistics.
* Daily examination of booking sheets at the central jail.

The Herald's editors have arranged for service by lawyers to back up reporters' requests for the release of information by the police. The lawyers also try to handle subpoenas issued by the courts, at the request of prosecuters or defense lawyers, to gain access to reporters' file and notes.

The newspaper has a policy of following up tips or complaints from citizens, such as the one given to Buchanan, on everything from illict drug trafficking to police brutality, failures of the justice system or outrages in the streets. The paper also keeps files in the newsroom for identification of people involved in crimes, as victims or assailants, including the latest city directories, tax rolls and other helpful data.

The FBI's Uniform Crime Reports

The FBI issues each year a thick book entitled Crime in the United States, which is crammed with disheartening statistics. While lists of cities with the highest crime rates are regularly compiled from the book's section called Index of Crime, Standard Metropolitan Statistical Areas," the FBI itself does not issue such a tabulation and discourages it as misleading for a number of reasons. However, the lists can easily be put together by checking the figures for the crime index total rate per 100,000 population.

While the list varies from year to year, three of the cities that have figured preminently among the "first 10" for some years are also the ones that attract millions of tourists annually - Mimai Atlantic City, New Jersey, and Las Vegas, Nevada. With the rate of crime in the average metropolitan area at the beginning of the 1980s set at 6,757.6 per year per 100,000 population, this was the rating of the three tourist centres. Miami, 11,581.8, Atlantic City, 11,481.3 and Las Vegas, 0,292.3.

The Rise in National Crime. The FBI report the decade 1971-80 showed a 54.8 percent increase in the number of serious crime committed since 1971 and an almost 10 percent increase from 1979 to 1980. In fact, the report showed that violent crimes over the decade surged by 60 percent and crimes escalated by 54 percent.

The Crimes Defined. The Uniform Crime Reports (UCR) uses these definitions of the eight crimes included in the index.

Murder and nonnegligent manslaughter The willful (non-negligent) killing of one human being by another. A total of 50 percent was attributed to handguns.

Forcible Rape. The carnal knowledge of a female forcibly and against her will. Assaults or attempts to commit rape are included, but not Statutory rape (with our force).

Robbery. The taking or attempting to take anything of value from the care, custody or control of a person or persons by force or threat of force or violence and/or by putting the victim in fear. Street and highway crime was put at 51 percent.

Aggravated Assault. An unlawful attack by one person upon another for the purpose of inflicting severe or aggravated bodily injury. Attempts are included.

Burglary. The unlawful entry of a structure to commit theft. The use of force to gain entry is not required to classify an offense as a burglary. There are three sub-classifications forcible entry, unlawful entry where no force is used and attempted forcible entry. A total of 67 percent of the reported burglaries occurred in residential property.

Larceny-theft. The unlawful taking, carrying, leading or riding away of property from the possession or constructive possession of another. It includes crimes such as shopliting, pocketpicking and purse snatching, thefts from motor vehicle, of motor vehicle parts and accessories and of bicycles in which no use of force, violence or fraud occurs. The volume of larceny-theft was 53 percent of the crime index total and 59 percent of the property crime total, with thefts from motor vehicles and the taking of motor vehicle accessories as the largest single crime, 36 percent.

Motor Vehicle Theft. The theft or attempted theft of a motor vchicle.

Arson Any willful or malicious burning or attempt to burn, with or without intent to defraud, a dwelling house, public building, motor vehicle or aircraft, personal property of another etc. The monetary value of property damage due to reported arson was very heavy, the most frequent target being structures which comprised 54 percent of the total.

The FBI reported that 10.4 million arrests were made in 1980 of all criminal infractions except traffic violations, with persons under 25 comprising 70 percent of those arrested for Crime Index offenses. However, only 19 percent of the reported index crimes were cleared during the year, the FBI said, the rate for violent crimes being 44 percent and for crimes against property 16 percent.

The Police Reporters' Task. This statistical pattern vividly illustrates the magnitude of the task crime poses for the news media in general and police reporters in particular. For in any self-respecting community, unfavourable publicity affecting the business community always produces dismay. And this is particularly in places like Atlantic City and Las Vegas, which are dependent on attracting millions of visitors to try their luck at the gambling tables, and Miami, as well as other Florida cities, in a state that annually draws 35 to 40 million tourists annually.

But not many newspapers in such areas try to bury the news or omit it entirely. As one editor put it, "This is not something we can keep a secret. We have to face it report on it and trust that our citizens will be sufficiently angry and determined that they will insist on federal and state action to help reduce the threat of crime."

That, in fact, is a substantial part of the anticrime movement throughout the country today.

Stories of the Police Beat

With violence rising in many American cities, large and small, a part of the police beat assignment necessarily has to do with delving into the causes of crime.

In states along the Atlantic Seaboard and the Mexican border, the FBI points out that much crime is drug-related. The drug traffic in itself is so huge as to be almost uncontrollable. In addition, there is continual warfare between narcotics smugglers and loosely organized gangs that vie for local control of illicit drug sales. No large city is immune from this type of mob violence, whether it is New York, Chicago, Los Angeles or Miami.

Then, too, there are major problems related to the massive influx of Cuban and Haitian refuges and millions of illegal immigrants from Mexico. It is no accident the New York police have found that hardened criminals let out of Cuban jails, who joined the mass movement of more reputable Cuban immigrants, were settling in the least accessible areas of the Bronx and preying on their countrymen and others. But in the 1980s, the move to the north had ebbed and most Cuban emigres were settling elsewhere.

Still, the police story can't be told entirely in terms of major drug busts, Mafia type gangland murders, large-scale robbies and other big-time crimes.

Edna Buchanan's bylines, for example, appear on all kinds of stories for the Miami Herald—fires, police shootouts, features and investigations. Within about one month, the following two accounts were among the interesting and detailed stories, most of them on Page 1, her assignments produced.

A Fire Story. Buchanan received a call from one of her sources at 4 a.m. that several people, all members of the same family, had died in a fire that destroyed their home. It was a stromy night, but she phoned a photographer to meet her and got rolling in her car in the middle of a thunder-and-lightning storm.

"The fire was more than 40 miles away," she recaleed, "and I got lost in south Dade Country farmland in the rainy dark before dawn. I was driving with my gas indicator on empty"

Finally she reached a gas station and was able to get to the firefighters, who had been on the job and had returned to the firehouse, before the shift changed in Leisure City. Then she drove to the charred ruins of the home and talked with investigators, cops, neighbours, friends and relatives of the bereaved family.

"I set out at 9.30 a.m. to return to the office and write for the early edition," she went on. "Back at the office, I interviewed the medical examiner by phone and talked the cops into giving us a rough drawing of the layout of the house and the body positions. In the meantime—in case of argument or disagreement—I got the floor plans of the house from the courthouse. After polishing and writing through for later editions, I left the Herald at 9.30 p.m."

> A smoldering fire from a worn air conditioner wire ignited a sofa, raced across wall paneling and gutted a Leisure City home in an inferno that killed five children and their small dog Wednesday.
>
> The parents, Redland Construction Co. superintendent John Paul Dixon, 54, and his wife, Barbar, 38, and their two other children, Delbert, 3, and Tracy, 19, were cut and burned but survived.
>
> "A $ 10 smoke detector would have saved five lives," said Metro firefighter Anthony Spadaro. He carried two dead girls, five and six years old, from the house.
>
> He found them in their bed, "beautiful little blonde girls in long nightgowns. One was resting her head in her hands like she was sleeping." Two baby dolls lay nearby.
>
> A neighbour tried to rescue the children but was driven back by two snaring and snapping family dogs, a boxer and a bird dog, who tried in panic to protect the burning house.
>
> Flames shot from every windows the doors were ablaze and a huge column of smoke rose skyward when the firefighters arrived at 2.54 a.m. The trantic parents and screaming neighbors shouted that five children were inside.
>
> There was no sigh of life within the modest 10year-old, four bedroom home. Rescuers were forced back by flames and heat so intense that it melted the aluminium trim on the house.

> A huge pumper equipeed with 3,000 gallons of water arrived at 3.03 a.m. The flames were knocked down and fire fighters were able to enter the house in five minutes.
>
> It was too late for those inside.
>
> A windows screen lay atop his body in a back bedroom. His hands were cut. His pet dog, a miniature dachshund, lay dead at his feet.
>
> Wanda Dixon, 6, and John Dixon's granddaughter, Misty Hogan, 5, died in their beds. Two more little girls, sisters Paula and Reba Dixon, three years old, died crouched, wedged in corners, trying to escape the flames....

It is reportorial detail that makes this story. It takes the reader to the scene, of the plight of the shattered family devastatingly real, adds poignant evidence of firefighter's observation that a smoke detector could have saved them all.

A Cop's Last Night on the Job. This was a different story, about a violent final night on the job. It is also came alive through Buchanan's drive for detail and more detail. Here is the start of that story:

> After a rough and tumble ten-year-career as a Metro cop. Officer James Melvin shot a man Sunday, his last night on patrol.
>
> Melvin, who is moving away from Dade County to South Carolina, wounded one of three burglars he caught in the act, police said.
>
> "He was upset. He wanted to get through a quiet evening his last night on the road," said Metro Police spokesman Pete Cuccaro.
>
> But Melvin, who has won honors for bravery and heroic rescues in the past, was too

> conscientious a cop to ignore a suspicious truck during his final hours on the job, superiors said.
>
> The truck was a pickup, parked at the rear of the Service Merchandise Mart and the vacated former Treasury Store, at SW 160th St. and US 1.
>
> The truck was loaded with thoursands of dollars' worth of stolen equipment, stereo and electronic, police said.
>
> As officers searched the darkened building, they spied two men, identified as Richard Yound and Ernest Holcomb, both 22, hiding in the ceiling work, police said. They added that both refused commands to surrender.
>
> Concerned, Young shouted an obscenity and rolled to one side, reaching into his waistband, police said. Thinking he was reaching for a gun,
>
> Melvin fired a shot, striking Young in the leg. Young is listed in good condition at Jackson Memorial Hospital....

Following up a Story

Police reporting elsewhere in the United States differs only in degree from the intensive work that is demanded of the men and women on the police beat in Miami and other metropolitan centres. The same watchfulness, the same effort, the same dedication and the same professional knowledge and skill are called for the people who handle police news in every city and town, regardless of size.

The routine may differ, depending on circumstances, but the stories are seldom if ever handed to reporters with a flourish and a bow from the participating police officers. If there is one lesson that beginners learn very early on the police beat, it is that they have to struggle—and sometimes even fight—for every fact they get. There is a limit to what even the best police sources can do for the news media, and reporter know it.

A Double Slaying in Kansas. Even if there isn't anywhere near as much crime in Kansas as there is in New York, Illinois, Florida or California, people in Kansas are just as concerned about the rise of violence on the Great Plains as other police news has to be carefully scrutinized.

Anita Miller of the Topeka Daily Capital only a year out of the William Allen White School of Journalism at the University of Kansas, may not have had either the reputation or the experience of Edna Buchanan of the Miami Herald, but she worked with the same care and efficiency in developing the facts behind a double slaying. It was sensitive story, to begin with, and Miller explained why:

> My story was a second day story. The first story was sketchy because police hesitated to say anything, since one of their own officers was involved.
>
> It was a double slaying. A girl had been fatally shot by her former boyfriend, and the boyfriend then was fatally shot by a police officer in the parking lot of a major shopping center in Topeka.
>
> I didn't write the first-day story but I felt a follow up was necessary because there wasn't much of a hint as to how the woman and man were associated. She was only 17 and he was 19.
>
> I happened to know one of the victims and I knew where the two had gone to school, so I began calling people at the school, including teachers, students and counselors. My main goal was to find some friends who might have been with the couple prior to the shooting, or knew what the girl was doing at the shopping center and how the man knew she was there.

> Digging for facts on a story like this was really frustrating. For every ten calls I made, only one would come up with good, current information. I was careful about taking down what each acquaintance said until I had a clear picture in my mind of what the girl was really like and the chain of events that led to the shooting.
>
> I didn't use information unless I felt comfortable with the people and had a good idea that they were telling me the truth.

Results of the Follow-Up. When Miller finally wrote her story for Capital she had checked all the facts she used. She didn't do a sob story-it isn't in her nature. The story is straight throughout, with no flourishes and no attempt to do anything more to set out the facts behind a tragedy. Here is the substance of the story she wrote.

> A 17-year old Topeka girl who was fatally shot Thursday night at the White Lakes Shopping Center parking lot had recently stopped dating the man who shot her, acquaintances said Friday.
>
> They asserted Linda M. Schneider, 324 Woodbury Lane, had dated Mark. Thompson, 19,919 S.E. Consuelo, about a year until they broke up two months ago.
>
> "When they broke up she went to St. Louis [and stayed with relatives] to get away, "Stacey Moore, 4012 W. 28th, said. "Then she moved back here with her parents about four weeks ago."
>
> Thursday night Miss Schneider was at White Lakes Mall attending her first session at the Barbizon School of Modelling since her return to Topeka from St. Louis. One friend said Miss Schneider had wanted to be an airline stewardess.

> Topeka police said Miss Schneider was fatally shot in the head by Thompsons at 8.59 p.m. as she ran toward two police officers just south of the Sears Automotive Center outside the White Lakes Shopping Center complex.
>
> Police said after the girl fell, Reserve Patrolman Gaylon Thompson, 27, a two-year member of the reserve force had fired in self-defence.
>
> Acquaintances of Miss Schneider said she had been invited to attend a party at a friend's house in central Topeka after her class Thursday, but Thompson was not allowed inside when he went to the house. However, he learned that she was at White Lakes and drove there, acquaintances said. The slayings followed.

Are Police Reporter Insensitive? People unfamiliar with newspaper work in general, and police reporting in particular, often assume that journalists are insensitive to all the tragedies about the on many occasions. A few maybe, but most reporters could be deeply affected if they weren't able to seal off their personal feelings by casting a protective shell about their emotions. This, perhaps, may give the appearance if insensitivity to human suffering, but appearances are often deceiving. Miller summed up her own position this way:

Talking to close friends and the family of a dead person really bothers some reporters, but it has never upset me much. Before I start an interview, as the people involved if they want to talk to me. I think it is important to give them a choice. If they refuse, then I don't pressure them. It's always necessary for me to remember that I'm approaching them at a sensitive time and try to be understanding. If they won't talk, there's usually someone else who will be able to give me the information.

The columnist Jim Bishop, once a police reporter on the New York tabloid the Daily Mirror, which went to the journalistic boneyard in the 1960s, put the case this way:

> "I was a crime reporter... A callus grows on your brain. The heart becomes a cool stone. There is a shade of cynicism on the retina." And then, he added, there comes a time when the reporter reads something about the piteous victim of a crime and this happens: "Your throat slams shut and you throw the book on the floor..."

The Miranda Rule

Under the Miranda Rule, the police are obliged, with certain exceptions, to notify defendants of their right to remain silent and to obtain counsel. The notification must take place upon arrest. It became law when the Supreme Court in 1966 reversed the conviction of Ernesto A. Miranda, a 25-year-old mentally retarded Arizona truck driver, because he had not been warned of his right to counsel or that his statements might be used against him before he confessed to raping an 18-year-old girl. Miranda had been serving concurrent sentences of 20 to 30 years.

Chief Justice Earl Warren held for the 5-4 majority that police must inform criminal suspects, when arrested, of their right to remain silent and to obtain counsel. While the Miranda ruling remains on the books, it has been weakened by subsequent high court decisions. In 1971, statements made by an accused person before being informed of his rights were admitted under cross-examination. Four years later, statements made by an accused person after being informed of his rights were admitted as rebuttal testimony. And in 1976, the Miranda rule was held inapplicable to grand jury testimony.

Arrest Procedures. In brief outline, is what happens when an arrest is made.

* The suspect may be brought in on a complaint or a warrant or he may be seized at the scene of a crime. But until formally charged and booked, he cannot be said to be under arrest.

* The booking consists of recording the suspect's identity, address and vital statistics in a large record together with

the alleged crime, time and place of the arrest and the name of the arresting officer.

* The suspect is searched, his property is enumerated, sealed and given to the property clerk for safekeeping.

* The Miranda card, notifying the suspect of his constitutional rights, is read to him. He is informed that he may remain silent, that he may consult a lawyer or, if he doesn't have one, a lawyer will be provided. Before he can be questioned by police, he must sign a paper waiving these rights.

* If he signs, the police question him and put together a formal arrest report. In any case, he is photographed, fineprinted, told he can make a telephone call and then he is put in a detention cell.

In some cities, notably New York, there is an arraignment either in a day court or in Night Court, as soon as possible after a formal complaint is drafted by a member of the prosecutor's office. The suspect then is given a chance to enter a plea. If the plea is not guilty, the presiding magistrater or judges sets bail.

Some defendents—depending on the charge and on their record, and on the amount of security company after the hearing and thereby obtain release. If they can't raise bail, they are held in jail.

The prosecutor's office must now determine whether the evidence against the suspect is strong enough to warrant holding the suspect on a felony charge, in which event a case must be presented to a grand jury and an indictment must be returned, or whether to proceed to trial in a lower court on a misdemeanor, a lesser charge.

It is at this point that the courts take over. If it is decided to proceed with the misdemeanor charge, generally the trial is scheduled in a lower court without a jury. But if the felony charge holds good, and an indictment is returned, the suspect must await trial before a judge and a jury. Or, through their lawyer, suspects may plea bargain with the prosecutor's office and conset to a guilty plea on a lesser charge.

In any event, once an arrest has been made, the police and court procedures are intricate and time-consuming. Generally, if the case warrants it the reporter who was in on the arrest follows through to at least the preliminary hearings in the lower courts. Once an indictment has been returned, particularly in larger cities where there are regular court reporters on daily assignement, they take over the story.

Guide to Crime Reporting

Some reporters often have to go behind the news. The following safeguards are, therefore, in the coverage of the administration of justice.

Arrests. It is a serious matter to report that a person has been placed under arrest. When such a report is made, the exact charge against the arrested person could be given and it should be documented by either a record or attribution to a responsible official. If such documentation cannot be obtained, the reporter had better to check the facts. The person in question may not have been under arrest at all. There are euphemisms in police work such as "holding someone for questioning, " asking witness to appear voluntarily to cooperate with an investigation" and simple statements which indicate the person is being detained but may or may not be subject to arrest. In many states an arrest is not formally accomplished until a prisoners is booked. The news, in any case, must be handled with care.

Accusations. It is commonly written that someone is being" sought for robbery," suspected of arson" or "tried formurder." Thisisjournalistic shorthand, which has gained acceptance through usage, but it is neither precise nor correct.

Persons are "sought in connection with a robbery, unless a charge has actually been made, in which case they are "charged with robbery." Persons under suspicion are not necessarily going to be charged with a crime and it is generally not privileged matter to indicate that suspicion is attached to any individual by name. Where the police suspect someone, but lack proof, that person may be held as a material witness—which is far different from being accused of a crime. Therefore, cases of suspicion are not usually given too extensive and detailed news treatment if no privileged material is available for use. The practice of reporting that a defendant is being "tried for murder," while widely used, is obviously prejudicial and could be more accurately, if less drama stated, as "being tried on a charge of murder, "or" on a murder indictment.

Confessions. The use of the word "confession" to describe stastatements made by a person to the police or to prosecuring authorities is dangerous when it is not a matter of public record. The fact that a police chief or a prosecutor has claimed to have a confession, except in open court, may be used only at the risk of the news organization. Most press-bar voluntary agreements forbid the use of confessions until they are admitted in open court. The records are full of supposed confessions that backfired later for a variety of reasons and of persons who admitted crimes they could not possibly have committed. Unless and until it is established in fact that a person has confessed, approved procedure for reporters is to use such terms as "statement," "admission," "description" or "explanation." They convey the shade of meaning that is warranted by circumstances and do not subject the news organization to unnecessary risk.

The reporter must always remember that under the law individuals are presumed to be innocent until they have been found guilty.

Investigations. Certain stages of police investigations require secrecy in the public interest. This also pertains to some of the aspects of prosecutions and trials. The secrecy of the grand jury room and of a trial jury's deliberations are soundly based on public policy. Except under the most extraordinary circumstances, no reporter and no news organization have any right to interfere and few have ever attempted to do so.

Often, during the course of investigations, reporters are confined to listing the identities of witnesses who have entered or left a police station or grand jury room, if the names can be obtained. They have every right to try to interview such witnesses, if the circumstances are favourable, before and after appearances of this kind. But it is the business of the prosecution, defense lawyers and the witnesses themselves to decide whether or not they should talk.

For this reason investigations in their earliest states, are likely to produce a crop of speculative reports without much asis in fact unless editors insist on sounder reporting. Clever, publicity conscious investigators can often hopelessly prejudice the position of hostile witnesses and others who oppose them if the news media do not hold rigidly to their code of presenting both sides of the story. That is why no claim by any investigators, regardless of their position and personal prestige, should be accepted and published at face value without some effort by a reporter to determine the soundness of the statements that have been issued.

Cases of Violent Death. Nowhere is there a greater tendency to jump to conclusions in the field of crime reporting than in the initial reporting of a violent death. The amateur reporter is invariably in a hurry to characterize the event as a suicide or a murder when it may be an accident death. It is advisable, therefore, to report only what is known and avoid speculation in the absence of an official verdict by a coroner, medical examiner or some other competent authority.

An apparent suicide is one of the most difficult crime stories to handle. If the police report that a man was found shot to death with a bullet in his right temple and a revolver in or near his right hand, the story should be written in exactly that way. In the case of a police finding that someone "jumped or fell" to his death, the reporter should not go beyond the facts but use that phrase. If a woman is found dead in bed with an empty bottle labeled sleeping tablets sleeping tablets beside her, no conclusions should be drawn.

In all such cases, it is proper to note any other circumstances that have a bearing on the story, particularly as to whether notes were left. It may not always be proper to publish such notes, even if the text is made available by the police, unless the material is privileged.

Moreover, unless there is a formal announcement of suicide by a responsible authority, the news account can do no more than to note that an investigation is being made to determine whether the death was a suicide.

When violent death occur without any indication as to whether they may be accidents, suicides, murders or combinations of all three, the story should report the identities of the victims and the manner of their deaths. It is usually fruitless to try to unravel such a mystery in a newsroom. That is the job of the police and the prosecuting authorities. In the absence of any word from them, a factual account of the event must suffice.

A murder investigation often tempts reporters to venture into recalms for which their profession has not really equipped them. Because a few reporters have achieved fame through phenomenal exploits, all reporters are scarcely justified in trying to play detective when a newsworthy personage has been "done in." Not many even attempt to do so because there is simply not enough time for the routines of both journalism and police work on a fast-breaking story.

Precautions. There are a few fundamental precautions of which reporters must take account.

The first is that police and prosedcutors rarely will give thm information on a silver platter. That means a tremendous amount of interviewing and research must be done in a very short time so that a coherent story may be written.

The second is that there can be no guarantee of police accuracy, in fact, an impressive body of evidence can be amassed to the contrary. That means police versions of names, addresses and other facts must be checked.

The third is that police and journalistic terminology are not necessarily identical. The legal term for a slaying is a homicide, but many news organizations loosely and incorrectly refer to such crimes automatically as murder. In a grand jury indictment the homicide eventually may be defined as first or second degree murder, depending on whether there was premeditation, or first or second degree man-slaughter, depending on whether there was provocation or negligence. Since manslaughter is not murder, care must be used in defining a homicide. Indictments charging murder have been found to be deficient in the past, so writers should be precise in their statements whenever they refer to the legal basis of any charge.

Assessment of Blame. Whenever there is a fist fight, shooting or collision involving police action, it is only human to wonder what happened and who was at fault. Often a trial can determine this, therefore, most reporters use as many versions of the incident as there are witnesses if such extensive treatment is warranted.

Such accounts begin with a statement that two men had a fist fight in a night club, or that there was a shooting match, or that two automobiles collided. The body of the story then documents the non-committal lead, giving such versions of the event as are necessary. The attribution of documentation of this type always presents a problem for writers who want to avoid using "he said," or "she said," or "the police said" in every sentence.

There are several ways of doing this. One is to quote the various versions, if they are briefly enough. Another is to write, "The police version of the incident follows," and then report it without further attribution. In any case, unless there is some official assessment of blame, it is usually not necessary for the reporter to try to act in such matters.

Identification. The identification of persons in crime stories sometimes leads to trouble, no matter how carefully it is checked. Confusion of persons with identical last names, mistakes in middle initials, mix-ups in addresses, misspellings of names and police errors all conspire against the reporter. There is no real safety in the familiar formula "The suspect gave his name as..." or, "the prisoner was identified as ..." If the identification is incorrect, the reporter and the news organization are in trouble.

It is usually a good rule, in stories that warrant it, to include material showing how the identification was made—by papers in the person's possession, by friends or relatives, or by other means. If there is any doubt, the reporter will find it does no harm to add a clause or even a sentence indicating that the identification was partial and remained to be checked. No news organization need regard itself as an oracle whose word is final, when the public knows that many things are possible between the commission of a crime and the conviction of a defendant.

Civil Disorder

The coverage of civil disorder imposes major responsibilities on journalists. On the one hand, they must exercise the greatest care not to spread rumors. On the other, they must expose themselves to danger if necessary to determine the magnitude of any street incident. But whatever they do, they must always be conscious that careless reporting or the provocative appearance of still or television cameras can cause untold harm in a tense situation, particularly in the crowded inner cores of many American cities.

Restraint in Conduct. The conduct of the journalist at the scene of action must be circumspect. A hard-hatted, swaggering white reporter in the center of an angry black community can provoke trouble. A television cameraman training his instrument on a floodlighted crowd, is likely to get more action that be bargains for when fighting has broken out all around him. Nor is there any great sense in sending an armored truck bearing the name of a news organization into a trouble area. These are the things that cause the news media to be blamed for spreading disorder. Complete coverage is desirable at all times, but no one is thereby justified to pay on a circus like performance.

Restraint, such as was maintained in the face of wholesale disorders by street gangs in Detroit, is a necessity in reporting policy.

Defining a Riot In both written and oral reports of any incident, every effort should be made to arrive at accurate evaluations. An isolated act of vandalism, or a street fight between two teenagers in the midst of a' crowed, must not be called a race riot. And if shooting is heard in a crowded neighbourhood at night, it is not automatically' "sniper fire", until an investigation determines that snipers are at work. Nor are all fires the work of arsonists. Looking, too, should be carefully defined. Great damage can be done if radio, television and published wire service and newspaper reports exaggerate a few small incidents. Consequently, in the early stages of any civil disorder, the basic rule is to work and report with the greatest restraint.

Necessarily, once a news organization's editors have evidence to show that they are dealing with a riot of major proportions, there is no justification for not making a complete report available to the community at large. When reporters see arsonists setting fire and looters carrying merchandise from wrecked stores, these things must be communicated. Yet, the need for restraint and patient inquiry cannot be abandoned even in such circumstances. For when shooting breaks out, the reporter is never justified to leap to conclusions that all the damage is being done by demonstrators or that race is aligned against race, littery police and National Guardsmen have been known to fire away at almost anything that moves, sometimes with unfortunate results.

Reporters have to be more patient and more circumspect.

Short Takes

These are the basics of covering the police beat:

* Police reporters check police and fire department radios, arrest records (where available), departmental liaison officers and associated sources. When they spot a story worth going out on, they call their city desk and make suitable arrangements.

* Police reporters do a lot of interviewing at the scene of a crime, a faire, an accident or other incident on a police beat. The heart of their work depends on a good deal of accurate detail and good quotes.

* Police reporters can't afford to be a part of then big blue machine. They must maintain their independence and investigate at once any story that indicates police negligence.

* Some stories, in which important angles are left hanging, must be cleaned up with second-day and sometimes third-day reports. A once-over-lighty isn't sufficient.

* There is no such thing as going with first police reports without checking the facts. Police reports themselves may not be accurate.

* Sometimes it pays to go deeper into a story that indicates a profound human conflict. Such stories may be told at first in three or four paragraphs. But if the police reporter suspects a much better story lies behind the initial report, he or she should try to sell the idea to the city desks and get help.

* There are restraints on the coverge of crime news. All suspects must be read their Miranda rights - their right to remain silent and to be represented by a lawyer. In some states, under voluntary Press Bar Guidelines, there are agreements that reporters will not use a defendant's prior police record and other damaging detail in the arrest report. What can and cannot be used should be checked with the city desk.

* Police reporters must be familiar with the department they cover, its regulations and procedures, and must have a good working acquaintance with criminal law.

* The greatest care must be taken in reporting arrests. Sometimes people are detained for questioning, asked to give help to the police or help as material witnesses. But these actions are not arrests and it is libel *per se* to report that such people are under arrest. The test for an arrest is twofold: *(1)* The subject must be bookeu and formal

charges must be lodged, and *(2)* both the booking and the charge must be attributed to a responsible police official.

* Similarly, in the event of a civil disturbance, no reporter should call the exchange of a few blows a riot. And particular care should be exercised never to term a disturbance a race riot, which is a major civil calamity.

* Reporters should beware of announcing confessions. Generally, what is done is to report that a suspect has made a statement, made admissions or given an account of the crime to the authorities, and the source of that intelligence should be named and identified by department and rank.

Let alone all newspapers, even the big newspapers of India do not have the resources to cover all the courts of their main circulation area. Reason: there are too many courts. Newspapers neither have the time nor the space to cover every thing that happens in the courts. Papers cover only those stories in which their readers are interested.

A country governed by laws needs many courts, each with a different jurisdiction. The emphasis of the news media is on Criminal Courts, High Courts and the Supreme Court.

The media are, less interested in covering Civil Courts. One of the reason for this lack of interest may be that the Civil Courts are jammed with cases, the suits remain pending there for several years and it is assumed that in the mean time, members of the public would lose whatever interest they may have showed initially.

Nonetheless, you go through the old files of a newspaper, you will find that the volume of Court reporting has increased in recent years. One of the reasons for the increase may be that the courts are now getting more active in the field of social justice. Public interest litigations are also increasing. As the number of petitions increase, one notices a corresponding increase in the coverage of courts and the judgements they deliver.

Who Are Court Reporters

There are only a few big newspapers in India who have full time correspondents exclusively for their court beat. These correspondents generally have adequate legal background. Other newspapers mostly hire stringers to cover court stories. Many of the stringers are professional advocates. Mofussil correspondents, who are mostly part-timers, also cover court stories in their respective areas. These part-timers come from teaching, law and other professions. A newspaper which does not have a full time law reporter may send its regular staff correspondent to cover an important court story.

Knowledge of Court Jurisdictions, Procedures and Hierarchy

The first time that one covers the court beat as a Court reporter, one usually feels lost amidst the technicalities and complex language. A trainee journalist aiming to be a future Court Reporter must at first acquire some understanding of the court jurisdiction, its procedures and its hierarchy. At the apex, we have the Supreme Court of India. Then there are High courts, Sessions Courts, Magistrate Courts, etc. Also, there are Tribunals, for example, the Tribunal for Central Government Employees.

If a reporter is acquainted with the jurisdiction of different courts, then one can easily locate the specific court for a particular matter. Similarly if one is familiar with the hierarchy in the courts, one can easily guess where the appeal would be filed.

Some Legal Terms

For a court reporter, some basic knowledge of some of the most frequently used legal terms is a must. The following are some of the legal terms used quite often in the news reports.

Adjournment Application	:	Request for more time for finding witnesses or important evidence or for other reasons.
Attachment Order	:	The court's authorisation to take and hold a person's property.

Bail Bond	:	A Security amount usually furnished to gurantee the appearance of an accused person in the court.
Change of Venue	:	Change of the place of trial.
Certorari	:	Writ from superior to inferior court requiring the records to be sent to the former for review.
Commutation	:	Reduction of sentence.
Concurrent Sentence	:	Court's decison that a convicted person serves only the longest of several jail terms import on him.
Contempt of Court	:	An offence against the court, punishable by a fine, or imprisonment or both.
Consent Decree	:	Court order to whch the defendant has consented.
Decree Nisi	:	Final judgment to take effect some time in the future.
Double Jeopardy	:	Plea that the defendant has already been tried for the same offence.
Extradition	:	Process of returning a prisoner from one country to another.
Habeas Corpus	:	Judicial procedure requiring production of a detained person in court to inquire into the legality of the detention.

Mandamus	:	Court's command to an inferior court, or ordering a person to perform a public or statutory duty. Requiring someone to perform an act.
Pardon	:	Action of executive relieving criminal from sentence.
Parole	:	Release on promise of reappearance at regular intervals or on call.
Plaintiff	:	Party who initiates litigation.
Reprieve	:	Delay in execution of a sentence.
Proceedings held in Camera	:	Proceeding held privately, *i.e.* not in public.

Professional journalistic practice requires each technical terms to be briefly explained when it is used in a story for the first time. A legal term, not explained in the story, confuses the reader. Except in professional or academic law journals, a news story must not be cluttered up with too many legal terms.

The English language is predominantly used in the higher courts of India. Therefore, for a reporter of a non-English daily, some knowledge of English language always helps.

News Sources

Much of a reporter's success in the coverage of the courts depends on one's contacts and sources, and one's ability to gain access quickly to records. For a reporter the key person in a court is the clerk of the court. A court clerk prepares and keeps the records. He can make available copies of transcript for a fee. Court reporting involves diligent checking of records. The judge who presides a trial is seldom one's source. But a reporter should, as soon as possible, introduce oneself in person to the judge. A court reporter should also have good contacts with the lawyers working on a case and if possible with the respective parties. Where a case attracts much public attention, reporters may be under pressure from rival lawyers for a more favourable description of their individual positions. The reporter must then ensure impartial reportage in all fairness to the proceedings in court.

It is not unusual for the parties and lawyers to approach a scribe and present their case afresh.. A young reporter should always try to seek some impartial legal source, usually a friendly lawyer, to learn what moves are likely to be made.

A court reporter should have adequate knowledge of different stages of civil or criminal proceedings. One should also know where an appeal can lie from the court one is reporting. When a reporter is assigned to cover a major trial, the first thing one should make sure of is that one has a seat in the court room. One should also have adequate communication links with one's newspaper or news agency office.

A reporter of a morning newspaper mostly does not face much problems in filing a court story, as one usually files the stories after the court retires 'for the day. However, for an aftemoon paper or for wire services, the stories must be filed during the day, *i.e.*, even sometimes when the court proceedings are on.

Trial Coverage

While taking notes in a trial coverage the reporter needs to have a sixth sense. Guided by this news sense, one could begin to take notes of important dates. When a reporter misses an important testimony, one can always regain lost ground during the recess by consulting one's colleagues in the court, or the court stenographer.

Writing with Quotes

In trial proceedings, wherever possible, the reporters must learn to quote the questions and answers or comments and remarks that arise in the course of the court's sittings. A story with quotes makes fascinating reading though sometimes, due to paucity of space, many comments may not be quoted in the news item. In the two examples that follow, we compare clippings taken from various newspapers, where the same story has been treated differently, *i.e.* with and without quotes.

Example—I. (Story without quotes)

New Delhi, 3 February—A three judge Supreme Court bench comprising Chief Justice M.N. Venkatachaliah and Justices P.B. Sawant and S.N. Singh, today, summon'ed three police officers of Etah district to appear before them on February 7.

The three police officers including SSP S.N. Singh and SP Jamal Ashraff, have been directed to appear before the court to explain the alleged inaction of the UP police in pursuing prosecution of a man and his family members for selling off his wife into the flesh trade.

The court ordered senior counsel Yogeshwar Prasad, who appeared for the state of Uttar Pradesh to produce tomorrow the records relating to the investigation by the police.

Nasrin, the victim, was allegedly sold off to flesh traders by her in-laws and husband five years ago. Her mother Shakila Bano learnt in November last that her daughter had not vaished mysteriously as claimed by her in-laws, but was actually in the red light district of Kasganj. in Etah district.

The same story with quotes, published in The Hindustan Times, New Delhi, 4 February 1994.

New Delhi, Feb. 3. The Supreme court today pulled up senior police officers of Etah district of Uttar Pradesh and asked them to appear-in-person before the Court on Monday to explain their inaction in implementing the Court's order asking them to produce a 21-year old girl, who was sold off into flesh trade by her husband and his family.

"As a result of police inaction, the girl, Nasrin alias Rani, has been destroyed totally and is a mental wreck and cannot even recognise her own mother", the Chief Justice, Me. Justice M.N. Venkatachaliah, who was heading a three-judge bench, observed.

The Chief Justice, Mr. Justice Venkatachaliah, warned that if the officers were found guilty for not taking timely action on the Court orders they would be sentenced to substantive prison terms for contempt.

The officer including one Senior Superintendent of Police, Superintendent of Police and one former Superintendent of Police, who has now been transferred to Ghazipur district were summoned to appear before a three judge bench comprising the Chief Justice, Mr. Justice Venkatachaliah, Mr. Justice P.B. Sawant and Mr. Justice S. Mohan.

The UP police was also pulled up for not producing the records today...

The Court rejected all excuses for delay, in producing the records as "red herrings" for their inaction.

Mr. Justice Mohan, another member of the bench, said that the very fact that the records had not been produced, despite the Apex Court orders, was proof of contempt of court. At this stage, Mr. Justice Venkatachaliah observed that the suppression of the records was deliberate.

The Chief Justice, Mr. Justice Venkatachaliah said that if this was the fate of the orders of the highest court one shudders to thinks of the plight of the public before the police.

When the judges asked the counsel who had the custody of the records, he replied, "Stenographer of the SP". At this stage, the Chief Justice, Mr. Justice Venkatachaliah observed that "this is not the way to treat the highest court of the land. I know the mentality of the police from the way they come to court, enter courtrooms and sit in the court. They are an irresponsible lot".

The counsel, Mr. Yogeshwar Prasad pointed out to the Court that the orders passed by the Court on Dec. 15, 1993 asking the SP to produce the girl had reached his office on Dec. 21, 1993. Since the SP was on leave since Dec. 20, 1993 another officer was asked to carry out the orders of the court.

As a result, the girl was produced before the Court on Jan. 6, 1994. She was recovered by Rajasthan police from a village in Rajasthan...

Example—II (Story without quotes)

New Delhi Thursday. In a case of custody death in Lodhi Colony police station, a Division Bench of the Delhi High Court comprising Mr. Justice Y.K. Sabharwal and Mr. Justice R.L. Gupta today said that they would inspect the lock-up where the incident took place for deciding whether or not to institute a judicial enquiry....

The petition has been filed by the borther of Vikal Kumar, for monetary compensation alleging that the man was wrongfully confined and tortured to death. The petitioner has also called for prosecuting the erring CBI officials.

According to the police, Vikal Kumar had committed suicide by making a rope out of the coir mat in the lock-up. The said articles, the police respondents claim, are lying in Lodhi Colony police station.

The same story with quotes published in The Hindustan Times, 14 Jan. 1994.

New Delhi, Jan. 13: Two High Court judges will visit Lodhi Colony police station on Monday to find out whether a Finance Ministry employee committed suicide or was tortured to death inside the lock-up.

This unprecedented decision was taken by Justice Y.K. Sabharwal and Justice R.L. Gupta on a petition filed by the dead man's brother who alleged that Vikal Kumar, 33, was tortured to death by CBI officials on Feb. 23 last year to save some senior Finance Ministry officials..

Vikal Kumar, an assistant in the Finance Ministry, was arrested oy Inspector S.K. Paschim of the Anti-Corruption Branch of the

Bureau on Feb. 23. The allegation against him was that he was blackmailing businessmen on the basis of forged income-tax raid notices. He was trapped on a specific complaint of the owner of Hotel Rajdeep, Karol Bagh.

Vikal Kumar, as per the police records, was brought to the Lodhi Colony lock-up at 10 p.m. on Feb, 23.

At 3 a.m. the next day, Inspector Rajbir Singh Jakhar, the then SHO of Kotla Mubarakpur, found him hanging by a rope inside the lock-up. They called up the Lodhi Colony SHO who cut the ropes and took Vikal Kumar to the AIIMS where he was declared brought dead.

Vikal's father, Yad Ram, said his son had been tortured to death while the CBI and police officials maintained that he had committed suicide by making a rope out of the mat and hanging himself with it.

The post-mortem report said the death was caused by "asphyxia as a result of antemortem hanging by ligature". The SDM, Mr. Z.U. Siddiqui, who conducted the inquest, concluded that it was a suicide although he noted that there were swellings on the soles of his feet, external injuries on his hands and bluish colour of irregular shapes on several parts of the body.

"It is quite possible that he must be highly depressed and stricken by remorse and that is why he committed suicide by hanging", said Mr. Siddiqui, in his report dated Aug. 18 last.

Justice Y.K. Sabharwal and Justice R.L. Gupta, who heard the petition of Vikal Kumar's brother today, however, tended to disbelieve the claims of the police officers and said it was a case of custody death. "The dispute is whether it was suicide or death on account of torture".

They said..., "we feel it appropriate to first inspect the lock-up in which Vikal Kumar died and then consider whether to direct an enquiry or not".

The judges then ordered Mr. Ramesh Sharma, a Joint Registrar in the court, to go to the police station and take the coir mat and the rope in his possession.

The judges then said they would like to visit the lock-up on Jan. 17 at 4 p.m.

PRECAUTIONS IN WRITING COURT STORIES

While writing stories one must be cautious in avoiding any contempt of court. Sometimes, a reporter files the court story without comments and sometimes with one's own or someone else's comments.

We now give some illustrations of newspaper coverage of the courts:

Story without comments published in The Hindu, New Delhi, 19 January 1994: New Delhi, Jan. 18.

The Chief Justice, Mr. M.N. Venkatachaliah, Mr. Justice S.C. Agarwal and Mr. Justice S.P. Bharucha, were on the Bench.

The Bench made these orders during "mention time" on a request by Mr. K.K. Viswanathan, counsel for the accused petitioner for urgent orders of "stay" of execution of sentence of death of the accused pending the disposal of his Special Leave Petition (SLP) against his conviction and sentences of death by courts below.

Story with comments published in The Hindustan Times, New Delhi, 14 January 1994.

There was a mixed reaction by leaders of the three major political parties—the Congress, BJP and the Janatadal—to the Delhi High Court order quashing the Delhi Government notification on holding elections for the Municipal Corporation of Delhi at present...

Story with comments published in The Pioneer, New Delhi of 20 February 1994.

Even as one policeman after another presents himself before the apex court to receive what may be described as the harshest reprimand in recent history, serving and retired police officers feel that angry outbursts of judges and chief justices, however justified, will not ensure more efficient law enforcement...

Former Director General of the Border Security Force, K.F. Rustamji, believes the kind of language used by the court could have an adverse impact on the way in which the police will respond to situations in future...

Story with comments published in the Hindustan Times New Delhi, 14 January 1994.

The High Court lawyers will strike work tomorrow to protest against what they call, violation of code of conduct by a high Court judge, Justice Sagar Chand Jain.

Justice S.C. Jain vehemently denies all the allegations against him.

The Bar's allegation is that Justice Jain was hearing a company case in which his son was a counsel and this was violative of a code of conduct for judges whereby a judge cannot and should not hear a case represented by his or her kith and kin.

The case in question was, in fact, represented by Mr. Huzefa Ahmadi, son of Justice Aziz Ahmadi of the Supreme Court. The Bar Association alleges thafMr. Ahmadi (Junior) was an associate of Mr. Pradeep Jain, Justice S.C. Jain's son.

The Delhi High Court Bar Association, at an executive committee meeting this evening, decided to go on a day's strike to protest against this alleged violation of code of conduct for judges.

Justice Jain, however, says he was not aware of the fact that his son's name was also in the vakalatnama filed by Mr. Muzefa Ahmadi. He said his son has never appeared in his court for this case.

Justice Jain said as soon as he came to know about the fact that his son's name appeared in the vakalatnama, he ordered the case to be listed before another judge...

"It is blackmail", the judge said.

Contempt of Court

The law relating to contempt of court can be braced from the Contempt of Court Act, 1971 and from various case laws. A contempt can be civil or criminal offence.

Civil Contempt

Civil Contempt means wilful disobedience to any judgment, decree, direction, order or other process of a court, or wilful breach of an undertaking given by a person to a court. There will be no civil contempt where there is ignorance of the order of a court leading to unintentional breach.

Criminal Contempt

Criminal contempt mainly means publication of any matter, or tne doing of any other act, which *(i)* scandalises or lowers the authority of any court; or *(ii)* prejudices or interferes with the due course of judicial proceedings.

Scandalising The Court

Under the law, publication of matter which creates doubts about the ability or fairness of a judge of a court is prohibited. A newspaper should not impute of improper motives to a judge. In 1971, in the case of Daphtary vs. Gupta, the Supreme Court decided that to express an opinion that a judge "toes the line" of another is contempt. Similarly, the expression that a judge pronounces his judgement under the influence of liquor or lure of wealth is also contempt. Casting defamatory allegations against a judge or judges, with or without reference to particular cases, is contempt because it creates distrust in the popular mind and shatters confidence of the general public in the judiciary. However, it should be made clear that the Contempt of Court Act, 1971, is basically designed to protect the judiciary from unwarranted allegations, and not to safeguard corrupt judges.

Prejudicing Fair Trial

Court reporting prejudicing fair trial may be of various forms. It is contempt *(i)* if a newspaper report deters a person from giving witness in a court; *(ii)* if the report offers threats or is written in abusive language compelling a party to discontinue the court proceedings; and *(iii)* if the report discusses the merits of a case pending in court.

In the United States, in the famous Sheppard Case (1966) the judgement pronounced by a court was reversed 12 years later on the ground of prejudicial publicity.

Facts of the case were that Dr. Samuel Sheppard had served nearly ten years on his 1954 conviction of a charge of murdering his wife. Later in 1966 the court held that due to virulent publicity and a "carnival atmosphere" a fair trial was not possible. The U.S. media. persons were warned that trials were not like elections, to be won through public meetings, radio, and newspapers. The media was also asked to show the increasingly prevalent habit of making unfair and prejudicial comments on pending trials.

The Dr. Samuel Sheppard case, as reported in Plain Dealer, Cleveland, U.S.A. (17 November 1966) gives an account of the reporter's experience of the proceedings in the court room:

Samuel H. Sheppard was found not guilty last night, in the 1954 slaying of his first wife Marilyn.

Sheppard gleefully slammed his hand down on the trial table after Common Pleas Judge Francis J. Talty read the verdict.

Sheppard had to be restrained in his joy by Defence Counsel F. Lee Bailey and co-Defence counsel Russel A. Serman.

"Sit down!" ordered Bailey, Sheppard sat down and burst into tears. A woman in the back row screamed, "Thank God"!

Other women could heard screaming in the corridor outside the second-floor courtroom in the Cuyahoga County Criminal Courts Building.

Sheppard's second wife, Aiane, covered her face and sobbed softly. She was sitting in the second row of the seats in the small courtroom jammed with nearly 60 spectators, 27 of them reporters.

As the jury was dismissed, Sheppard broke for the rear of the courtroom, thrusting a sheriffs deputy aside. "I'm going to see my wife", he said.

He leaned off the bar rail and embraced his wife, she threw her arms around him. "Oh, baby", he sobbed. "Oh, baby" .

Leaping and pushing his way through the crowd that had amassed in the corridor, the former osteopathic neurosurgeon shouted, "He's my man!" and clasped the stocky Bailey around the neck.

Bailey, who had worked to have Sheppard freed in 1964 on a writ of habeas corpus, looked on and beamed. This was the moment he had waited for - for 1,827 days, he had told the jury, ever since he became interested in the celebrated Sheppard case in 1961...

Marilyn Sheppard, 31, died with more than 25 bonedeep wounds in her head. She was four months pregnant with her second child.

Asleep in the next room was the Sheppards' 7-year-old son, Chip, now a 19-year old freshman at Boston University. He testified in the current trial that he never awakened the night or morning of the murder.

Sheppard told authorities in 1954 that he was attacked and knocked out twice by one or more unknown assailants when he rushed to the rescue of his wife and later when he pursued a shadowy form to the beach behind the Lake Road home.

Sheppard was found guilty of second degree murder in 1954 after a 65-days trial, Sheppard served nearly ten years before he was released from prison on $10,000 bail by a U.S. district court in 1964...

The United States Supreme Court's attack on prejudicial publicity has had its effect on the coverage of the mass media in most cases since.

In Britain in the Michael Fagan case (1983), The Sunday Times was fined by the court because the paper published certain particulars about the accused when the trial was pending. The case was related to Michael Fagan who was alleged to have intruded into the Queen's bedroom.

In another English case, RV.S. Thomson Newspapers (1968) it was held that to publish a criminals antecedents, during the pendency court proceedings against him, is contempt. There are definite reasons why trial by newspaper is prohibited. A trial by newspapers may influence the minds of witnesses. It may also compel a party to withdraw the suit. It may prejudice public mind against the administration of justice. It may also deter other people from filing suits in the court of low.

JOURNALISTIC DEFENCES

According to Sec. 5 of the Contempt of Court Act, 1971 a person shall not be guilty of contempt of court for publishing any fair comment" on the merits of any case which has been "heard and finally decided".

Now two questions arise. What is "fair comment" and what is meant by "heard and finally decided?".

Fair Comment

There is no single formula to decide the fairness of a comment. The matter depends on the facts and circumstances of each case. To comment on the correctness of a judicial decision, whether on law or facts, is not contempt. Similarly, to point out inequality of sentences in two different cases of the same nature, is also not contempt. However, while commenting on the merits of a case if improper motives are imputed to the judge, then the comment ceases to be fair. Similarly, to express that the judgement was arbitrary or the judge was incompetent is also contempt.

Heard and Finally Decided

A fair comment on the merits of a case can be made when it is heard and finally decided. A case cannot be said to have been finally decided until the period of limitation for filing appear has expired. Where an appeal or revision has been filed the comments on the merits of the case should not be published until the appeal is finally decided. P.M. Bakshi states in his book Press Law that in practice no one waits for the expiry of the limitation period.

Ignorance of Pendency

If a court story interferes with the course of justice, but its reporter had no reasonable ground to assume that the proceedings were pending, then one will not be guilty of contempt of court. Prior to the enactment of Contempt of Court Act, 1971, ignorance of pendency was not a defence or excuse.

Fair and Accurate Report

According to Section 4 of the Contempt of Court Act, 1971, fair and accurate report of the court proceedings is lawful.

However, a report will be contemptuous if it has been prohibited by the court or is forbidden by any law.

Truth No Defence

In case of Perspective Publications *vs.* State of Maharashtra (1971), the Supreme Court has held that though truthfulness of a statement is a good defence in an action for libel, it is no defence when it comes to contempt of court.

Academic Writings

Academic writings or a report written academically on a point of law is not a contempt of court, just on the ground that the law discussed is at issue in a court.

STORY REPORTING

Human Interest stories are those which present a bit of life's fabric rather than record major "hard" news. Yet these items about people and animals and things a bit" off heat" fulfill a valuable news media need. They provide spice, the desert for the daily news diet.

Those worthy of the human interest classification produce a chuckle, a sigh, a lump in the throat, a tear.

The format-limitless. Here all is sacrificed to a simple, usually unadorned telling. For if the event lacks puch; the cleverest of writers can't create it. Possibly this is the secret—in the best human interest stories the writers stand aside and let the story come through.

The writer's major contributions, then, are *(1)* being constantly alert for items that merit human interest treatment and *(2)* using imagination in selecting the method of presentation, choosing the one which will best tell the story. This requires writing skill of the higest order.

Of Zoos and Guns

Note how Charles Maher of The Associated Press did just that in this brief item. His play on words grows naturally out of this news event.

BY CHARLES MAHER
The Associated Press, Oct. 28, 1960

LOS ANGLES, Oct. 28. The zoo knows it and gnu knows it: It takes a he-gnu and a she-gnu to produce a new gnu.

That's why Griffith Park Zoo is making a deal with the Fresno Zoological Society.

Griffith Park has several she-gnus but no he-gnus. At Fresno, she gnus are rare but there are no he gnus to spare.

The news is that the two zoos will be making guns by matting gnus. (Written by gnus man Charles Maher).

Daddy's A Hero

The Seattle Post-Intel ligencer gave Mel Meadows' feature on a minor human tragedy best page one play, and for good reason. Meadows humanized deftly this father and son so they come through as people, not merely a prisoner, a statistic. This is just another reminder that we all live on the "people" level with our personal problems and joys. Well written copy aimed at this appeal seldom misses.

Meadows intelligently wrote this from the child's viewpoint, "Eight months is forever". Even so, one understands the heartache of the parents, the all-too-brief happiness. The story gains by its simplicity—he developed only three central characters and let the little drama unfold easily, chronologically. He wisely withheld until the end why Billy and his mother are separated from daddy.

A Night for Drama Lovers

Accuracy is to a reporter as piety is to a clergyman. But accuracy involves more than getting facts straight, spelling names correctly, giving disputants fair treatment. It includes evaluating a news event insightfully so this event may be reported in its proper context.

Carl Gartner must have asked himself "What is this really all about?" when he covered the appearance of the wrestler Gorgeous George for the Des Moines Tribune. Obviously, the Tribune drama critic saw this as a spectacle, a performance. Why not treat it thusly? The strength of this whimsical article lies largely in his light -handed reminiscences of other dramatic performances at the KRNT theater and his gay phrasing, which appears throughout the piece. Even though a highly featurized style was used, the report includes the essentials the outcome.

Winnie Ille Pu

To write interesting features one must assume an attitude proper to the news event. He then must translate that mood clearly, appropriately, accurately without submerging the event into a morass of stylized jumble.

Todd Simon interwove imaginatively Lain phrases, numerals, references into his story about "Winnie Ille Pu." Even to one who does not appreciate the subtleties of Latin, the piece communicates clearly. Note the crowning stroke in this delightful story: Simon's by line appears at the end.

BY TODD SIMON

The (Cleveland) Plain Dealer, Dec. 28, 1960

This is a little bear tale. It begins at the end and goes frontward, being rather vice versa by nature.

THE END

And so you can buy the Latin version called "Winnie Ille Pu" some time between the ideas of January and the calends of February, if you still love the small bear and didn't find Gaesar's Gallic War too traumatic an experience in your youth.

Right now there are no copies, but after doing a double take, the Dutton publishing house is scurrying to print up a big second batch of them.

The Public Book Mart, somewhat stunned, sold CXXV copies and couldn't get more no matter how it hollered. Dutton had underestimated the egg-head-edness of the public.

It was a sneaker. Unballyhooed and brought out too near to Christmas, "Winnie Ille Pu" was gobbled up like Saturnalia cakes. It could have been the top juvenile book of the gift season.

DIVIDED INTO PARTES TRES

Who were these customers grabbing for it? The bookseller found they were divided, like Gaul, into partes tres:

(I) People who had been reared circa MCMXXVI and would like Pooh Bear whether he lived under the name of Sanders or under the name of Ursus Pu.

(II) People who met Pooh when young and whose children are currently hating Cicero in school.

(III) Some who thought it chi-chi; "Who ever heard of translating a book INTO Latin, instead of out of it?"

Publix Book Mart sold XXV then L, then a second L. Both it and the publisher were obstupefacti, as the Lating Winnie would say. Os hians, pedibus planibus, we dare say. We dare say it because that's how our Latin dictionary talks when it means open mouthed flat footed.

The owner of the Publix Book Mart read a halfcolumn review—in Latin!—in the London Times literary supplement in September. Being no bear on Latin but a shark at spotting a good, off beat commercial possibility he sent for the American edition. The London Times had reviewed an edition by Methuen & Co. Ltd.

BY TODD SIMON

Sell us Anything

The Holy Bible remains as many writers model for literary excellence. It is little wonder, then, that reporters have attempted to adapt parts of the Bible to news events. Virtually always the result has seemed forced, often because no realistic relationship existed between even and Biblical reference. In other instances the event was lost sight of, buried under an illfitting literary style. Some have suffered from the opposite failure to retain the writing theme throughout.

Robert W. Wells of The Milwaukee Journal selected the birth of the Christ child for the theme of his "last minute shopper" article. His allusions are entirely natural, thanks to his keen observations and imagination. Fiction you say? Not on your life. This happens and happens and happens. Therein lies much of its charm. Any writing which strikes a memory chord common to the many has stroked writing's most responsive key.

Word selection, restrained use of repetition, real life experiences add to the warmth, the humanness of this witty morsel.

BY ROBERT W. WELLS

The Milwaukee Journal, Dec. 23, 1960

And it came to pass, the season of the last minute shopper having come, that it was Friday. The time of desperation was upon the land and 10, there was wailing and gnashing of teeth.

The wise shoppers departed homeward, trampling each other, striking out joyfully with the elbows, bearing with them gifts of exceeding worth, to be paid for noman knew when. The pleas to do such shopping early had resounded loud in the land, being cried from the housetops and trumpeted from the loudspeakers.

And it happened that the wise shoppers had heeded these exhortations so that in the time of desperation their teeth should remain ungnashed and their garments unrent.

But it was not so with the prodigal shoppers. In the time when the wise ones had been trampling each other and striking out joyfully with the elbows, the unwise men had stayed behind in their tents, sulking or playing at sheepshead, hardening their hearts against the prophets who cried woe.

Woe to those who wait until the last minute to seek out gifts of plastic! Woe, and again woe, to those who delay the assembling of presents for the little ones, following those instructions laid down by scribes gifted in tongues, none of them understandable.

But the last minute shoppers heeded not the warnings, and it came to pass that it was the Friday before the Sunday and they were cast down into the pit, which was loud with the sound of gnashing incisors.

And their women berated them, saying: Go to the market place, thou clown, and return not without golden baubles to lay at my feet or the skins of minks for my shoulders. For my neighbour's husband has met with the money lenders and is in hock to them forever and why should the wife of my neighbour have a chance to lord it over me when the gifts are opened?

And so it was that the prodigal shopper appeared at the gates, wild of eye and tremling, crying aloud to the merchants.

Sell me anything, he was crying, sell me whatever is left. Sell me cashmere with collars of animal skins. Sell me, oh, merchant, whatever you have not yet unloaded. For I have not heeded the warnings of the prophets and the sands are running out and I am not ready.

Sell me sequined babushkas. Sell me toys with three screws missing. Sell me the gifts the wise shoppers cast aside as unworthy, for there is no time remaining.

For while I was sulking in my tent playing sheepshcad, the hour has waxed late and to. I have been found wanting.

And it came to pass on the last Friday before the Sunday that is called Christmas that there were legions of such prodigals abroad in the land, each trampling the other and striking out with his elbows.

And the wise men heard the noise and saw the confusion and were exceedingly content.

Old Times in a Picture Book

Every mortal doubtless harks back to joyful times when a less complex universe seemingly rendered life less challenging. Only fleetingly may man re-experience anything akin to the lost past. Robert J. Lewis did. And at a time when doubtless a million others bypassed this, "pleasure" with oaths for an inconveniencing snowfall. Possibly Mr. Lewis' Deeper messsage suggests we need that alert to savor "Old Times in a Picture Book." At any rate his story for The Washington Evening Star gave thousands a chance to reminisce.

Imagination? Doubtless. Yet it was all there for anyone to see, to recored. This four-mile forced walk home in deep snow would embitter most. Not Mr. Lewis. He saw this as a rare opportunity, a delightful experience. His story literally reflects enjoyment with each step. And why not?

The description is clear, accurate, and interesting, primarily because it deals in specifics: initials in a heart (per. 9-12), a display window (par. 15), a neighbour by name (next to last paragraph), etc.

BY ROBERT J. LEWIS
The Washington Evening Star, Jan. 27, 1961

I Walked all the way home last night.

The cars couldn't take it, physically or spiritually. So they deserted the town and left it for human beings. Pedestrians, remember?

It was old times in a picture book.

Snowflakes in your face. A blanket of them, dry and squeaky, underfoot. The lights glowing brightbeckoning beacons, inviting and gay. The air crackling and tingling the skin.

But the city is magically warm, for all that. It's full of the nostalgia of things-asthey-used-to-be. And as they could be again.

It's a sidewalk world. The boulevardiers are out in force. Snow narrows up the walking space. The paths are cozy. You have to say "Excuse me" as you pass others going in the opposite dirction.

And you learn so many things as you walk the 4 miles, all the way home.

LOVE IN BLOOM

Love, for example, blooms in a driving snowstorm. Your know that, for sure.

Do you believe that people draw hearts in the fleeting snow, shot through with an arrow and labeled with initials like "E.R" and "W.M."

You do, indeed, because you see them there on Connecticut Avenue, just above R.

Gentle flakes, silent and growing deeper, soften the outlines of those sentimental graven hearts. Soon they'll give way to a bland, poker-faced billow of white.

But they prove while they're still there that walkers in love were out this night, thrilled, no doubt, as you are by a city miraculously changed and made better.

All the usual hetic quests are forgotten. Nobody even seems to be hurrying home any more. What are all these people doing downtown?

They're window-looking for one thing. The cruise clothes are marvelous this winter.

LABSTER, OYSTERS AND SNOW

And, somehow, flakes of snow are drifting into the display space of Harvey's Restaurant. There they nestle among the bright red lobsters, unshucked oysters and the usual garnish of tomatoes—intruders in a work of art.

As you walk you wonder.

Why is the city different.

How has six inches of snow changed it so much?

Tire chains of a passing taxi tinkle an answer. The muffled rasp of a distant snow shovel add a word or two.

The city's reborn, they seem to say.

It's a place for people again. It's smaller.

It's cleaner.

It's quieter.

It's snug and bright.

It's fun to walk things just echoes of other words you've been hearing lately? That downtown should be refashioned in scale for walking human beings?

A tougher stretch is ahead—the hill from Florida avenue to California street. Here the sidewalk disappears altogether. But soon you're up the hill, and on your street.

As you reach your house, after those four miles, a real surprise. Your neighbour, Dr. Stone, is shoveling a path across your sidewalk.

Good cities make good neighbours. That figures, too, you guess.

INVESTIGATIVE REPORTING

Public Service Journalism

Andy Knott, a hard-driving six-footer with the energy of a threshing machine, became an investigative reporter of the Chicago Tribune soon after his graduation from the University of Tennessee. For three months, he worked undercover as an Emergency Medical Technician for five private ambulance companies in Chicago. Then he wrote a six-part series for the Tribune entitled Ambulances—Unsafe at Every Turn," Which disclosed scandalously poor maintenance of may private ambulances and widespread abuse of patients. The result major reforms, made mandatory by new state and city laws and regulations.

Andy Knott's campaign, based on his own investigative reporting under the guidance of the Tribunes seditors, is one example of the manner in which public service journalism works in the United States. Others of major importance have been a campaign by the Charlotte (North Carolina) Observer against brown lung disease, created by the cotton dust that is responsible for the deaths of thousands of textile workers; the Nashville Tennessean's crusade against a resurgent Ku Klux Klan, based on undercover work by a reporter who became a Klan member, and the Philadephia Inquirer's campaign against the reckless disposal of hazardous waste chemical products.

There are many others of current interest in which newspapers, both large and small, have taken unpopular positions based on principle and carried out investigations against the angry objections of powerful adversaries. The record shows, as well, that the broadcast medial also are going into the field with signal results, as the popularity of the CBS programme 60 Minutes demonstrates.

How Campaigns Begin Many campaigns are quite deliberately planned to meet a long-felt community need. Others develop naturally out of news breaks that point to the probability of dangerous abuses. Often, they come about by accident, as witness the following:

A woman wrote a letter of protest to the Detroit News, touching off its campaign to free four men who had been wrongfully convicted of murder in New Mexico. A congrssional secretary confided her woes to a symathetic stranger satd next to her on a bus, who happened to be a Washington Post reporter, and who proceeded to break the congressional sex scandals. A photographre in Buffalo happened to take a picture of a city truck unloading supplies at a private contracting job, thus revealing a major municipal scandal that rocked City Hall. A penciled notation on a card, found by a reporter for the Seattle Times, resulted in clearing a University of Washington professor of charges of Communist activity. A wrinkeld news paper clipping about an Air Force lieutenant who was losing his commission because some of his relatives were left-wing sympathizers led to a great television expose by Edward R Murrow.

A few campaigns, usually the most exciting of all, are brought about by the reporters themselves who delve into a suspicious situation long before their editors are aware of it and, in effect, commit the paper to a public service campaign. This was the story of the Watergate investigation of the Washington Post, brought about by Bob Woodward and Carl Bernstein. It was also the way Andy Knott's campaign bgan against ambulance dangers in Chicago, although in his case the ditors grabbed up his idea quickly and supported it.

The Ambulance Story. Knott had been pitching several investigative ideas at his boss, Bernard Judge, the Chicago editor of the Tribune, from the time he joined the staff. Finally, Knott came up with a proposal to look into the private ambulance operation, which had brought a Pulitzer Prize a decade previously to William Jones, then a Tribune investigative reporter and now the magazine editor. The plan was to take another close look at a much-criticized service, and both Jones and Judge approved it.

The first thing Knott had to do was to qualify for certification as an emergency medical technician (EMT). Under Illinois law, this meant more than 100 hous of classroom work at a local junior college, three hours of field training and at least 10 hours of work in a hospital emergency room. The reporter completed the course successfully.

Support by the Paper. The most important factor Knott had going for him was the full support of a powerful paper. It meant—win, lose or draw—that he would never be defenseless. If he was hurt, he would be cared for. If he got into legal trouble, he would be defended. There was no advance guarantee that he'd find anything wrong-the ration of successful investigations to failures is about one in five in the United States—but he knew that a washout wouldn't cripple his carrer. He was just beginning.

Was there personal danger? He didn't know. But he realized that it would be no fan riding a racing ambulance through heavy traffic. There were risks and they were a part of the job.

Under the guidance of William Reckentwald, a senior Tribune investigator who also had worked on the original story, Knott took these additional steps while he was studying to be an EMT:

1. Examined ambulance company records in Springfield, the state capital, and learned that the private firms billed the state $2 million a year in the Chicago area.
2. Checked into Dun & Bradstreet corporate records.
3. Reviewed records of suits in United States Tax Court in Washington Federal court in Chicago and Cook Country Circuit Court.
4. Made himself familiar with all state and local laws bearing on private ambulances, emergency vehicles and good samaritan laws.
5. Used his first name, Tom, to put together a background as Tom Knott of Georgia, plus references that weren't

> checked; obtained a "hard card," (chauffeur's license) plus the necessary certification from the Illinois Department of Public Health and the Chicago Board to Health.

Then knott wrote of his employment:

> I got a job at the first place I applied and was working on an ambulance less than a week after I first walked in the door. I stayed there about a week and a half. The company was reputable and we used it as a benchmark to judge other companies.
>
> The second company, where I stayed three weeks, was located on and served the South Side of town. I alternated north, south and west to reduce the risk of running into people from other companies.
>
> Quitting one job and moving to the next was not always accomplished with the greatest of ease. It was easy to get a job, for sure, but it was hard to just up and quit The hours were exhausting. Most EMTs in Chicago work 60 hours a week, ten hours a day, six days a week. In all, I worked more than 400 hours. After each day, I would return home and write a long memo on the day's activities. These were painfully detailed memos and added up to more than 250 pages by the time I started writing my six-part series.

It was unusual, to say the least, for so young and relatively inexperienced a reporter to be put on a major assignment of this character. But, in the Woodward Bernstein manner, it all worked. Knott recalled:

> Although I wanted to do this story very much. I was not quite prepared for the loneliness of the task. Because I was considered young and green,

> my editors were very concerned about my I performance. When the investigation began, only five people knew of it. When I went undercover, I just disappeared from the office. My peers at the Tribune knew I was doing an investigation but they didn't know what it was absout. I had very, few people to talk over my problems and concerns with and, to make matters even tougher, I was under strict orders to limit my social life severely. The editors were afraid bar talk might get me into trouble.

Writing the Story. It all turned out well. Knott did all his six articles before the series went into print. With all his findings and his background of investigation, this is how he led off his first story.

> I'm exhausted after a long, tense day of high-speed ambulance riding through the streets of Chicago.
>
> This day began at 7 a.m. when we finally limp back to the garage 13 hours and two ambulances later, we have no beacon lights, no siren, no power steering, no shock absorbers. The brakes are in terrible shape.
>
> My partner, Bob, who is driving, isn't doing much better. He stopped twice to drink beer today and he says he's "popping" Valium to keep going.
>
> At one point, I thought I'd be killed. With a beer can in one hand and the other on the wheel, he almost lost control of the ambulance as we wove at high speed down a South Side street.
>
> We were "running hot" at the time—lights flashing and siren blaring—even though it was a

non-emergency call, I don't know how last we were going. The speedometer didn't work.

On this day also saw fraud and theft. And I can't foreget how we terrifet the lunchtime crowds as we zipped down busy Michigan Avenue on the wrong side of the street.

I'm expecting more of the same tomorrow and I'm not sure how much anger I can take it.

Today was by no means my worst day. What I've described happened again and again in the 500 hours. I worked undercover as a certified emergency medical technician (EMT) or five of the city's private ambulance services.

Many of the ambulances are dangerous. In my three months on the, our service to the sick and injured was rarely efficient or safe.

The poor condition of many.ambulances was the most immediate mass fault we discovered. The Chicago Board of Health is required to inspect them annually. That check is no more than a.

But so many elements of ambulance service are bad that it's hard to say what is the "worst". The problems, which will be examined in detail in subsequent articles, include the following.

Vehicle condition: Tires were bad. Brakes were mushy. Safety lights and signals didn't work.

Some ambulances had structural damage or body corrosion. Rain leaked through the roof; road prime came through holes in the floor.

One ambulance I worked in caught fire from a short circuit in the writing while we were carrying a patient. Another fish-tailed and nearly rolled over because its shock absorbers were shot. Another had 3 to 4 inches of play in the steering wheel, making accurate steering difficult.

Patient care, Patients in private ambulances were cursed, threatened and subjected to rough treatment. A mental patient was allowed to wander unattended. Another had bronchial trouble but was subjected to an EMT's cigarette smoke.

Worst of all was the time when we were transferring an ill man from a hospital to a nursing home and an EMT told me "if his heart arrests, don't do anything. Let his dies if his heart stops in the ambulance, just don't tell me.."

Equipment condition: Ambulances I worked in were usually short of bandages, sterile water to cleanse wounds, gauze, oxygen, splints and neck braces. One didn't have any first rate linen.

Soiled linen was used repeatedly. Some ambulances did not carry fire extinguishers or oxygen tanks, both required by the city, or spare tires.

It took an extra 30 minutes to get a woman with a ruptured stomach lining to a hospital because we didn't have a stair chair to get her down a narrow stairway.

Running Hot: Private ambulances consistently run hot, with lights and sirens going, when there is no emergency. On runs I made, it might have been necessary only one time of every five times we did it. At other times, lives were needlessly endangered.

> The practice resulted in the death of a 19 year old EMT in September after he'd been on the job only two weeks. The ambulance he was riding in and a car collided at a Park Ridge intersection and the ambulance rolled over. Police said the ambulance was running hot on a non-emergency call.
>
> EMT attitudes: Most EMTs in Chicago are underpaid, ($3.50 an hour is typical) or they work on a piecework basis, which foraces them into a frantic pace. The quality of care suffers as EMTs, brutalized by the system, transfer their frustrations to patients.
>
> Though I saw some good EMTs at work, too many were inept. One didn't even know how to take blood pressure readings.
>
> Nothing in my training fully prepared me for what I saw....

Results. Once the Tribune's series ended, changes were swiftly instituted. Governor James R. Thompson signed a bill into law in September 1981, making it mandatory for every ambulance in the state public and private—to undergo inspection twice a year. The Chicago City Council at the same time moved to righten local inspection and regulation laws affecting private and public ambulances. EMT training also was required of ambulance company dispatchers.

The campaign was a classic instance of cooperative effort between a young reporter, directed by knowledgeable editors, and public authorities who acted decisively as soon as the results of a newspaper investigation were brought to their attention.

An Investigation of Local Industry

It requires courage, clout and a lot of money to take on a dominant industry, on which the prosperity of a whole region of the country depends. This is what the Charlotte Observer did when it investigated the incidence of byssionsis, or brown lung, the disease caused by inhalation of cotton dust.

The Observer was well aware at the outset that the powerful textile industry, largest in the Carolinas, would fight its inquiry and its findings.

But more than 391,500 Carolinians work in the textile industry, one third of them in plants that process cotton. At the time the series was published, 18,000 Carolina workers had been disabled by cotton dust, but only some 320 had received compensation.

This was a typical reaction from one of the leaders of the $17 billion industry, W.B. Pitts, president of Hermitage, Inc., who wrote:

How shameful it is for the Knight family and its organ, the Observer, to take the side of OSHA and the oppressive bureaucrats against the magnificent southern textile industry: It is sickening to see the gutless minions of the news media siding with a few crybaby Americans who obviously are looking for a handout from the very hand that fed and clothed their families.

Taking the Public's Side. Nevertheless, the Observer continued its long inquiry, in which 15 members of its staff participated, and blasted open its campaign against brown lung disease. This is the lead on a summary of the 22 articles. It was written by a staffer, Bob Drogin, who then was 27 and had only been on the paper for three years.

> Cotton dust is a killer in Carolina mills.
>
> Already 18,000 Carolina workers are disabled by byssinosis, or brown lung, the lung disease cotton dust causes. Only about 320 have received compensation.
>
> Now six years after the officials oredered mills to clean up, about 115,000 of the Carolinas'

391,500 textile workers remain exposed to dust in cotton mills. Health officials say at least 10,000 North Carolinians still work in dust levels that can kill.

It is a case of deadly neglect.

According to the last week's Observer series on brown lung in the Carolinas:

* At least five textile companies didn't tell some workers they had been diagnosed with brown lung.

* Companies have contested 80% of the 936 North Carolina brown lung compensation claims and virtually all of about 200 South Carolian claims.

* Both industrial commissions have ignored state laws requiring companies to report on workers diagnosed with occupational diseases such as byssinosis. The North Carolina Commission has violated its own rules by approving company written agreements in which workers forfeited all future claims.

* The commissions have approved compensation in only about 320 of 1,136 claims filed. Settlements often didn't cover lost wages and medical expenses. Some workers died waiting for compensation.

* Some doctors who advise the commissions on brown lung cases also see patients for textile companies; one former South Carolina medical panel member was a consultant for two textile firms...

The End of a Campaign Editor Richard A. Oppel recalled that within less than a year after the series ran, North Carolina textile workers had received $4 million in compensation for byssinosis, more than had been paid out in the previous nine years. And one mill worker in South Carolina, disabled by brown lung, was awarded $86,000 compensation.

Commission files in both states were opened to the public in response to the Observer's editorial pressure. The North Carolina Labor Commission increased its inspection staff by 11 people and the state's Industrial Commission put on three additional deputies to speed up compensation decisions.

The campaign won for the Observer the Pulitzer Prize gold medal for meritorious public service. The jorors called it an example "of how a newspaper can effectively and dramatically use its editorial resources to expose and draw public attention to an important and previously ignored problem — in this case a disease that disables and kills thousands of workers."

Exposing the Ku Klux Klan

J.W. Thompson, a career Army man who took early diability retirement as a sergeant and earned his living as a cabinet-maker, was a member of the Ku Klux Klan for a year. When he quit, he resumed his true identity, Jerry Thompson, an investigative reporter, and wrote a series of articles on his experiences for his newspaper, the Nashville Tennessean.

It was a courageous thing to do. As John Seigenthaler, publisher of the Tennessean, wrote some months after the Thompson series was published, "Jerry Thompson always was in danger of discovery and lives today under police protection."

Inside the Klan. This was how Thompson wrote the lead for his Klan series:

> The Ku Klux Klan today holds a strange, disturning attration for frustrated, fearful middle-

> income men and women—and a dangerous potential for violence and terror.
>
> I know, For the last year, I have been a Klansman. I have worn the white robe and hood. I have twice taken the oath pledging my life to the Klan. I have twice been "naturalized" into separate Klan empires. I have paid my Klan initiation fees and my Klan dues.
>
> I have fired Klan crosses, collected contributions at Klan roadblokcs, marched in Klan street demonstrations and helped disrupt public order at a public meeting with shouts in a Klan chorus. I have attended KKK den meetings where men armed with pistols and automatic rifles mounthed their routine racist rhetoric: "The niggers and the Jews are ruining the country."
>
> Clad in Klan garments, I have picketed the President of the United States, demonstrated against a TV station showing a documentary about the KKK, and been jeered by black citizens. And I have concealed the pistol of an ungarbed fellow Klansman beneath my flowing robes when he thrust it at me as a policeman approached.
>
> Through it all I was acting out a role—working as an investigative reporter for the Tennessean, striving to discover just how dangerous the Klan is, endeavoring to penetrate the secrecy veil that has obsured much of the Klan's life since its founding in Pulaski, Tenn., more than a century ago...

The Findings. These were Thompson's conclusions buttressed **by an independent outside investigation by other Tennessean reporters and a photographer:**

1. The Klan must be disarmed. Many Klansmen routinely carry guns on their public marches and demonstrations. State and federal laws need to be strengthened so that police can deal with this growing threat of violence.

2. The Invisible Empire of the Ku Klux Klan, headed by Bill Wilkinson of Denham Springs, La., grows more dangerous each day, with a paramilitary training camp near Cullman. This militant faction of the Klan, of which I am a member, bears close scrutiny by the authorities. The Justice Department agrees and has asked federal agencies to cooperate in an effort to combat the danger of violence posed by Wilkinson's group.

3. The rival Klan faction, of which I am also a member, the Knights of the Ku Klux Klan, headed by Don Black of Birmingham, is less militant because it is losing members. Still, its wizard, Black, is vehemently anti-Semitic and equally hostile to blacks. A Texas branch of this Klan also operates a paramilitary training team.

Unhappily, despite the expose, very little has been done either to disarm the Klan, close its training camps or reduce the threat of violence. But the Tennessean and Seigenthaler, its publisher, have never regretted going into the investigation. Nor has Thompson been sorry that he gave a year of his life to the inquiry.

A TV Investigation

Because television is a visual medium and TV reporters work under severe limitations of time, the investigative job for TV has to be done differently. A two-part series on space weaponry by David Andelman, which was broadcast on successive nights on The CBS Evening News with Dan Rather, illustrates the essential points of difference.

Beginning an Investigation. As was the case with Andy Knott's investigation of ambulances for the Chicago Tribune, David Andelman developed the idea for his CBS investigation. He wrote:

> This series grew out of some reading I'd been doing on this subject as much as a year before. At the time of the launch of the first space shuttle, I became further intrigued with the uses of military shuttles that were to follow, all of which were shrouded in the deepest secrecy. Looking into the uses of the military space shuttles led me to the much broader question of the nature and use of space weaponry.

CBS Evening Ncws liked the idea and Alan Weisman was assigned as producer.

Investigating a Top-Secret Subject. Andelman went on:

> We began by extensive phone work while a researcher dug up everything published on this subject over the past couple of years (much of which turned out to be somewhat unreliable). In the course of our phoning, we realized that the issue was extremely broad, but potentially far more serious than we had thought. Weapons decisions taken quietly today appeared likely to be nearly irreversible, committing the U.S. and by corollary the Soviet Union to MX-type missile programmes perhaps 10 years down the pike.
>
> We decided, therefore, to outline a three-part series (this way ultimately reduced to two parts), then sat down to figure out whom we should talk with on camera (of 25-30 people we had consulted by phone or in person). We settled on six key interviews. I took off across the country to do them (two were in Washington, three in California, one in Boston). Weisman began to work up a series of graphics that were, after all, the heart of the piece, and he rounded up obscure

footage of some of these weapon prototypes in action.

I shipped back the interviews as they were done, Weisman transcribed them, looking for the best "sound-bites. " By the time I had returned to New York, he had already sketched out an outline of the two parts (where the sound would go, the graphics, etc.) we began work on the detailed scripts. We had been consulting by phone in the evenings after each interview.

The scripts must have go through five or six drafts, each draft being pared down (with 22 minutes in the CBS Evening News, our early drafts would have eaten up a third of each show) We then spent a day doing the very complex on camera bridges (shot with two cameras in the main control room of the Evening New's we used it a sa "set," the computer graphic animations we had prepared rolling on the main monitor behind me as I began talking).

Both pieces were finally screened for the executives of the CBS Evening News and Dan Rather, too. Dan made some very useful suggestions on where both pieces could be trimmed, there were some negotiations back and forth, and finally both pieces ran on consecutive evenings.

Broadcasting the Investigation. The first of the two Andelman pieces on space weaponry was in effect a primer on space weapons, what they are, how they may be used. The "lightning bolt"—a laser beam of intense light—was one of the potential weapons included, but there were others just as exotic. The principle, however, was to introduce the millions of viewers of the CBS Evening News to a complex subject that was going to cost taxpayers a lot of money—much more than most of them realized.

Here is the audio part of the second piece, with the graphics and other illustrations in the video part of the script omitted:

RATHER: Speaking of missiles, the Defense Department has just sent Congress its so—called "definitaive report" about research into direct energy weapons, particularly laser weapons. The report is classified, but sources tell CBS News it recommends increased funding to determine just how effective lasers could be against a variety of targets. As David Andelman reports in Part Two of his investigation into the movement toward militarization of outer space, firing lightening bolts through the atmosphere is an idea whose time is coming—rapidly.

DAVID ANDELMAN: Since the early I 960s, the United States has been developing lasers for use by the military. Prototypes have destroyed revolving targets, and airborne targets, and have even been installed in planes for air-to-air combat. But using a laser to fire at a target in space presents some different problems. A land-based laser firing at an orbiting satellite would need huge power and clear skies to hit its target. Without sufficient energy and the large mirrors needed for aiming, the beam would disperse as it passes through the clouds and end up too weak to effect the target. But a laser in space with enough power and precise aiming could conceivably hit a Soviet ICBM as the ascending missile broke through the clouds.

FFOBERT FOSSUM (Defense Research Project Agency): Specifically, we would have in orbit a sequence of lower-altitude battle stations, say on the order of 20, or that order of magnitude number of of battle stations. At anyone time, several of these would be within visible range and laser-weapon range of a mass attack. A taraget assignment would be given. One must then acquire on the battle station that particular target, then track the target because both the target and the battle station are moving.

The laser would not fire at the missile's warhead. The beam would lock on to the second stage, the booster, bathing it with intense light, heating it during the ascent and before the warhead has a chance to arm itself.

SENATOR MALCOLM WALLOP (R-Wyoming): I honestly believe, from what I have seen with my own eyes, that we could put together and orbit this prototype satellite within the next four to five years.

ANDELMAN: But the skeptics abound. They say the idea is far more costly than supporters think, that conventional weapons could do the job just as well, and that the Russians could simply harden their missiles or trick the lasers into firing at the wrong targets.

WOLFGANG PANOFSKY (Stanford Research Laboratory): You can deploy deceptive screens and alternate targets which fool the sensors and/or serosol sprays which hit the target. You can do all sorts of things with very little weight.

ANDELMAN: Nevertheless, companies like TRW, Rocketdyne, Hughes and United Technologies are hard at work perfecting the mirror's tracking system and energy sources for the battle stations. Funding for laser technology now runs about $200 million a year. But the Defense Department, in a top-secret report to Congress, is now requesting an additional $250 million over the next five years.

The Soviets too are spending a lot of time and a lot of money developing directed-energy weapons. But there is no hard evidence that they are any closer to an operational system than the United States. And as research of all sorts continues, so does the crucial. question: is the dawn of space weaponry the end of the old arms race or merely the beginning of a new one?

FOSSUM: We have avoided for various policy and national reasons the idea that we should go to space with weapons systems. It is almost investible in my mind that we will have to consider going to space with weapon systems at some time in the not-too-distant future.

WILLIAM PERRY (former undersecretary of Defense): I think it would be an extremely desirable objective for the United States to try to nip this space war in the bud, to stop it before it starts. It is still early enough to do that. Now, four or five years from now the Opportunity to stop it may be gone. That is, the advances made by both nations by then may be so great that it is a clock whose hands cannot be turned back any longer.

ANDELMAN: We're really at a crossroads right now.
PERRY: I think we are. I think we are.

ANDELMAN: In accepting the Albert Einstein Peace Prize recently, George Kennan, one time U.S. ambassador to Moscow, remarked that the arms race had reached such grotesque dimensions as to defy rational understanding. The Soviets and the United States, he added, are like victims of some sort of hypnosis, men in a dream, like lemmings headed for the sea. And perhaps he might have added out into space.

The Mirage Bar Story

The investigative art is by no means confined to men, although they are usually given the fattest assignments and the most prominent roles. The great exception is Pam Zekman, the Chicago Sun Times's crack investigative reporter, who has run a dozen major inquires with dramatic results. She was the proprietor of the Mirage Bar, which was run by Sun Times reporters to prove that thieves sell stolen goods with impunity. The accumulated the evidence and brought about major reforms in the city's penal system. Although it is taken for granted that reporters will adopt disguises for good reason to obtain necessary results, always with the consent of their paper, the Mirage Bar story didn't with a Pulitzer Prize because some of the board members thought it was "too deceptive."

This raises the issue in journalism of where righteousness ends, in adopting a disguise, and where unethical deception begins. It always has to be decided on a case by case basis by the news organization involved, and there are no set rules by which to judge such a moral issue. In the Mirage Bar case. however, Zekman certainly lost no prestige, in fact, she and here colleagues did win a number of prize and industry wide accolades.

Other women who have done first rate work on investigations, and who have shared Pulizer Prizes include Ann deSantis of the Boston Globe, Lucinda Franks of UPI and Myrta JJ. Pulliam of the Indianapolis Star. The evidence is abundant, regardless of disguises, that women investigators do their jobs with as much skill and spirit as men.

The Bolles Case

The case of Don Bolles of the Arizona Republic should serve as a constant reminder to all journalists both of the dedication and the courage that are required of investigative reporters who venture into dangerous situations. The reaction to his muder in downtown Phoenix, while he was on the trackk of gangland connections with official Arizona, should also serve as an inspiration.

After Bolles was killed, 36 reporters and editors from different news organizations came to Arizona and many of them spent up to six months in the state, under the leadership of Bob Greene of Newsday, to try to finish the work that the Arizonan had begun. It was a unique cooperative ~ffort, financed in part by most of the 20 news organizations that were represented, to show that no investigative reporter could be harassed or slain without inviting the most serious consequences.

The series of articles produced by the Investigative Reporters and Editors Inc., as the group called itself; was published and broadcast in whole or in pan by a number of the participating organizations, but not in Bolle's own paper. The charges of links between buşiness and politics and organized crime in Arizona, in a number of instances, bore out allegations that he had first made.

Campaign Objectives

It used to be said that the primary objective of most campaigns was to put wrong dores in jail and get innocent persons out of jail. These, naturally, are the most spectacular results of campaigning. But there are many others, as this discussion has made abundantly clear. It sometimes happens that without any decalred intent, a major public service is performed because a news organization and its staff do their work of informing the public under extreme difficulties and in superlative fashion. This often occurs in the coverage of natural disasters or civil disorders. It results occassionally wh‸n a reporter, out of sheer conviction, risks life and limbto get story that can be obtained in no other way.

In some campaigns, the news stories are quite factual and restrained in tone but the alarm is sounded on the editorial page with thunderous emphasis. This was the case in the successful effort of the Winston-Salem (North Carolina) Journal and Sentinel to prevent strip miners from tearing apart the beautiful hill country of northwest North Carolina. One of the major editorials took this approach:

> The rolling hills and valleys in northwest North Carolina are among the most beautiful any Where. But the land in Ashe, Alleghany, Wilkes ans Surry counties won't be beautiful much longer if strip-mining gets a foothold in the area.
>
> Strip-mining might get that foothold if land-owners and concerned citizens in the norathwest aren't careful. The Gibbsite Corporation of America, which has obtained options on thousands of acres in the northwest and in southwest Virginia, is conducting studies to see if gibbsite—a mineral found in the area—can be extracted easily and cheaply from the soil for use in producing aluminum. If the studies prove that strip mining would be profitable, Gibbsite apparently will exercise its options...
>
> One weapon against an unwelcome intruder is a public outcry. Such a protest helped Orange County keep Texas Gibbsite think twice.
>
> If the people of the northwest should allow stripmining to get a substantial foothold and if

> large parts of that scenic country side become a virtual wasteland in a decade or so, they will have nobody to blame but themselves.

The point cannot be overemphasized. If a campaign is to mean anything, it must be undertaken with vigor and supported by the resources of the entire newspaper—from Page 1 to editorial, from pictures to cartoons.

This is something that few broadcasters have learned to date in their laudable efforts to emulate the crusading press; it is one thing to do an effective documentary, it is quite another to arouse the public without the editorial intervention of the management itself.

Does Campaigning Pay? There have been few campaigns of consequence that have added substantially to the circulation of a newspaper becomes as wealthy almost overnight as Woodward and Bernstein.

The record shows depressing instances in which campaigners for worthy causes in the press and broadcast media have lost circulation and advertising, become the targets for boycotts and even lost their jobs. The expose is not the royal road to success, by any means.

The Arkansas Gazette paid for its championship of school intergration in Little Rock with heavy monetary losses and the eventual resignation of its editor, Harry Ashmore. Several newspapers that ran campaigns against unscrupulous used car dealers lost automobile advertising. And in a classic case, the Wall Street Joumal lost its General Motors advertising becuase it published information about new models before the auto giant was ready; however, GMJ soon came back into the paper.

One discouraged small-city editor, who tried and failed with a perfectly good campaign, even thought of giving up crusading altogether because it was so little appreciated. And J. Montgomery Curtis, while director of the American Press Institute, once came across and old Marine editor who refused point-blank to have anything to do with a campaign to improve his community, saying "Son, the durn town ain't worth it."

True, crusading isn't easy. Nor can anything of consequence in a community be accomplished quickly or cheaply merely by viewing with alarm. Most campaigns are won simply by hard, consistent work, backed by a determined editor and publisher. Such was the case in the Lousivilee Courier-Journal's drive to tighten Kentucky's laws against strip-mining, which took four years before the Kentucky legislature finally passed what was then called "the toughest strip-mining legislature in America." More often than not, even a modest crusade takes a good deal longer than either editors or reporters anticipate at the outset.

The issue is not whether crusading joumalism pays but whether it is necessary. The answer must be overwhelmingly yes.

Toward the Future

If anything at all is certain about the concluding years of the 20th century and the opening of the twenty first, it is that American society will undergo drastic changes and journalism will have to reflect them. In no sense can it be said that social and economic pressures on this nation are likely to decrease; the outlook is quite the opposite. Even such necessary and long-delayed political reforms as government consolidation, an equitable taxing system and the elimination of towering injustices in the treatment of the sick and the needy, helpless children and the elderly may have a chance of success.

The nation will have need of a more efficient and broadened system for the dissemination of news, ideas and opinions. What we are seeing today in the adaptation of newspapers and wire services to the computer age and the development of the electronic media is only the beginning of the changes that are ahead for journalism. It is useless to speculate on whether there will be giant screens for TV across our living room walls, instant production of newspapers in the basement whenever we want them or production of voluminous statistics from distant data banks at the touch of a finger. The genius of science, interacting with the laws of supply and demand, will determine how much instant journalism we can live, what form it will take and how much we can actually absorb.

There are several things that are more important to the journalist than research and development, much as they are needed in a profession that has been backward for too long in such matters. The first and greatest of these is the continued protection of the freedoms guaranteed in the First Amendment, which are under increasing challenge in times of social change and worldwide political upheaval. For without a free press, the journalist becomes a mouthpiece for government, a lackey of the powerful, a robot who performs mindless duties in a graceless style.

While it is a temporary relief to have the United States Supreme Court strike down judicial gag orders and other prior restraints on publication, no journalist can feel secure if reporters sit in jail in violation of judicial orders to disclose their sources to the authorities and act, in fact, as servants of the government. It is a disturbing, even a threatening trend.

Second only to the perpetuation of the rights of a free press is a reconsideration of the substance of journalism. And that bears upon the preparation and the beliefs of those who are intimately concerned with the identification, gathering, distribution and presentation of the news. Because, whatever definition may be offered, news actually tends to be what the journalist says it is. And the current defintion of what the journalist treats as news is simply not good enough. Television and radio will have to be something more than glorified bulletin boards; newspapers; wire services and news magazines will be obliged to shape their reports to a greater extent towards areas that more deeply affect the public interest.

Finally, journalism must stand for something if it is to continue to be respected in a democratic society and given constitutional protection it is enough to be the harbinger of bad tidings; in primitive societies, such messengers were killed and journalists, in modern times, have frequently felt the sting of public animus merely because they did their duty. No less than the holding of public office, the difficult task of informing the public is a trust. It is therefore inevitable that the concept of journalism as a public service is bound to increase in strength. Today, it is a trend. Tomorrow, it will be a necessity.

Important Salient Features of Campaigning and Investigative Reporting

1. Campaigns must have the wholehearted support of the news organization—newspaper or magazine or broadcasting station—or reporters will find themselves helpless to continue. Even though one reporter may be the main investigator, the whole organization must give the inquiry its backing. And if legal trouble results, the reporter must have a proper defense, supported by the management.
2. Campaigns based on the premise that the press in the watchdog over the public's business should show results. If there is a need for an inquiry, however, it should be undertaken whether there is any advance guarantee of results or not.
3. Reporters undertaking investigations of crime or suspicious organizations are always in personal danger and they and their editors must realize it. Don Bolles of the Arizona Republic was murdered during his crime inquiry. Jerry Thompson of the Nashville Tennessean remained under police guard for a long time after he became a Klan member for a year and then wrote an expose.
4. It is manifestly true that not every campaign or investigation that is undertaken will pay off in a dramatic way. The radio of success to failure is about one in five in the United States.

5. TV investigations, because of the visual nature of the medium, usually take a lot longer to complete than newspaper inquiries. On network TV, with the exception of special programmes like 60 Minutes, the time allowed for national coverage is relatively modest. TV reporters usually have to do a much tighter job of writing than their colleagues in print.

6. The substance of many an investigation is based on examinations of public documents such as land sales, tax records and court actions. The objective, in examining such data, is to determine first of all if there is a pattern of suspicious circumstances that might indicate wrong doing. If the pattern exists, it should be followed up with a detailed inquiry.

7. A campaign or an investigative report should be written in a caim, restrained manner. This is not the place for hype. The lead ought to indicate broadly the nature of the inquiry and the prinicpal results, the reason the investigation was undertaken, the length of the inquiry and the participants.

8. Whether campaigns are undertaken in the public or private sector, they ought to be so fashioned and so directed as to serve the public interest. In most investigations, both news organizations and reporters will find it to their benefit to work with prosecuting authorities. Except when the prosecutor's office itself is involved in an investigation, it seldom helps to fight the people who will eventually have to decide whether sufficient evidence exists for criminal charges.

ELECTIONS REPORTING

Journalism and Social Science

If all editors have not hailed the development with hosannahs, and if all journalists have not hurled themselves headlong into the breaking statistical waves, that is only characteristic of the innate skepticism of the profession. However, progress is being made.

There are, throughout the land, a modest number of reporters who have the qualifications to conduct a reliable scientific study of public opinion, who are adept at analyzing masses of statistical data and who are not afraid to work with computers and learn computer language. There are, as well, an increasing number of editors who are willing to employ them, news organizations that use their work regularly and sophisticated public officials and business and industrial leaders who know how to evaluate polling results.

Whom Do Polls Influence? Social science has shown us that, except in cases where public opinion is almost evenly divided, polls in and of themselves seldom can make perceptible changes in the mass mind. This is, of course, also true of much editorial opinion published in newspapers and newsmagazines and broadcast locally or by the networks. What polls can do in the vast majority of cases, is to reinforce opinions that are strongly held.

Whom, then, do polls influence mainly? As nearly all responsible social scientists agree, the people who commission polling research are the ones who are most likely to change their opinions and their public positions to conform to the public opinion findings. This is more true, naturally, of the vendors of commercial products than of others. And yet many a political leader and nearly all recent American presidents have been powerfully influenced by the findings of their private poll-takers.

While the "bandwagon vote" conjured up by James A. Farley has little substance—even though the old master of the first two Franklin Roosevelt presidential campaigns fervently believed in it—many a politician still clings to the notion that last-minute voters will flock to his or her standard just to "ride with a winner." And they try by every conceivable device to create the impression that they are certain winners.

The main reason for this exercise in atmospherics is to keep wealthy corporations, individuals and labour unions in a mood to continue to make large financial contributions to particular campaigns. Senator Hubert Horatio Humphrey was convinced to the end of his days that a California Field Poll, which showed Jimmy Carter ahead by 25 percent before the California Democratic primary of 1976, prematurely dried up contributions and crippled a last minute TV effort in the state by the Humphrey forces. Humphrey lost the primary by less than 5 percent.

Where the polls do have an enormous influence on voters is in the network projections of winners, based in part on the random sampling of voters' choices gathered immediately after they cast their ballots. In the 1980 presidential Carter conceded defeat while the polls on the Pacific Coast were still open. The result, according to most reliable political estimates, was that a certain number of voters didn't even go to the polls in that area. Although this could not have changed the outcome of the presidential election, it could have had an effect on other close races in states in the Pacific time zone.

Polls: Their Nature. It is not in politics alone that poll-taking is of importance. The Nielsen ratings, to a very large extent, determine what we see on television. Nielsen and other commercial poll-takers are well into the critical surveys of whether old products should be changed or withdrawn and whether new products can be sold.

Polls also are taken on every conceivable subject. Within a few days in a recent year, poll-takers covered these issues.

* An Opinion Research Corporation Poll showed 75 percent of respondents mistrust big business.
* A Harris survey showed 62 percent of respondents mistrust big government.
* A United States Census Bureau study indicated that American women will continue to outnumber men for the rest of this century.
* A New York Daily News Poll determined 77 percent of respondents had lost trust in public officials.

* And a Los Angeles Times survey disclosed that most jurors in a poll were against judicial press gags.

That was, by the way, only a small sampling of the American news media.

The Researchers. It merely proves, if proof were needed, that the public opinion survey and social statistical analyses have become the basis for a major industry.

Within a little more than a generation, the news media, the universities and the commercial polling organizations have established a formidable network for measuring the frequent and sometimes dizzying shifts in public sentiment. However, it is still true as it was a century ago when Lord Bryce wrote that "the obvious weakness of government by public opinion is the difficulty of ascertaining it." Wide differences of opinion may be caught very quickly, it is true, not when the margin of error approaches 3 percent on either side, most poll-takers agree, however reluctantly, that the acceptable margin of confidence usually has been reached.

No one, therefore, can quarrel with Winston Churchill's celebrated dictum "Nothing is more dangerous than to live in the temperamental atmosphere of a Gallup Poll, always taking one's temperature, There is only one duty, only one safe course, and that is to try to be right and not fear to do or say what you believe to be right."

Two of the pioneering polling organizations still remain in the forefront of public opinion research—George Gallup and his American Institute of Public Opinion and Elmo Roper's organization. Among the other, Louis Harris and Daniel Yankelovich are both prominent and widely used.

Of equal importance are the university research centres and the numerous social science researchers in academe, who are so often sought out to help with the various types of polls and other statistical studies. Among the oldest are the Michigan Survey Research Center and the National Opinion Research Center.

Finally, some of the stronger and wealthier news organizations are doing much of their own work, as witness the rapid adaptation of social science methods by the Knight Ridder Newspapers. Others have joined forces and thereby shared costs as well as services, the CBS News-New York Times polls being one example. Then there are the statewide polls, some going back for many years including the Des Moines Register' s Iowa Poll, the Minneapolis Tribute's Minnesota Poll, the New York Daily New's New York State Poll and the Mervin Field organization 's California Poll.

Measuring Public Opinion

Everybody recognizes the importance of public opinion in an open society but few agree on what it is or how it operates. Nor is it easy to define, even by social scientists.

What is Public Opinion. In a far smaller and less complicated United States nearly a century and a half ago, Alexis de Tocqueville called it the "predominant authority' , that acted by , 'elections and decrees". In a moment of disillusion with the vagaries of the British Public, Sir Robert Peel was less admiring to him, it was "that great compound of folly, weakness, prejudice, wrong feeling, rightfeeling, obstinacy and newspaper paragraphs which is called public opinion." In the early 1920s. Water Lippmann argued that it was "primarily a moralized and codified version of the facts," and that "the pattern of stereotypes at the center of our codes largely determines what group of facts we shall see and in what high we shall see them." In our own time, a social scientist, W. Phillips Davison, has concluded that public opinion should be treated as a "consensus that influences the behaviour of individuals who contribute to the consensus... a form of organization [that] is able to coordinate the thought and action of a large number of people."

Of one thing there is no doubt. Whether it is the "predominant authority." a "great compound of folly," a "pattern of stereotypes, " of a "consensus," the measurement of what is called public opinion has become of transcendent importance in modern mass communications. It forms the basis of much advertising and merchandising practice, determines what shall and shall not be seen on television, locates new enterprises as varied in character as food markets and newspapers, provides trends for the illusion of trends in political campaigns at all levels of government and dominates the coverage of national elections. Journalists have not been able to escape the implications of this expanding activity. It has placed them squarely in the middle of the computer age.

Since newspapers have taken up "precision journalism, " polling assignments have become a part of the regular routine. The Chicago Tribune, for example, has found that nine of 10 persons surveyed in Chicago favoured mandatory hand-gun registration. The Dayton (Ohio) Journal Herald forecast the outcome of a city tax referendum with less than 2 percent error. In a survey of "white flight" to the suburbs as a result of school integration, the Milwaukee journal found that the trend was exaggerated. And the Associated Press, in one of a number of surveys, looked for a relationship between caner death rates and the rate of spending for research.

The Rise of the Pollsters. The practice of poll-taking goes back to 1824 when a Harrisburg Pennsylvanian straw poll indicated Andrew Jackson was ahead in the presidential campaign. Over the course of the next century, such news papers as the Boston Globe and New York Herald conducted street corner polls. And at the beginning of the 20th century, advertisers began experimenting with market surveys, the true forerunner of the modern public opinion poll. The first "social scientific" poll of public opinion was conducted in 1907-1908 by the Pittsburgh Survey, with the support of the Russell Sage Foundation. Another first was the Kansas City Star's quadrennial selection of "sample precincts," from which it would calculate the winner of the presidential election and banner the result soon after the closing of the election booths in the land.

But none of these was as spectacular a success — and failure — as the Literary Digest Poll which began in 1916. For most of the presidential elections through 1932, the Digest sent out postcards to millions of persons and predicted the outcome with reasonable success. By 1935, there was so much concern over polling that a bill was introduced in Congress to prohibit the use of the mails for polls and stop this "vicious practice." The bill failed. But in the same year, Elmo Roper began his poll in Fortune magazine and the first Gallup Poll was issued by George Gallup's newly founded American Institute of Public Opinion.

In the 1936 presidential campaign, the Literary Digest calculated on the basis of more than 2 million postcards received mainly from telephone users and automobile owners, that President Roosevelt would lose to Alfred M. Landon, his Republican challenger, by 42.9 percent of the vote to 57.1 percent. The outcome gave Roosevelt 62.5 percent of the vote, which enabled him to carry 46 of the 48 states. The Digest Poll thereby racked up a polling error of 19.6 percent, the largest ever known for a presidential election, and the magazine went out of business. The Gallup Poll based on a scientific sampling of a few thousand respondents, called the election correctly but itself registered an error of 6.8 percent, larger than any it has since made. Of course the difference between the two was that the Digest sampled only prosperous people in a time of depression, those who had phones and cars, while Gallup reached a better crosssection.

Despite a relatively good record set by Gallup. Roper and other pollsters, the polling industry had to struggle for years to overcome the Digest debacle. Just as it was regaining public confidence, however, it came a cropper in the 1948 presidential election, when President Truman upset the favored Thomas E. Dewey. The picture of a grinning Truman holding up the Chicago Tribune, with a banner headline proclaiming a Dewey victory, is a favourite in every journalistic album ofthe era and one the pollsters will never forget.

In 1948, Gallup was in error by 5.3 percent, Crossley by 4.7 percent and Roper by 8.4 percent and all understated the Democratic vote by these respective amounts. The Social Science Research Council blamed errors of sampling, interviewing and forecasting. Gallup himself argued that he failed because he stopped polling "about 10 to 14 days" before Election Day and thereafter Democrats who had been "leaning" toward Dewey changed their minds. He changed his sampling methods and began polling up to two days before Election Day.

The pollsters had some rough times after the Truman disaster, and some bright moments as well. In the close presidential race between Senator John F. Kennedy and Richard M. Nixon in 1960, both relied heavily on private polling advice, Kennedy on Louis Harris and Nixon on Claude Robinson of the Opinion Research Corp. Kennedy always gave credit to Harris for the findings on which his successful campaign was based. In the 1968 election, last minute Gallup and Harris surveys indicated that there was a trend toward Senator Hubert H. Humphrey, the Democratic candidate, that was reflected in Nixon's narrow victory.

Luck as a Factor. All poll takers are well aware that they ignore the usual 2.5 to 3 percent margin of error in any national survey at their own peril. And this was particularly apparent in the exceedingly close 1976 presidential election, when most major polling organizations came up with predictions of 1 percent or less in favour of jimmy Carter, George Gallup, the dean of pollsters, picked Ford by the same figure. However, Gallup and others covered themselves —pointing to the margin of error and said the election was "too close to call."

The only one daring enough to make an unqualified forecast was Burns Roper, for the Public Broadcasting System, whose final survey Carter 51 percent, Ford 47 percent and the minor candidates 2 percent. He came within 1 percent of complete accuracy, the final vote giving Carter 51 percent, Ford 48 percent and minor candidates 1 percent. Said Reporter "Polling is part science and a helluva lot of human judgments. Fortunately, we made the right ones. "And Gallup commented drily. "The plain fact of the matter is that you have to be lucky. You have to repeal the laws of probability."

Yet, poll-taking and election forecasting have become so deeply imbedded in the American political system—and in American journalism as well- that they have continued to develop despite all setbacks. Their credibility has suffered from time to time, particularly when hired pollsters of some repute issued findings that tended to support the positions of those who paid them. Yet on the whole, this has not seemed to affect their public acceptance.

As a result of their 1976 experience, most poll takers were overly cautions in the 1980 election and called it a tossup, a close election and some even refused to predict a winner because their samplings showed such an even division. The only major poll-taker to break out of this bind was Louis Harris, who went on national TV in the closing hours of the campaign and forecast a large Reagan victory. A few hours after the polls opened, the news leaked out of Washington that Patrick Caddell, President Carter's private poll-taker, had told him that he could not win.

The Reagan landslide was thus a surprise to almost everybody in the polling business except for Ronald Reagan himself and his closest advisers. They had assurance from their private polls that the victory would be theirs and that it would be very large indeed.

Reasons for Forecasts. It may well be asked why the news media go in so heavily for surveys of public opinion with the reporting of politics and government, and elections in particular. One very good reason is that such forecasts, and the basis for them, are a part of the legitimate business of political reporters and their news organizations. An even more compelling reason is that no news organization worthy of the name can act as a mere recording device that plays back speeches and rival claims but does not undertake to evaluate them. When the public asks, "Who's ahead?" the question is worthy of a serious reply by trained reporters commentators.

Polling Techniques

The oldest, least sophisticated and least dependable type of public opinion poll is the reportorial survey in which an editor sends several staff members out to talk to almost anybody they think will give them a good quote. Before the rise of the feminist movement, it used to be called the man-in-the-street poll, and it is still used by editors here and there.

The notion is that any reporter, unschooled in the simplest statistical procedures, can talk to 20 or 30 persons and come up with a valid reflection of the view of the community. Such exercises, no matter how carefully reporters go about their work, come near the truth only by the sheerest accident. The sample has not been picked at random according to the rules of probability and therefore can't be truly representative of the views of all persons in the region under consideration, known in statistical terms as the "universe."

The Random Sample. Many journalists still believe that a random sample consists of picking anybody you want to talk to on the street. The folly of that approach is readily apparent in a place like New York city, for example, where people picked at random at the fashionable corner of 50th Street and Park Avenue, in front of the Waldorf Astoria Hotel, will be no more typical of New Yorkers as a whole than those selected at the corner of 125th Street and Lenox Avenue, the cross roads in Harlem.

The definition of a true random sample specifies that everybody living within a given "universe", that is to be surveyed must have an equal chance of being selected for interviewing.If the selection is properly done, the sample need not be large. As statisticians are fond of pointing out, if an experimenter draws 100 balls from two casks of black and white balls, one with 100,000 and the other with 1,000 and each divided into a ratio of three black balls to seven white balls, the likelihood is virtually the same that the drawing will yield 70 white and 30 black balls from each cask. Thus, Gallup's usual random sample is about 1,500 and his and other national polling samples during a political campaign run to no more than 3,000 persons.

In any event, reliable research and news organizations always go to considerable trouble and expense to develop; a random sample that will represent the "runiverse" whether it is a village, a country, a state or the nation as a whole. In some instances, a "universe" may consist of groups of people taken by irregular areas depending on the type of survey and the desires of the person in charge.

The Probability Method. The most difficult, time-consuming and costly technique is the probability method. It is also the most widely accepted.

In this process, nothing is left to chance that the sample will be truly selected at random. Trained interviewers are given a list of carefully prepared and pretested questions, certain addresses in specified areas, a list of selected apartments in such buildings and a group of persons to be interviewed in order (the oldest male, the oldest woman and so on) at certain times of the day or evening.

They are given a choice if the address turns out to be an empty lot, or an apartment is vacant, or the type of person to be interviewed isn't available after repeated calls. Then the interviewers are given a list of alternatives, the whole following a statistical pattern developed will in advance.

Various refinements are applied to increase the representative nature of the sample, including stratification. This means simply that where the "universe" includes several identifiable groups of persons, samples will be drawn separately from each group to make certain they are properly represented. This helps maintain the accuracy of the sampling process, whereas clustering—interviewing several designated types of persons in one house or apartment—tends to reduce it.

A Question of Confidence. Using statistical tables of probability, polling organizations invariably determine the size of their samples on the basis of what is called a "confidence level" - in other words, a test of accuracy. If Gallup sample totals 600 persons, for example, he calculates that the chances are 95 in 100 that a poll which divides 60 percent in favour, 40 percent opposed (or the reverse) will be within four percentage points of the true figure. This means that the number in favour will be somewhere between 56 percent and 64 percent. By doubling the sample to 1,200, Gallup holds that the error factor (using the same 95 in 100 criterion) is reduced to 2.8 percent. Doubled again, there is a further decrease to 2 percent.

It isn't any great mathematical feat, using statistical tables and relatively basic mathematical procedures, to work out the confidence level for any sample size and confidence level. Most surveys make it their goal to operate within 4 percent error at the 95 in 100 confidence level, which means a sample of 600 persons is adequate. At 3 percent, a sample of 1,067 is needed, 2 percent, 2,401, 1 percent, 9,605. These figures assume, of course, that there is an absolutely true sample based on probability. As for the size of the "universe" involved, those figures don't make much difference until they get below the 10,000 level.

For many years, it seemed to many that it was sheer madness to try determine national trends by polling a handful of citizens in a town, a few score in a state, and between 1,200 and 3,000 nationally. And yet, barring technical and human failures that now are usually kept to a minimum, the system works. The Bureau of the Census has been using the probability method of random sampling for years to determine population growth (the house to house enumeration process occurs only once a decade).

Sampling Techniques. The basis of most sampling techniques consists of maps and other data from the Bureau of the Census. If these are reinforced with city directories or comparable tabulations, the raw material for establishing a sample is in hand.

In the probability method, the primary sampling units may be drawn at random (using a table of random numbers) from a list of all the countries and metropolitan areas in the United States. These are then further reduced to urban blocks and rural segments, also selected by the random process as it is known in statistics. Next, within each selected block or segment, every dwelling unit is listed and a fixed number is selected at random. Finally, in the selected dwelling unit, all adults are enumerated, from each, one person is chosen, again at random.

The sample thus selected has a high probability of reflecting all the characteristics of the "universe" from which it is drawn. Factors of age, sex, economic status, ethnic and religious group and other relevant items are all represented in the sample. It is in this manner that interviewers are provided with their list of persons to be located and asked the precise list of questions drafted by the polling organization.

In telephone polls, which are faster and cheaper, the number of names in a telephone directory in a particular city is divided by the size of the sample (600, 1,067,2,401 or whatever). The quotient shows the number of names to be skipped, from the beginning to the end of the directory, to produce a true random sample. Then, the designated telephone numbers are called by researchers. To cover unlisted numbers, some social scientists advocate adding one digit at the end of each telephone number on the list.

The Uses of Polling. It is a familiar argument among pollsters, particularly those with an academic background, that the poll is more sinned against than sinning and that news organizations misuse polls by attempting to extract more information from them than they are able to give. To a certain extent this may be true. However, as long as polling organizations offer their wares for sale and as long as they announce certain results within a given range of probabilities, it is only logical to hold them responsible for their output.

No one can claim absolute accuracy for any public opinion study, whether it is done person-to-person, by telephone or questionnaire. The allowance on percent error on either side is fairly standard in political poll-taking, but the public tends to overlook it in a close political fight when there is perhaps only a 1 percent difference between the chief rival candidates. Moreover, some polls are put to grotesque uses toward Election Day when one side or the other will claim victory on the basis of a lead of as little as one half of 1 percent.

While political polling is a hurry-up-job with a considerable element of risk, and while TV ratings are also under constant criticism for the same reason. the social issues type of poll can be much more leisurely and often just as useful. The Detroit Free Press, in a study of black attitudes after the Detroit riots, took three weeks. A University of California study of the Watts riots took two years to produce. The Miami Herald took a considerable period for its inquiry into the militancy of blacks in the Miami area. And academic studies always take a great deal longer.

Depth Interviews. There are some practical minded social scientists and political experts who have faith in a few depth interviews - solicited from various types of persons at specific locations - as a means of judging the mood of a particular "universe," which may be a small voting unit or even the entire nation. Such depth interviews may be conducted for two or three hours and encompass a variety of subjects. It is hardly fair to say that this kind of work is a protection of the man in the street interview, done at a highly sophisticated level. These depth interviews require a rare combination of journalistic skills and social science background, plus shrewd political judgments.

One of the most successful practitioners of the art was the political analyst Samuel Lubell, who did most of his own interviewing and calculated his own results. Lubell might select for a depth interview a man who resides in a low costing housing development and works in a factoty, a housewife who lives in the center of an area torn by controversy over school busing or another emotional issue, a farmer in the center of the Midwestern grain belt, a small home owner and other such typical American citizens. Out of the mix of their opinions and his own judgment, he shaped his conclusions.

Is the United States Overpolled? Although a Gallup survey has indicated that six out of seven Americans over 18 have never been interviewed in a poll, polling organizations agree that there is rising public resistance to their surveys. The work not takes much more time, it is more costly and more people simply don't want to be bothered. The reason is evident. In addition to polls by the government, universities and the news media, more than 1,000 commercial organizations are now in the business—which means the public is being asked to do a lot of the pollsters' work for free. "Perhaps," one pollster suggested, "we are not treating the respondent with respect as a human being".

Checking Trends. The use of selected national or state voting units is a favourite indicator of political trends. Every major polling organization has a well guarded list of such precincts, picked because they have accurately reflected the outcome of elections over a period of years. Of course, in landslides such as 1964 and 1972, it is easy to pick a winner by using the results in the model precincts and projecting them. Sometimes it can even be done before the polls close by taking a random sample among voters as they emerge from casting their ballot. But in a close election model precincts are a risky guide.

Among newspapers, it is a time honoured custom for political writers to publish their forecasts on the Sunday or Monday before election. Necessarily, this is nowhere near as informative as it used to be because the publication of weekly surveys before Election Day has taken the edge off what used to be "the last word. " Once again. it is no big deal to call a one sided election as for the close ones, predictions continue to be a gamble regardless of when they are made.

Polling Standards. Here is a checklist of the information that should accompany any poll.

1. The sponsor of the poll.
2. Exact wording of all questions.
3. Definition of the population sample.
4. Sample size and, where needed the response rate;
5. Allowance for sampling error;
6. Proportion of "don't knows" and others in sample who may not vote;

7. Method of interviewing and, where done;

8. Time period for interviewing.

Predictions

Any election forecast should have suitable qualifications throughout, even though the result may seem to duplicate many years of similar pre-election accounts. This is a sample of the usual type of forecast lead.

Mayor Hammond Garvell appears likely to win re-election on Tuesday if the vote is as large as expected.

A sampling of typical voter opinion, plus talks with professionals in both parties and the findings of private polls, indicated today that the mayor was expected to defeat his opponent, Hereford Cates.

But even Mayor Garvell' s closet aides emphasized that as an independent running for re-election, he must count on a heavy turnout at the polls-always a sign in this city that the independent voter is making his influence felt....

"Foregrounding" Politics. A considerable segment of political writing in newspapers and newsmagazines and analytical comment on television is based on the summation and interpretation of coming events. The holding of conventions, listing of known candidates and issues and analysis of rival claims are subject for reports of this type. Another is the planning for a campaign during a given period and the conclusions that may be drawn from it in terms of objectives.

Best known of all is the pre-Election Day summation giving the times places and candidates involved in the voting the registration figures, probable vote totals, analysis of issues, weather and whatever conclusions the writer or analyst wishes to make. On television, this type of information can only be give the voter all the material he needs to make a decision on numerous candidates, propositions and referenda. This, certainly is the place where a good newspaper is priceless and the electronic media are at a complete disadvantage.

Covering Elections

The early part of the 20th century was the golden age for political reporters. They were regarded as seers in their own right the travelling companions of the great and near—great, the oracles who-in their own time at their own pleasure—gave the people the Word Arthur Krock of the New York Times, Charles Michelson of the New York World, Edward Folliard of the Washington Post and their associates were national figures. However the coming of television changed all that.

The Reporters' Job. Today, the exposure of TV and its astronomical costs limit political campaigning in all except the marathon races of presidential years. The wise candidates try to save their principal pronouncements for TV and get by the rest of the time with a stock speech. But they are constantly on the move.

Consequently, political reporters for major news organizations outside TV are up against an almost impossible job. Their work is so concentrated that they have little time to talk to the candidates or their managers, let alone the voters. In a national campaign, if they try to see anybody at an airport or train or motorcade whistlestop, they risk being left behind. Nowadays candidates will cover several states at a time in a single day. And because most candidates rely on the basic speech that isn't news after the first few times it is used. Except in the hands of experienced reporters who know how to dig for the unusual in a political campaign coverage tends to become a humdrum affair. More and more, it is the analysis that counts with many a newspaper.

Team reporting based on surveys of public opinion is being used by news papers that can afford it. And where research is needed one'or two reporters may be assigned to do a lengthy background report on a candidate or an issue. Much of the news, therefore becomes a matter of reportorial initiative rather than the rewriting of political handouts or the stale coverage of last night's TV appearance. For newspapers and wire services, it is more of a challenge and, on the whole, it leads to better reporting over a period of time.

The Political Routine

The electronic revolution that is reshaping the news media has enabled political reporters and commentators to use new and far more effective instrument in their work. At the beginning of the century, the task of obtaining and analyzing registration figures for all but the smallest elections was so time consuming that only a few great newspapers and the top echelons of wire services made much of an attempt to do it. Now the computer has made statistical analysis of registration figures almost a routine matter. This, plus social science's new knowledge of the habits of the nation's voters, has given public officials, journalists and office seekers alike new insights into the operation of the machinery of self-government.

There is no excuse today for any political reporter who does not know the geographical social and ethnic backgrounds of the various areas of the nation. Nor can the journalists who cover politics ignore the need for a broad academic preparation for their work. It all may seem very glamorous to the beginner, who sees television floor reporters running around national conventions and buttonholing the elect of the country for interviews in front of the ever-present minicams with their instant replay videotapes.

Actually, that is only a small part of the job. Regardless of electronic advances in journalism, a certain amount of routine remains for every political reporter, and it has to be done well. For coverage begins with registration and proceeds through the nominating process preconvention maneuvers, the conventions themselves or the primary elections that have replaced them in many states and then the coverage of the campaigns for all major candidates. What is involved here is a lot of traveling, interviewing research and writing at all hours of the day and night, the reporter doesn't exist who can cover politics on a regular basis within the neat framework of a seven or eight hour day.

Covering Political Conventions

The old tradition of the "Smoke filled room", from which candidates like Warren Gamaliel Harding emerged and were thrust upon an astonished electorate in presidential elections, has been shattered by the growth of television. While many a politician sighs and wishes for its return the "smoke filled room" is now a part of history. Undoubtedly there will be what are known as "brokered" conventions of the two major political parties in the future, as there have been in the past but it will be next to impossible to keep the wheeling and dealing secret.

This is the main reason for the dramatic changes in the national political conventions at which presidential candidates are nominated. At the 1960 and 1964 conventions of both major parties, the presence of television cameras and TV reporters and commentators led to continual disorder as publicity conscious candidates and delegates crowded each other for exposure.

That, however, was but a foretaste of what was to come at the disastrous 1968 Democratic National Convention in Chicago, when masses of antiwar activists, seeking to punish the Democratic leadership for the escalation of the Vietnam War disrupted the proceedings with riots and other demonstrations before the television cameras. The Chicago police, surging to attack the demonstrators helped produce what turned out to be a political disaster for the Democratic nominee, Senator Hubert H. Humphery. He was defeated by former vice-president Richard M. Nixon, the Republican candidate in the November election.

Both parties tried, without much success to reduce the confusion on the convention floor in 1972 by attempting to restrain television coverage. In 1976, finally, despite the use of hand-held minicams and videotape TV people were ordered from the floor of the Democratic National Convention several times in order to disperse the crowds around the cameras.

Calm, order, and dullness were the rule of the day at the 1980 conventions. At the republican convention, Ronald Reagan, the frontrunner during the primaries, was nominated in what amounted to a coronation. At the Democratic convention, with the exception of a 1st-gasp effort from Senator Edward M. Kennedy, who made a brilliant speech, President Carter wrung an easy renomination from the reluctant Democratic leadership and went down to overwhelming defeat in the November election.

Election Day. The proceedings on Election Day, once so boisterous in the average American city are reasonably quiet today. In big cities, with few exceptions, there is almost a holiday air with banks and bars closed and often schools as well. It is seldom that there is news of such chicanery as stolen ballot boxes, the multiple voting of floaters and other tricks of the bad old days. If an election is being stolen the few remaining political bosses try not to make a public announcement of it. Trickery at the polls, in consequence, is rather difficult to detect except in illinois, as the 1982 gubernatorial election showed.

This does not mean that news staffs have an easy time of Election Day, however. On the contrary the arduous business of interviewing voters after they have cast their ballots now begins with the opening of the polls. And as the voting progresses, the news no longer is based on an hour-by hour estimate of how many have voted but on projections at sample precincts of the standings of the various candidates. Of course not every news organization is equipped to do this, because it takes a major outlay of funds and commitments of staff and electronic gear. But those that do can make an Election Day story much more exciting than it has been in recent years.

Election Night. The important thing about Election Night work is the effort that goes into organizing it. In the press and in the electronic media the news staff that generally does the best job is the one that prepares for it with the greatest care. Sometimes the preparations for an Election Night begin as much as six months in advance. During the final weeks, the compilation of background figures, campaign materials data covering everything from biographies to party platforms and the outlining of actual assignments are almost as important as the day to-day cover age of the news. No good news organization goes into Election Night without complete, pretested planning and batteries of the best calculators and computers available with trained personnel to run them.

Election coverage is the kind of thing the American news media do best. Once the polls close and the first figures start flowing from the newsrooms, partisanship is nearly always forgotten by the working journalists and all effort is concentrated on reporting who won how victory was achieved and what it means. The union of wire services and the three major television networks for Election Night coverage has reduced the public's uncertainty over the outcome in all but the closet elections.

Tabulating the Vote. The public's attention is riveted on the television screens on Election Night and the announcements as soon as possible of the winning candidates. The electronic performance is risky, but it is in the journalistic tradition, Gradually, the major television news organizations have learned the bitter lesson that newspapers absorbed in the years before the electrpnic media took primacy in such spot-news reporting. They have become far more careful with the announcement of who won—and why—and have generally adopted a stance of responsibility that befits the journalist far better than a wild-eyed claim of exclusivity. Their cooperation on presidential elections is in the public interest.

Even though television is first with the results and often first with the announcement of the winners, it cannot—by its very nature provide the detailed tabulations of the voting down to the smallest districts and the totals amassed by every candidate in the various races. That is something good newspapers have always done superbly and they still continue to do so. Without this kind of service, it would be difficult for a democratic system to operate as well as it does.

Handling the Figures

The basis of any voting announcement. whether it is given by the wire services television or rival media, is the vote total itself, the number of districts it represents and the identities of these districts. No fragmentary vote is worth anything unless the source is identified, so that it can be compared at once with previous records. Thus, any voting result that is important enough to be made known should contain the number of voting districts, the area and—if possible—his time as follows.

442 out of 1,346 election districts in Great Bear Country, on the state's northern border, gave these totals at 10.32 p.m.

Iones (D)	60,024
Smith (R)	50,555

26 election districts in the 64th Ward, in the heart of Central City's south side, gave these totals at 9.30 p.m.

Brown (D)	2,022
Green (R)	2,366

The names of election units change, of course, from one place to another, but whether they are wards or districts the practice is the same. On the basis of a sufficient cross-section of the voting, and a knowledge of past performance in the same area, a projection of the figures can be computed and an indicated voting result can be given. Thus, on the basis of a 25-percent voting return, an experienced political analyst can calculate what will happen and make an announcement that reads something like this:

> On the basis of returns from one-quarter of the city's districts two hours after the polls closed, Smith led by 40,622 to 32,634 for Jones, his Democratic rival. This gave him an actual plurality of 8,028 over Jones and an indicated plurality of more than 30,000 if the same vote ratio continues.

Political analysts know if it is possible for the same ratio to continue. They have all the statistics of past performances and they have tabulating machines and computers, with operators, so that it takes little time to work out a proper projection in all but the closest contests.

Where cities are heavily Democratic and rural districts are overwhelmingly Republican, as is usually true in such states as Illinois, New Jersey and New York, the initial returns from cities, being tabulated faster, often show Democratic candidates far in the lead. But this is where the analysts take over. They point out that the early figures may be misleading. As the return scome in from rural areas, they make projections of the vote to see if the usual Republican majorities are being piled up; if they are, then it is a relatively simple matter to match this projection against those of the cities and arrive at a tentative winner if the swing between the candidates is wide enough. But where the difference between the candidates" vote percentages comes to 3 percent on either side, the familiar danger point for most statistical compilations, the wise analyst concludes that it is best to await virtually complete results.

It has happened, although rarely, that candidates have conceded defeat on the basis of projected returns and gone to bed, only to find upon arising in the morning that they have won because of a surge of late returns in their favour. And sometimes, when only a handful of votes separates winner and loser, a recount may reverse the result. So caution in close elections is an article of faith in every newsroom on Election Night.

The stories of the election results—written and verbal-are based on the tabulated figures, and the majorities and pluralities are calculated accordingly. (A majority is the difference between candidates where only two are running; a plurality between two candidates is the difference where more than two are in the race. A candidate may have a plurality over the second person in a three-way race and a majority over the combined total of the opposition.

Anchor persons on TV need judgment, stamina and verbal skills to a high degree, but they don't have to worry too much about organizing their remarks. Newspaper work is different.

The key to the successful newspaper story on Election Night is the organization of the piece. It should be assembled in such a way that it need not be completely rewritten every time a voting total changes. Often figures are left out of the lead for this reason. The lead is merely based on the fact that one candidate is leading, the actual returns being given immediately afterward in tabular style so that they can be changed quickly by substituting an insert.

Qualifying the Story. Until a vote is decisive, it is well in reporting on Election Night to use such qualifications as, "On the basis of scattered returns," or, "Partial and unofficial returns showed Smith had a narrow lead 30 minutes after the polls closed." Until the election has been decided, a careful writer qualifies the lead in this manner:

> Robert J. Epperson apparently was elected mayor last night by an indicated plurality of 40,000 votes.
>
> Although no concession of defeat came from his rival, Arthur Ahlgren, Epperson claimed victory on the basis of returns from half the city's districts which gave him a commanding lead....

Sometimes, in a close election, a candidate may be the victor on the basis of final and unofficial returns and the loser may charge fraud, demand a recount or both. Circumstances dictate how the story should be presented, but it is only logical to report that one candidate has scored a victory that is being contested. The charges of fraud should be used in a lead only when there appears to be some basis for them.

When elections are very close, news organizations sometimes have to wait until the entire vote is counted before declaring a winner. In rare cases, the decision has to await the filing of official returns a week to 10 days after the election. But generally, an election is considered final when the rival or rivals of the successful candidate concede defeat.

There have been instances in which a candidate conceded defeat only to learn, when complete returns were in, that he had won. But that doesn't happen often..

Styles vary in the reporting of election results in newspapers. Some carry the actual figures in a box preceding the story, where readers can see them before they look at anything else. Others like to use a lead saying who won, and then immediately summarize the salient figures, even though television has already done the job. Here is a general style in use on many newspapers and wire services, which is also familiar to television audiences who have heard it present—tensed and read by exhausted second-string announcers late at night after the first team has gone home.

Arthur J. Wintage scored victory last night over his Democratic opponent, George Berling, who was seeking a third term as governor.

The Republican triumph in the state, which ran counter to a nationwide Democratic trend, was the result primarily of deep inroads that Mr. Wintage made into normally Democratic pluralities in Central City, largest municipality in the state.

Governor Berling conceded defeat at 11:15 last night. The concession followed a conference with Gunnar Dahlquist chairman of the Democratic State Committee, and Mayor Franklin Quest of Central City.

At 12.32a.m., with nearly complete statewide returns in, 10,132 out of 11,110 districts gave:

Wintage (R)	Berling (D)
2,834,263	2,378,767

Nearly complete returns from Central City at that hour indicated that Mr. Wintage, 54-year-old industrialist from Willow Grove, had cut the usual Democratic plurality there to less than 400,000 votes. Four years ago, Governor Berling was able to carry the city by almost 700,000 votes...

The unofficial results, reported on Election Night by the news media, are seldom upset by challenges, charges or recounts, but the final result must await the official canvass. When there is an election upset, it is major news.

Basics on Polls and Elections

Here are some of the main things to remember about reporting on public opinion, polls and elections:

* Polling is based on the scientific use of statistics and must always include an announced probability of error, based on the number of people involved in the sample and the method of interviewing. No poll is ever going to be perfect.

* The least effective, and least scientific, poll is the one in which a reporter asks any dozen or so people for an opinion. That kind of poll is useless scientifically.

* A proper poll is based on the selection of a true random sample, in which everybody in a given polling area or group has an equal chance of being interviewed. The usual national telephone sample is about 1,500 which has a 3-percent margin of error on either side, in 95 out of 100 instances.

* The two main methods are *(a)* probability, in which the interviewer is given specific instructions on exactly where to go and whom to interview, and *(b)* the quota method, in which the interviewer is told the types of people to interview (young, old, men, women, etc.) and the number of each and left to his or her own devices. The probability method is generally used.

* Polling reports should include the population sample, the size and response rate, the wording of questions, the poll sponsor, allowance for error, the time period for interviewing and when the interviewing was done.

* Any poll that shows a narrower percentage of support between two candidates than the margin of error for the poll itself is not really worth much. It shows an election too close to call.

* In writing about elections, any partial vote total must include the number of voting districts reporting, the area, the time, the partial totals and the part of the vote that is still missing as to area and, if possible, past voting performance.

* Until an election has been decided by the concession of one or another candidate or the completion of the vote, all reporting of returns must be qualified. Vote projections, as used by the networks and major newspapers, should be announced with the margin of error involved.

* In very close races, the official retums—which may take a week to 19 days—are often the decisive count. It the case of recounts, court actions may be involved, and the final decision could take months to determine on Election Night on the basis of projections of partial returns and should be so labeled.

CRIME REPORTING

Crime reporting is not separate from the objective, interpretative and investigative form of reporting. Here it is separately dealt with because it is a separate and important beat in all big and medium level daily newspapers.

There is a tremendous public interest in crime stories and no newspaper can afford to ignore them without damage to its circulation and credibility. Attempts made by some newspapers to keep crime out of their columns, proved to be counter productive and were soon abandoned.

Crime is a part of life and it is a newspaper's duty to'inform the readers of what crimes are going on in their city, state or country.

However, crime reporting should not aim at satisfying morbid curiousity or sensation mongering.

Although crime reporting is usually assigned to one of the junior reporters in a newspaper, it is a highly responsible and specialised job. The reporter should not only have the ability to shift the grain from the chaff, and the truth from lies, he should also have good contacts in the police and other departments of the administration as well as a working knowledge of the penal codes and law on libel and other relevant matters.

Besides, he must observe a code of honour. He should be as objective as is humanly possible and avoid resorting to sensationalism or cheap gimmicks to catch the attention of the readers. He should not suppress news of public interest. Nor should he seek to settle personal scores with police officers or lawyers or judges. And he must be careful that in the course of this work, he does not unnecessarily invade a citizen's privacy.

There has been much criticism of press reporting of crime and not all of it is baseless. Some reporters have been found quality of unethical standards, thus causing much pain and sorrow to their victims or their families and friends.

In the case of the brutal murder of two Bombay nuns, some newspapers published totally baseless allegations conveyed to them by irresponsible police officials that the nuns were in the habit of receiving male visitors. The reports offended all decent citizens, particularly the members of the Christian Community.

A leading newspaper once published a fictitious report about a couple having been waylaid by a gang on the national highway. The report said that the husband was beaten up and the women was molested. The story was subsequently found to be incorrect, the product of the imagination of a reporter anxious to get his by-line in the paper.

Reports glorifying the activities of criminals or making heroes of them should be discouraged as much as a resort to sensationalism.

The crime reporter must never violate standards of decency and good taste.

Crime as News

There are several types of crime news-murders, fires, accidents, robberies, burglaries, fraud, blackmail, kidnaping, rape, etc.

Fires

The reporter must get his facts correct about the essential elements of a fire story the number of persons killed or injured, the extent of damage to property, the loss of valuables, etc. He must also find out if the fire brigade responded in time or was guilty of delaying the fire-fighting operations through sheer lethargy or incompetence or a lack of water supply. He should question eye-witnesses about any acts of bravery or cowardice. All these are essential ingredients of a fire story.

The lead in a fire story would normally suggest itself. If, for instance, lives have been lost, it needs highlighting in the lead. Where possible, list the names of the dead and the injured.

Example. A major fire caused extensive damage to New Delhi's Vigyan Bhavan, the premier venue of international and national conferences, on Monday night. A chow kidar on duty received minor burns.

According to preliminary investigations, the fire broke out in the kitchen and soon spread to other rooms on the ground floor. The chowkidar raised an alarm which alerted the head clerk on duty who informed the fire brigade and the police. Ten fire tenders soon arrived on the scene. However, their fire-fighting operations were hampered by lack of water in the hydrants. By the time water tankers rushed to the site, the fire had engulfed a large area and damaged files, furniture, curtains and ceilings.

The police suspect electric short-circuit as the cause of the fire.

Homicides

In cases of a major murder, the reporter should rush to the scene as soon as possible after receiving a tip and gather all the relevant facts. In nine cases out of ten, crime reporters in, say, Delhi, depend on police information bout murders and there is a time lapse before they can begin their investigations.

This often hampers their search for the truth. The reporter must, in any case, exercise great care in how he handles the story. Otherwise he runs the risk of causing offense.

In reporting dowry deaths or alleged dowry deaths, for instance, the reporter should refrain from levelling uncorroborated statements by one party or the other. He must therefore get his facts correct-by talking to the investigating police officer, the girl's in-laws and her parents, and, if possible; the neighbours.

Example. A 25 year old housewife, Sushmita Malik, died in Pant Hospital on Monday morning from burns received in a kitchen fire. The housewife's parents allege that she was murdered by her in-laws who had been dissatisfied with the dowry she brought at the time of her wedding a year ago.

However, the husband, Keshav Malik, a garment merchant in Chandni Chowk, and his father who were in the house at the time of the accident maintain, that Sushmita's sari caught fire when she was lighting a stove in the kitchen. Since the kitchen door was closed, they did not hear her cries for help.

The police are questioning the women's relatives as well as neighbours and are reluctant to offer an opinion until the investigations are complete. At the insistence of Sushmita's parents, however, they have registered a case against her in-laws.

Accidents

Most accidents are reported on the basis of police bulletins or information supplied 'by police spokesmen. However, wherever possible the crime reporter must rush to the scene of a major accident to give authenticity to his story.

Example. Three members of a family-husband, wife and daughter-were killed on the spot when a speeding truck remmed into their car on the road to Indira Gandhi International Airport on Sunday morning. A fourth member of the family had a providential escape. According to the police, the truck driver lost control of the vehicle and swerved sharply to the right and hit the car coming from the opposite direction.

Those killed are Ramkishore Singh, a businessman of Agra, his wife, Sumitra Devi, and their daughter, Sapna. The second daughter, Tanuja, had a miraculous escape and suffered only minor bruises on her arms and legs. She was treated at the Safdarjung Hospital and allowed to go home.

The truck has been seized by the police but the truck driver, Milkha Singh is absconding.

REPORTING OF TOUGH STORIES

The group of convivial reporters, news agency writers and editors sipped on cold drinks, fruit juices or upon good Tunisian wine. The day's official newswriting seminar had been over hours ago. But the group lingered in the hotel room, reluctant to give up the good conversation and comradeship of the day. Outside, a full, silver-bright Tunisian moon came up, and the night breeze rattled in the palm branches. There was a pause in the conversation.

"You Know," mused one of the African journalists, "I wish there were some way to do a lot of stories I feel I can't do. You know, the kinds that can upset officials, that really tell people what is going on." Everybody nodded in agreement. Journalists all, whether from the developed world or the developing nations, they were united in trying to figure out ways to cover the "uncoverable."

"Why don't we exchange some ways we cover tough stories?" one asked.

What follows in this chapter are a few of the suggestions reporters and editors brought up to help others cover major stories of a "sensitive" nature which need to be done. Even where journalists are part-and-parcel of the government press system, they often yearn to be allowed to tell some stories which in one way or another menace highly placed officials, the ruling political party, or other important interests in their country. Frequently such stories don't really undermine a national governmental or threaten the legitimacy of the party in power.

But it is a fact of life that national leaders, both in developing and developed countries, have contrived to have a near-paranoia that they will be made to look foolish or that the programmes they hold dear will be downgraded publicly in the press. Almost every successful journalist, where ever he or she may practice reporting or editing, must develop adroit and tactful ways of getting stories into print about sensitive matters. And it was the consensus of the group of journalists that night in Tunisia at a non-aligned nations news workshop that in almost every country, there are ways to publish stories which at first may seem unprintable.

Of course, in a regime which has absolutely no freedom of expression, the journalist has no latitude in what he or she can write. But most Third World Journalists, and even quite a few from the Second, or Socialist, World, say they have had some success in covering the "uncoverable". The readers of this chapter, knowing their own situations, will know whether they may apply some of the methods used. Even if they can't directly use what is suggested, the discussion of how to write about difficult and sensitive subjects may stimulate them to think of new ways to better inform their readers.

The main reason persons in power refuse to let certain stories be done is that they believe such stories menace them in some way. When a reporter or editor believes that a certain story is needful and believes it will be difficult to get in print, he or she needs to ask why it may appear threatening. What is the menacing thing about the story? Few persons like to be attacked with a broadside which questions their authority, intelligence or goodness. Reporters who adopt confrontational tactics and who are plainly hostile are not likely to get very many stories—especially in countries where there are many controls on the press.

News sources and government officials frequently complain that members of the press are mainly in the business of digging up negative, controversial news and have their eyes closed to news at the other end of the scale—news which recounts positive activities and achievements. Journalists frequently reply that news sources and officials want only self serving publicity releases which plaint them as saints or super brains. But if we are to consider how to get into print stories about sensitive topics, we must pay attention to the sources of the news and to those who have the power to say "publish it" of "kill it."

This high importance given to the negative, atypical and aberrational in western journalism lends some weight to the criticisms by news sources. We referred to this problem in the chapter on investigative reporting. But we only take time here to point out that many journalists feel they have wasted their time if they have investigated a situation, hoping to find corruption, crime, incompetence or the immoral- and they have instead found honest people doing a good job against heavy odds. This is a strange blindness. It can be highly newsworthy to find upon occasion that government really works, that someone is doing a good job, or that a leader is honest and sincere. Journalists take a cynical view of human nature and reply that the public is only interested in reading who gets caught being a scoundrel, or in finding out that evil rules the day. But positive news can also have readable elements of conflict against adversity of the exceptionally competent or empathetic leaders, or in stories which celebrate the struggle of ordinary people to survive in harsh environments.

Probably the underlying idea of how to cover the "uncoverable" story is to be able to persuade those in power that the stories do not question their legitimacy or the national interest. Getting the sensitive story printed is not easy you will win some and lose some. But each one printed is a victory.

The reporter must realize that much hostility toward him or her results from the self-righteous attitude of the press which in some countries reserves for itself the self-appointed job of judging who is good and who is bad, and what the best interests of the nation are. The press has the luxurious position of standing back and weighing and measuring performance of government, business, etc., while not dirtying its hands with the hard task of leadership. We can imagine the screams of outrage which would result if the national government, for instance, set up teams of "investigative reporters" to delve into the operations of a major elite newspaper. "By what right do you appoint yourselves judges of how we decide what goes into our paper?" the furious publisher might ask. "Who gave you the moral sanction to sit in judgement of how we serve our readers and advertisers, or how can you tell us what is the common good?"

If the reporter or editor can attempt to put himself or herself into the position or persons attempting to run a country, community, business or other organization, this effort will result in more understanding and empathy with these news sources. None of what is said here should mean that journalists should not work hard to do accurate stories about their community and nation. We only say that they must report the scale of human activity, not constantly merely headlining and giving prominence to failures and "bad" news.

The Third World reporter especially needs to approach news-gathering affirmatively with sympathy toward sources, since they are frequently inexperienced in leading and must face many problems more established countries have already dealt with.

The reporter practicing her or his craft must constantly be aware that if sources feel they are being used or manipulated, they are likely to get angry and uncooperative. Each reporter must answer in his or her own conscience about approaches used in covering stories and dealing with sources. Some of the ways mentioned in the rest of this chapter to get sensitive topics into print may border upon manipulation. If the source, or person in power senses the reporter is cold-bloodedly contriving these approaches, everything will be lost. Even in enunciating these methods of dealing with sources there is some danger for abuse. Each reporter must decide which methods are ways to work with sources and those in power.

Frequently the public official about to deal with a reporter on a story either consciously or unconsciously is asking several questions. When the reporter realizes that these questions lurk in the back of the source's mind, they can be dealt with.

One of the first questions a potential source or government official approving a story must ask is: "Will I lose favour with higher-ups, or will I be denoted, or lose my job?" In some countries, some stories may even result in sources being physically injured or killed. The reporter should always be conscious of such extremely dangerous situations. If the story is that dangerous to the source of information, it may be just as dangerous to the existence of the reporter. There is little satisfaction in being a dead hero, even if the story has been told. Hundreds of others will go untold if the reporter doesn't survive to write another day.

When the reporter seeks to do a sensitive story, he or she must be able to come up with answers about why the source should cooperate. Some appeals which can be made include that the story will help explain the work being done by source or government official. The reporter can also point out, by indirection, that the source's task will be made easier if a thorough story is done about it.

Especially in the Third World, solidly written stories about topics of public interest have educational value. The source may be able to give information through the story that the public badly needs. Many leaders have a strong desire to educate the public about what their programme or projectis about. The reporter can point out the educational opportunity the story offers.

An approach which is sometimes successful in persuading sources to give information about controversial matters is the assurance by the reporter that his or her story will give the source a chance to have his side of the controversy aired. Politicians especially want to tell their side of the story when the opposition has already had its say.

Some sourccs or persons in power have a genuine desire to talk about their projects out of altruism. They may truly desire to serve the people well, and a story which accurately reflects their programmes or activities will aid their unselfish desire to serve. The reporter or editor is of course a student of human nature. He or she realizes that most persons are a mixture of light and dark qualities, of selfish and unselfish motives. But there is no reason to assume cynically in every case that the source has only selfish motives or is an evil person. After more than 30 years as a reporter, writer and editor, this writer is convinced that virtue exists in about the same proportion among leaders and public officials as it does among private citizens andjournalists. No one has a monopoly upon being "good" or being "evil," "smart" or "stupid."

Occasionally the reporter will have to promise the source that his or her identity will not be revealed in a story. If the source believes the reporter can protect what needs to be told without direct attribution, some sensitive information may be forthcoming. But once a reporter or editor promises not to identify a source, that promise must be kept. If it is broken, the source's job or even life may be endangered. The reporter's ability to get further stories from the source whose trust was violated will be nil. Among journalists, reporters or editors who go back on their word to protect sources are considered to be the lowest of creatures. The end does not justify this means.

Third World reporters and editors must be especially careful in promising anonymity to sources about sensitive stories. In the first place, even when such sources are not identified by name, they can frequently be identified by name, they can frequently be identified because only a few persons may have knowledge of the sensitive matter. Many Third World countries are basically run by only a few hundred persons. It's easy to figure out who "leaked" what sensitive information. In small countries, too, readers (and higher officials) are exceptionally able at figuring out where information may have come from.

The reporter or editor may also keep in mind that he or she may be FORCED to reveal sources of sensitive information. We have seen many instances even in Western countries where reporters have been forced by the courts to reveal their sources or go to prison. There are even more persuasive ways to force reporters to tell where they got information in authoritarian regimes.

Some Third World journalists have had good luck in printing sensitive stories if they emphasize that a situation is a challenge, rather than being a serious problem. The very word "problem" has the oonnotation of being something negative and threatening to the persons hoping to resolve it. If they are told the' reporter wishes to deal with the challenge or opportunity of dealing with a situation, they may be opened toward seeing such a story in print. One Third World reporter had very good luck in using this approach to deal with the question of unemployment in his small country. He was able to get government officials to reflect frankly and openly when he posed the question about the challenge of unemployment, rather than about the horrible problem some considered it to be. But he was able to convey the needed information in his story.

A rather unusual method used with some success by another Third World reporter is to write graphically about another country's problems. He received permission to do a hard-hitting series about inefficient agricultural production in a neighbouring country. His readers were intelligent enough to see that the problems in the neighbouring country were almost identical to those in their own nation. The lessons being learned in the neighbouring country could be applied in their own nation without anyone criticizing the Minister of Agriculture.

"Pointing out another country's problems makes you reflect on your own similar problems," the reporter said. "I have also found this method to be about the only acceptable one for writing stories about governmental corruption. It is a no-no to write directly about corruption in my own government. But I am free to bring out the high costs of corruption in bribes and inefficiency—if I use examples which aren't too close to home."

Sometimes it is possible for a reporter or editor to persuade a source or powerful person that doing stories about sensitive subjects is really the source's idea. If the benefits of a reporting project are pointed out to the source or decision maker, sometimes .e or she will go along, even to the point of unconsciously thinking the stories were really his or her own idea. This ploy is probably manipulative. Another more sincere avenue of approach would probably be to see the source and reporter as working as partners to explore a sensitive subject. Reporters and editors need to be able to put aside their own conceits and ego-involvement in order to accomplish this.

Upon occasion, a reporter can disarm hostility in a public official by using what some writers call the Goals-Obstacles Solutions formula. When interviewing and gathering information, the reporter can first ask the source what his or her goals are. This approach has the advantage of relating more closely with the source. Then, the logical next step is to ask, "If those are your goals, what stands in the way of canying them out what are the obstacles?" And finally, many sources will open up when they are asked what solutions might be possible.

Not only does using the goals-obstacles-solution approach help to set sources at ease, it also gives a logical structure to the reports written by the journalist.

This writer has known hundreds of journalists over the years. One common trait many of these have had is that they are somehow mentally conditioned to look for failures of individuals or of the system. To some extent this is healthy, since many public officials and leaders will not call attention to failure. But if the journalist approaches each topic with the assumption that something is wrong, this negative attitude will be reflected in the resulting stories. Quite a few journalism and editors have a "good complex," just as do some leaders. These reporters and editors spout glib, superficial judgements of officials and persons in the news. It is common for us all to project our own shortcomings upon others. The journalist is tempted to do this when working with his or her sources. It is often easier to question the morality of others, rather than to look within our own hearts. It is easier to say what a bunch of incompetents run-such and a ministry, when our own newspaper may be botching up things just as much. The mature reporter or editor will recognize these temptations to project our own human weaknesses onto others.

Knowledge of our own shortcomings will help us temper our coverage of the problems of our country or of the lacks in those we deal with. The reporter will hesitate to expect perfection from others when he or she realizes his or her own imperfections.

Journalists have a heavy responsibility to know themselves. Since their attitudes are often reflected consciously or unconsciously in what they write, they must search themselves for prejudices and biases. They have them, just as do all other persons. Many white U. S. journalists have had to realize they have secretly thought that blacks were dumber, more primitive, less ablc to advancc and to be educated. Journalists frequently grew up immersed in such prejudices. When they began to cover the lives of blacks or problems of racial inequality, they had to become aware that they might have their own burden of prejudice to carry.

Frequently Western journalists have been liberal politically. It has been difficult for them to set aside their bias a consider conservative politicians. Can the liberal U. S. Democrat put aside bias, writing about the conservative Republican?

In the Third World, can the reporter from the predominant tribe of the country write without bias about members of the minority tribe? Can the black journalist put aside a heritage of wrong-doing at the hands of some white people to see that some white are not evil or exploitive?

As the reporter or editor gains in knowledge of his or her own biases, these can be guarded against in stories. The knowledge that we are fallible, prejudiced begins is soon reflected in our increased understanding and empathy of others facing difficult jobs or situations. Other persons sense seductively when we ourselves are non judgemental or sympathetic in our relations with them. Often the key to doing the controversial or sensitive story is the source's recognition that we will deal charitably with the source's shortcomings or the difficulty in solving a problem.

Some journalists will think that these comments are more appropriate for the psychiatrist's couch or the church service. The psychology of working with sources is given very little attention in the standard reporting texts. These frequently see the reporter-source relationship or the press-government relationship as a black-and-white dynamic. The press is good and all-knowing. The sources, government, private corporation reported upon is the "Bad guy" whose actions must be exposed and condemned. This adversarial relationship is responsible for hostility toward journalists. This writer is constantly amazed that there is even as much goodwill and cooperation shown to journalists. Each reporter working with sources must put aside smugness and self-righteousness that he or she is keeper of the sacred flame of morality and competence.

The reporters who frequently are able to do the sensitive story, or the controversial story, often are the ones who can show understanding and empathy. For every story successfully done by confrontational tactics and hard-nosed journalism, probably ten more are done by non-confrontational efforts and sympathy with the sourace. This doesn't mean that the adversarial relationship doesn't have its place. The journalist will at all times have to get the adrenaline up to do battle. But don't expect to be a winner every time when you irritate and anger those from whom you hope.

❒